"I DESIRE YOU, MY WIFE . . ."

"You can't possibly—"

"But you refuse me. Therefore I must hunt. Which means, I must seduce you."

"Seduce!" She found an extra inch to retreat.

He caught her earlobe between two fingers and tugged. "Seduction is sanctioned within marriage, you know."

She couldn't help it. She twitched sideways, away from his devastating touch. "You agreed to wait!"

He let his hand drop, relaxed again, but not a mite less dangerous. "Of course. Until you present your soft vulnerability. Willingly. Eagerly . . ."

"Eagerly?" It came out on a breath, a whisper. With just his eyes, his remarkable eyes and big body, his long legs dominating the space, his wide shoulders filling her vision, with just these things, without touching her, she was halfway to surrender. . . .

Forbidden Magic

Jo Beverley

A TOPAZ BOOK

TOPAZ
Published by the Penguin Group
Penguin Putnam Inc., 375 Hudson Street,
New York, New York 10014, U.S.A.
Penguin Books Ltd, 27 Wrights Lane,
London W8 5TZ, England
Penguin Books Australia Ltd,
Ringwood, Victoria, Australia
Penguin Books Canada Ltd, 10 Alcorn Avenue,
Toronto, Ontario, Canada M4V 3B2
Penguin Books (N.Z.) Ltd, 182–190 Wairau Road,
Auckland 10, New Zealand

Penguin Books Ltd, Registered Offices:
Harmondsworth, Middlesex, England

First published by Topaz, an imprint of Dutton NAL,
a member of Penguin Putnam Inc.

First Printing, November, 1998
10 9 8 7 6 5 4 3 2 1

 REGISTERED TRADEMARK—MARCA REGISTRADA

Printed in the United States of America

Acknowledgments

Thanks to all the people on the Internet who make a writer's life so interesting these days, and to all the experts there who generously respond when an author comes along hungry for facts. I sometimes think cyberspace defies logic and lives on dreams and faith. Perhaps it's another form of magic, but if so, long live magic.

Chapter 1

London, 1812

The sharp rap of the knocker almost made Meg Gillingham cut herself with her paring knife. It was Christmas Eve! Surely they'd leave them alone for Christmas.

A succession of noisy raps shattered that hope.

Her young sister rose, face shadowed by the same fears. Meg waved Laura back to her seat at the kitchen table, back to supervising the twins' messy construction of angels out of scraps. After nervously wiping her hands on her apron, she picked up the two heavy shawls she kept handy, and went into the cold corridor, heading for the front door.

She longed to peep out through the parlor window to see who was on their steps, but a door-shaking thumping, and a bellow of "Open, in the name of the law!" had her running to draw the bolt and turn the key.

She flung it wide to see icy fog swirling around Sir Arthur Jakes, their landlord, and even worse, portly, uniformed Beadle Wrycroft, with his rod of office.

Not on Christmas Eve! she prayed. *Please.* Sir Arthur had been so kind. He was an old friend of her parents. Surely he'd never throw them out of their home on Christmas Eve.

He clearly wasn't suffering for lack of their rent. His heavy caped greatcoat was of finest quality, as were his warm muffler, his thick leather gloves, and his high-crowed beaver hat. "At last, Meg," he said, clean-cut face rather pinched. "Let us in, please."

Meg swallowed, but could do nothing but step back and gesture them into the narrow hall. "You wanted something, Sir Arthur?"

Once she'd shut out the frigid air, he said, "My dear girl, it cannot have escaped your attention that you have paid no rent for over three months."

"But you said we weren't to worry!"

Her breath puffed, and she shivered, tucking her icy hands under her shawls. If Sir Arthur had come alone, she would have invited him into the kitchen, the only room with a fire. She rebelled, however, at inviting grubby, onion-reeking Beadle Wrycroft into the most intimate room of her home.

"My dear Meg, you must see that I meant only to give you a little time after your parents' shocking deaths. Time to seek help, to make arrangements." He shrugged without distressing his perfect clothes in any way. "It cannot be indefinite, particularly with winter coming on."

She glanced around, as if help or advice would appear like an angel. But the only angels here were the paper ones the twins had made, and neither they, nor the holly twigs filched from nearby gardens, offered any help or advice.

"Of course, Sir Arthur. I do see. You have been most kind. If you could give us just a little more time. It is Christmas. . . ."

"Now, now, Miss Gillingham," the beadle said, "Sir Arthur has indeed been kind. More than kind."

The benefactor raised a gloved hand to silence him. "And can afford to be kind a little longer. As Miss Gillingham says, it *is* Christmas."

Oh, thank heaven!

"But you must see," he added to Meg, "that this cannot be a permanent arrangement."

Meg did. She had lived on hope for months, writing first to a scattering of relatives, then to friends. She'd had a few kind responses, and even some small bank drafts, but no one wanted to take on a lively family of five.

Recently, she had resorted to charities, but since she'd managed to keep up appearances, such groups showed no interest. Perhaps if the Gillingham family ended up on the winter streets with just the clothes on their backs, the Gentleman's Society for the Relief of Indigent Orphans, for example, would take up their cause.

But any charity would split them up. At twenty-one, she would be expected to fend for herself. Seventeen-year-old Jeremy would be set to clerking. Laura, Richard, and Rachel would be sent to institutions to be trained for a trade. She should be grateful, but it wasn't right. It wasn't fair! They were the sons and daughters of a gentleman.

It was pointless, however, to try to conceal their desperate situation any longer. Their money was just about exhausted. The best she'd been able to scrape together for Christmas dinner was a rabbit. They'd fill up on Christmas pudding made in the summer, before her parents' death, but after that they'd be on soup rations, and inevitably, one day soon the money would be completely gone.

She looked down, hating it. "I really have no idea where to turn."

"Oh, my dear." At his kind tone, she looked up, hope sparking, but something in his eyes made her want to step back, to escape. She remembered now that years ago, Sir Arthur had changed from avuncular to a kind of sly suitor. It had made her most uncomfortable. He was looking at her that way now. Did he still want to marry her?

Her skin crawled. She remembered the way he'd touched her back then—kindly pats, but in the wrong places. She remembered, too, how he'd often embarrassed her by the things he'd said.

But if he offered to marry her now, she'd have to do it.

She looked at his handsome face, his elegant appearance, and tried to persuade herself that it wasn't such a terrible fate.

"Beadle Wrycroft," Sir Arthur was saying, "I believe we can dispense with you for today. I will sit with Miss Gillingham and see if we cannot find a way out of her predicament."

"You're too kind, sir, too kind." The beadle looked heavily at Meg and waggled a grubby finger. "You pay attention to Sir Arthur, Miss. 'Tis a sad truth that beggars can't be choosers. If you're without resources, you will all have to lower your standards and make do."

Meg bit her tongue. They'd been lowering standards and making do for months. Was it their misfortune that their decent clothes were not worn enough yet to give them a suitably tattered appearance?

But she forced a smile and thanked the beadle for his help. There hadn't been any, but he clearly appreciated being appreciated.

Left with her landlord, Meg led him into the chilly, neglected parlor. If he was going to propose, it seemed suitable, and if he was going to set a date for their eviction, she'd rather her siblings not learn of it tonight.

She saw Sir Arthur glance at the empty grate and shiver. It almost made her smile. Almost. He was going to propose, and she was going to have to accept. Then she'd be trapped with him forever, having to let him do what husbands do, and subject to his will.

Her shiver was not from the cold.

She directed him to a chair and took a seat as far away as she dared. "If you can see a way to help, Sir Arthur, I will be very grateful." There, that was encouragement, surely.

He sat. "There are generally ways, my dear. You have heard nothing hopeful from your relatives?"

"My father's only brother is a missionary in the east, and his only sister is the wife of a curate in Derbyshire. With six children of her own there is nothing she can do."

"Your mother's family? She never spoke of them."

"As far as I know, they did not communicate. I found an address for a sister in Kerry and wrote to her. I have received no reply."

"How sad to see a family divided. Do you know the cause?"

"No, Sir Arthur." Meg wished he would just ask her. She had to want him to, no matter how he made her shudder.

His pale eyes flicked over her, perhaps assessing her. They'd hardly spoken since her parents' funeral, and before that she'd been away for three years as a governess. Perhaps he was disappointed in how she'd turned out.

For her family's sake, she wished she were a beauty like Laura, but she accepted reality. With her sturdy body and plain brown hair, she was inescapably ordinary.

He didn't look disappointed, however. He looked . . . anticipatory. She supposed she should like being desired, but in fact she felt like a trapped mouse being eyed by a weasel.

"So," she said, a little too loudly, "can you think of a source of aid for us? A way to keep the family together."

His brows rose. "Four youngsters is a heavy burden to bring to anyone, Meg, but I might have a suggestion." He paused thoughtfully, and she wanted to leap up and shake it out of him. She'd do it. Anything had to be better than this.

"Companionship is so important," he mused, "and I live alone. Bed and board . . ."

She made herself smile. "Yes, I think so."

"I have always enjoyed your family. So lively. So warm. Perhaps I could take on the care and guidance of you all. If there was a closer relationship."

Meg knew her cheeks were turning red and hoped he took it for a pleased blush rather than a flush of agitation. "Relationship?" she echoed, since something seemed to be required.

"A warm and intimate relationship with a fresh, untouched young woman."

Now she could think of nothing to say, and waited for the fateful words, steeling herself to say yes, and to say it graciously.

He crossed his legs, unnervingly at ease. "I might— no, would—be willing to assist you all, to provide for your comfort and even the education of the younger ones—if Laura becomes my mistress."

The world stopped for a few missing heartbeats, then Meg exclaimed, *"Laura!"* A second later, at a higher pitch, she gasped, *"Mistress?"*

He smiled, and she knew now it deserved a shudder. "Is your nose out of joint, my dear? It's true, when you were younger I did find you somewhat appealing, but you are, what? Twenty-two?"

"Twenty-one."

"Still . . . But Laura. Ah, Laura . . ."

"She's *fifteen!*"

"A wonderful age."

Meg leaped to her feet, wanting to scream at him, to throw him physically from the house, but—hands clenched—she made herself pause. She understood his purpose. If she didn't agree, they would all be cast out on a frosty darkening evening into direst poverty. Perhaps even into death.

Should she even consider it? Would not Laura's situation be better if . . . ?

No.

Never.

But she needed time.

Time.

One idea occurred to her, disgusting her almost as much as Sir Arthur's proposal.

To do that, she had to put him off.

She faced him. Oh, she'd been right to think him a weasel. A smug, sneaky weasel, confident the mice were trapped.

"I cannot agree to this at a moment's notice, Sir Arthur."

"I cannot give you much time, my dear."

"At least till after the Christmas season!"

"Two weeks? Too long by far." He rose slowly, drawing out the moment. "One week. I will come for my answer on New Year's Eve. Yes. How appropriate. How delightful to start the new year with Laura in my . . . home. But for that indulgence I deserve one. Call your sister so I may enjoy her beauty for one moment."

If only she could refuse, but she would have to allow this. "You will not speak of . . . of what you said?"

"I'm sure you will be much better able to prepare her. To persuade her."

Meg felt physically sick, but she fought it, opened the door, and called her sister.

In a few moments, Laura hurried down the corridor, an enchanting vision even in a shawl made out of an old gray blanket. Her golden-brown curls were tied back simply, but clustered charmingly around her smiling face. Her skin was flawless, her eyes large, clear, and innocent.

Meg fiercely wished her sister were dirty and disordered, but Laura never was. Even in poverty and simplicity she shone.

"Oh, Sir Arthur," said Laura, dropping a curtsy. "Good day to you, and a merry Christmas!"

Sir Arthur, thought Meg, had a remarkable degree of self-control. Or was a deceptive weasel, depending on how one wished to view it. His smile was exactly what one would expect of an old family friend. "A merry Christmas to you, too. Working hard helping the twins?"

"And hard work it is! I'm sure the whole kitchen is glued by now." But she spoke with good humor and showed her dimples.

It was completely impossible to deliver her up to lechery.

Sir Arthur strolled over and raised Laura's hand for a light kiss. "Your sister and I have been discussing your predicament, and we hope we might have found a way to help you all."

"Really? Poor Meg has struggled along, but I know we can't continue like this forever. I have been preparing myself to become a scullery maid."

"This lovely hand"—he patted it—"could be much more pleasantly occupied than scrubbing and scouring, my pet, and I will see to it." He kissed it again. "Oh yes, indeed." Still smiling, he took a coin from his pocket and pressed it into her palm. "Buy yourself a little something pretty."

He strolled to the door, but he paused to look back. "A week, Meg."

With that shot, he left.

"A week?" asked Laura.

Meg was shaking and prayed Laura wouldn't notice. Laura must never know. "That's when he thinks he might have a solution for us. With the new year."

"Well, it will be nice if he finds something. I've never liked him, but perhaps I've misjudged him." She looked in her hand. "Oh, it's a crown!" She gave it to Meg, who wished she could throw it through the window.

"It will buy us enough meat to make stew for a week."

Meg noticed that her sister was, perhaps unconsciously, rubbing away his kisses from her hand. Oh,

Lord. What was she to do? For the moment, she had to get rid of her sister before Laura noticed something wrong. A crash and cry did it for her.

"Oh, those monsters!" Laura exclaimed and ran out to return to the twins.

Meg sat with a thump, soiled coin clutched in her hand. In all her nightmares of their fate, this one had never occurred to her. If it had been herself, if Sir Arthur had wanted herself as mistress not wife, she would have done it for the sake of the rest.

But not Laura.

Never.

Which left only one resource, the thing she'd avoided throughout these terrible months.

The wishing stone.

She put the crown in her pocket, then slowly, stiffly, went up to her parents' silent bedroom. How she missed them. How furious she was with their fecklessness! Had they never thought, through all the jolly years of living for the moment what would happen to their children if they died?

Apparently not.

She ran her hand over the worn green coverlet, remembering how magical it had been as a child—a field to people with toy animals, or to set a paper house upon. A battlefield for her brothers' toy soldiers.

She shook herself, carried over a chair to stand on, and reached up into one dusty corner of the bed curtains to unhook a matching, green bag. Awkward because of the weight, but also because the thing had started its magic, she clambered down, then collapsed onto the chair to gather herself.

It was humming. That's how she thought of it, though no one else seemed able to hear the noise. Perhaps it was more of a vibration, like being in a coach speeding over cobbles.

Whatever it was, she hated it. She quickly put the bag on the bed so she wouldn't have to touch it.

Or not yet.

It had to be done, however.

Resolutely, she loosened the strings and lowered the bag around the crude stone statue.

It was years since she'd seen it and it still shocked her. Seven years, in fact, for she'd been fourteen when her mother had shown her the *sheelagh-ma-gig,* and explained where it was kept, why it was hidden, and the powers it possessed.

Seven years since Meg had found out that she had the horrible gift of using the wishing stone.

Not all the women of the line did. Her Aunt Maira had lacked the skill, and had resented the fact that Meg's mother had refused to ask it for wealth and rich suitors. Apparently, when Walter Gillingham had fallen in love with Meg's mother and swept her away, Aunt Maira had believed she'd used the stone for herself.

That was the cause of the split. It was not something she could have told Sir Arthur.

How could she tell anyone about the *sheelagh*—pagan magic and improper as well?

The ancient stone figurine was of a woman, a naked, grinning woman. Between her spread legs, she held herself—her intimate self—wide as if she wanted to swallow up the world.

According to Meg's mother, these *sheelagh-ma-gigs* had been placed in the walls of Irish churches, which Meg found rather hard to accept. She'd refuse to believe it, except that her generally light-hearted mother had been deathly serious when talking about the wishing stone. She'd said some *sheelaghs* still sat in church walls near the door, and that people still touched them for luck when going in to pray to the Christian God.

Most had been removed, however, by people trying to get rid of pagan influences, or just out of decency. Usually they were smashed, but some had found their way into private hands. Meg's mother had had no idea whether they all had powers as this one did.

This *sheelagh-ma-gig* was a wishing stone, and to the women of the family gifted with the power, it would grant wishes.

At a cost. Always at a cost.

One cost was the unpleasantness of the process—a sickening pain which usually caused a faint. That discomfort was brief, however, and could be borne. The other

cost came because it was a mischievous stone which always granted the wish with a sting in the tail.

The classic story was of the young woman who wished
for beauty. She received what she asked for, and found
herself shunned by her jealous friends, pestered by ardent men, and unable to be comfortable ever again.

Another woman asked the stone for a particular man
as husband, seeking to steal him from a friend. Her wish
was granted when her parents arranged the match, but
he never stopped loving the other, and eventually they
ran off together to the distress of all three families.

Meg's mother had explained it all to her not long after
she'd started her woman's courses. That, apparently, was
the time when the magic would appear if it appeared at
all. She'd insisted Meg try it, at least once.

Even at that age, Meg had been wary of such a thing,
and already disturbed by its palpable power. She'd
searched for an innocent wish, a harmless wish, and in
the end she'd asked for a special cherry cake that the
local baker made.

It came within the hour, but in the hands of the
baker's pimply son who brought it as a courting gift.
Too kind to just dismiss him, especially when she had in
a sense summoned him, Meg had had to endure his doting company for months before she convinced him that
she was bookish and boring, and he went off to pursue
another.

So now she studied the stone warily, wondering what
she should ask for, and if it was possible to avoid the
sting.

Money?

That's what they needed, but it could come in many
unpleasant ways.

Security?

A charity school or even the workhouse could provide
that. Even Sir Arthur might, for a while at least.

To make the stone do her bidding she had to form
her wish exactly as it should be.

The future of her siblings. That's what she wanted.
Their future as the children of a gentleman. Especially
seventeen-year-old Jeremy with his gifted mind, who
should already be at Oxford or Cambridge.

She framed a wish and went over and over it. It seemed too much to wish for, an impossible wish, but it was what they needed, and she believed in the power of the *sheelagh*.

Then, when she was ready, she found the special red candles her mother had kept for this purpose, and the tinderbox. Once a candle stub was burning steadily on the bedside table, gilding the gloomy room, she took a deep breath and made herself put her hands on the grimacing statue.

The power rushed into her, and the grimace seemed to become a scream of victory.

"I wish," she said as firmly as she could, "that within the week, we shall all be provided for as befits our station, and with honor and happiness."

She could not let go. She knew that from the last time, but for a moment, she tried.

Then she made herself surrender, plunge deep into the stone's wild energy. The power engulfed her, bringing the remembered shivers and aches, the dazedness and breathlessness. Dimly, she thought she should have locked the door in case one of the others came in and found her like this.

She wondered, too, if the stone could kill, for she felt she might die. She'd felt the same way last time, though, and survived.

This was worse, though. Stronger.

Perhaps the power of the stone equalled the dimension of the wish. And she had wished for so much! Was it possible to wish for *too* much?

Panicked, she again tried to pull free. What if it never let go? What if it sucked all life from her. She couldn't! She couldn't bear it . . . !

She became one with the *sheelagh's* primal scream.

Sick and dizzy, she came to herself, shaking. She still couldn't take away her hands. The *sheelagh's* power ebbed, but slowly, almost reluctantly, as if it resisted releasing its victim.

Victim?

Why think that, when the stone offered their only chance of escape? When the power sank, instead of snatching her hands away, Meg made herself stroke the figure, and whisper, "Thank you," before freeing herself and pulling the bag back around it.

She had to take a few moments to steady herself, but then she blew out the candle, put it away, and hung the heavy bag back in its secret corner.

Now it was just a matter of time.

It would happen, she was sure. Within the week, the wish would be granted.

Time alone would reveal the price.

Chapter 2

Owain Chancellor opened the bedroom door, hoping Sax was alone. He usually got rid of his women before falling asleep, but every now and then one managed to linger. This morning, however, the Earl of Saxonhurst sprawled over the entire width of his enormous rumpled bed, his disordered tawny hair and sleek muscles making him look like a sated lion.

It probably wasn't hard for him to persuade his lovers to leave. They'd only have to once experience his greedy dominance of the whole bed.

Owain pulled back the gold brocade curtains at one of the long windows to let in crisp, wintery sunshine.

Sax stirred, muttered a sleepy complaint, and opened one eye. "What?" It was delivered flatly without a hint of alarm, but contained the trace of a warning. There'd better be a good excuse.

"A letter from your grandmother."

The other eye opened and the head turned to the mantel clock—the one set in the belly of a fat, white, oriental figure. It made Owain think of an enormous, grinning maggot. "You woke me before ten for that? It can only be a deathbed plea for mercy and understanding."

"I regret to inform you that the Dowager Duchess of Daingerfield is in her usual health. But I think you'll want to read this without delay."

Sax closed his eyes again. "What an extraordinary assumption."

Owain rang the bell and waited. Soon a powdered and liveried footman backed in bearing a tray containing a

silver coffeepot and accompaniments. He was almost
bowled over from behind by a huge, enthusiastic, ugly
hound, who charged in to rest his head on the high bed
by Sax's head, teeth showing as if he'd found the most
tasty meal.

"We in trouble, then?" the footman asked cheerily,
setting his tray down. The short stature, lively face, and
big eyes had given him the nickname Monkey, and truth
to tell, the dog looked to weigh more than he did.

Sax didn't open his eyes. "You will be, Monk, if you
sound so cheerful at this hour."

"Some of us 'as been up since dawn, milord. Can't
stay miserable for 'ours just to suit you. Message from
the dowager duchess, they say."

"Have *they* managed to read it yet?"

"Mr. Chancellor's not let it out of 'is fingers, milord."

"Plague take you all. I don't know why I had you
taught to read. Go away."

Cheerfully, the footman left.

Owain poured a cup of the blisteringly strong coffee,
and stirred in three lumps of sugar.

Sax inhaled.

His eyes opened, and he snarled amiably at the
hound's teeth, causing the shaggy tail to thump on the
floor like a drum, then he rolled to sit up, stretched just
like a big cat, and took the cup.

He wasn't actually an enormous man, and in fine
clothes he looked just elegantly well-built, but he was
all muscle like a healthy predator, and nakedness made
the most of it.

He drank the whole cup in silence and held it out to
be refilled, casually greeting the dog, Brak, with his free
hand. Only then did he glance at the letter. "Since
you're not a fool, Owain, I am visited by a sense of
deep foreboding."

Owain offered him the unfolded sheet of paper. Sax
took it but fingered it as if trying to sense the contents.
"The old monster can't affect my income or my freedom.
So . . . ? She's not trying to visit, is she?"

"To the best of my knowledge, the duchess is celebrating the season at Daingerfield Court."

"Thank God." He was coming to wakeful alertness

almost visibly, Owain thought, changing from lion to tiger to his most dangerous form—intelligent man.

Sax drained his second cup of coffee before finally opening the letter and reading it. Owain watched with interest, for he really had no idea how his friend would handle this predicament.

"Plague and damnation," Sax said at last, but dazedly. Braced for one of the famous Saxonhurst rages, Owain breathed a sigh of relief.

When Sax looked up, for once he looked rather lost. "When's my birthday?"

"Tomorrow, as you well know. New Year's Eve."

He almost levitated from the tangled sheets to pace the room, magnificently naked. "The old bitch!"

It was said angrily, yes, but with a hint of admiration. Sax and his grandmother had been waging war for fifteen years, ever since she'd taken over the raising of him. It was a war for power between two of the stubbornest, most arrogant people Owain had ever met.

And two of the fiercest tempers.

He should have known the storm would come, especially as Brak was already wriggling backward under the bed.

Sax wrapped a gold curtain around his hand and pulled, bringing the rail half off the wall. Another fierce tug had it down in a shower of plaster dust.

Owain sighed and tugged the bell-rope again. Then he picked up his friend's gold-and-black banjan and threw it to him. Sax put in on without comment, still pacing and almost growling.

"I think she's got you this time."

Sax casually backhanded a squat, purple vase to shatter on the floor. "Devil take her, she has not. I promised to marry by my twenty-fifth birthday, and I will. A Torrance breaks many things, but never his word."

"By tomorrow?" Owain said, trying desperately to keep some sanity in the room. "Can't be done. Why the devil did you make such a cork-brained promise?"

"Because at twenty I was cork-brained like most men. And twenty-five seemed a dim and distant future!" The matching vase shattered. "Back then I was sure I'd soon fall in love with the perfect, pretty maiden." He impatiently kicked a shard from his path. "I've certainly done my best to find her."

"I thought you avoided maidens like the plague."

"Only since I discovered that they're after one thing. A coronet."

After a moment's thought, he plucked a yellow china cow off the mantel and threw it to shatter on the floor at the feet of the bunch of servants who had burst through the door armed with brushes, cloths, mops, and expectant expressions.

One maid started to sweep up pottery fragments. Menservants hurried to deal with the curtain. Owain noted wryly that all the indoor servants except the cooks had felt called to the tasks. No one liked to miss a Sax-onhurst rage. He'd never grown accustomed to the way Sax let his strange bunch of servants intrude on his private affairs like meddling relatives.

"She planned it, you know," Sax said, ignoring his staff and still pacing. He was also ignoring the fact that his loosely tied robe was scarcely decent, but then all the servants had seen everything before. That didn't stop the maids from casting appreciative glances.

One, Babs, who made no attempt to pretend shame about her previous profession, pulled a sprig of mistletoe from her pocket and tucked it optimistically into the deep fringe hanging around the tester bed.

"She deliberately sent that letter to arrive today to give me a day of anguish before the hour of doom." Sax picked up the matching orange bull from the other end of the mantelpiece. "Susie. Catch!" He tossed it to the one-eyed maid who wore a patch. She shrieked and grabbed for it. Then, quite deliberately, she let it fall.

With a cheeky grin, she said, "I had a crown on that one."

"That's cheating, my girl."

"You must have caught me on my blind side, milord. But watch where you're marching." She set to brushing the sharp fragments out of the way of his bare feet.

Sax duly stalked through the cleared path, seized a very real saber from the wall, unsheathed it, and impaled a pink satin cushion on the point. He then tossed it up and sliced it in two as it fell so downy feathers burst out to fill the room.

Laughing, Owain leaned back in his chair, propped his feet on the bed, and surrendered. It was a performance, really, and they all knew their parts.

Sax only ever allowed himself tantrums in this room, so they didn't keep any of the good stuff here. In fact, the servants scoured London for pieces worthy of destruction and placed them here at the ready. As Susie implied, they had a lottery going belowstairs on which piece would be next for destruction.

The whole household regarded Sax's occasional fiery outbursts with a kind of proprietal pride. Owain rather enjoyed them himself. He had a guinea riding on his belief that a simpering shepherdess on a small bamboo table would survive till Easter. Sax was generally very kind to women.

His grandmother being the notable exception.

Cook had bet an equal amount that the table itself would go. It was an unfortunate piece lacquered in lurid green and pink. Owain watched his friend eye it and his sword. Could he destroy it without smashing the shepherdess?

Perhaps that's why Sax dropped the sword on the bed and turned instead to a large portrait of a very ugly, sour-faced monk. Would he . . . ?

He jerked it off the wall so the hook flew through the air, then smashed it over the back of a ponderous chair.

Owain offered a prayer of thanks. He'd been ready to smash the thing himself. How anyone could sleep, never mind make love, with that warty, scowling face looking down, he didn't know.

"A Torrance," repeated Sax, slightly out of breath, sweeping blond hair off his forehead, "breaks a great many things, but never his word."

"So it's said."

Sax turned on him. "So it *is*." He scanned the audience of servants. "Where's Nims. *Nims!*" he bellowed. "Come and shave me, you damned idler!"

Since most of the show was clearly over, the servants set to clearing up properly. But slowly, in case there might be an encore.

Sax's stocky valet backed in from the next room, agile despite a wooden leg, steaming water jug in hand, cloth over arm. "I'm coming, I'm coming! How could I be expected to be ready for you at this hour, then?" He looked around and rolled his eyes. "That much trouble, eh? Sit down. Sit down. You want shaving, or you want your throat cut?"

A gray-blue parrot flew in behind him and landed on Sax's shoulder. *"Hello, my lovely,"* it said in Sax's exact voice.

Sax relaxed and smiled, letting the adoring bird nuzzle around his ear. "Hello, my lovely." Then he sobered. "Devil take it. Knox will throw a fit."

Indeed, Knox the parrot was glaring at the servants. *"Women! Women! Road to hell."*

As Sax sat in a chair so he could be shaved, Babs sashayed over, taking a hazelnut out of her pocket. "Go on, Knox, you love me really."

The bird eyed her, swaying. *"Eve. Delilah."*

She offered the nut, just out of reach. "Be nice, Knox."

"Delilah!"

She waited, and when the bird muttered, *"Pretty lady,"* she gave him the nut and blew him a kiss. He turned his back to enjoy it.

"See," she said to everyone. "You can handle any male if you find out what he really wants."

"Babs," said Sax, "you're a walking warning to the males of any species. But how, I wonder, did you find time with Knox to train him?"

Babs didn't answer, but she winked at the valet. To Owain's astonishment, Nims blushed. Jupiter, but this place would drive him crazy if he wasn't already beyond hope.

"Shift yourself, Knox," said the valet, flapping a snowy cloth. When the parrot was safe on the back of the chair, he wrapped the cloth around his employer's shoulders and started to shave him.

"Start naming names, Owain," Sax said.

"Names?"

"Potential brides."

Knox jumped. *"Marry not! Marry not!"*

Sax rolled his eyes. "Names. And for heaven's sake try not to use words that'll set him off."

With a familiar feeling of being stuck in a mad house, Owain took out his notebook. Knox's previous owner had trained him to warn against involvement with women, particularly marital involvement. Sax was right. A bride in the house was likely to give the bird a fit.

"What kind of names?" he asked.

"Potential . . . partners in connubial bliss."

"What sort?"

Nims was stroking the sharp blade over Sax's cheek so he spoke calmly. "One who'll go through the ceremony with me tomorrow. Which means just about any of 'em."

Knox must have felt Sax's tensions, for he hopped onto his shoulder and rubbed soothingly against his ear. Sax relaxed and stroked the bird. "Who was the one who sprained her ankle outside the door a couple of weeks ago?"

"Miss Cathcart. You said you wanted to throttle her."

"I just wanted to twist her ankle properly for her."

Owain wrote on a clean page. "You want me to send a note to say you will call on Miss Cathcart's father? I'm not even sure they're still in town."

"Probably few of them are. Oh, 'struth."

He snapped his left hand and Brak slithered hesitantly out from under the bed, teeth still bared as if ready for the kill, but eyes anxious. The poor hound couldn't help it. He'd been born with a deformity of the mouth that made him look fearsome. Unfortunately, he was an abject coward, and even now was hesitating, sniffing the air for trouble.

"It's all right, Brak," Sax said. "Come on."

The dog shook his massive bulk and walked over to sit nobly by Sax, as if he'd never known a moment's fear in his life. He and the parrot eyed one another, companionable rivals for the attention of their adored owner. Owain wondered if Sax ever felt strain at satisfying their demands, and the demands of all the other loving charity cases around him.

Sax stroked the dog's head. "Most people will be at their country estates for Christmas. Why the devil was I born at this time of year? I can't see how the dragon could have planned it, but it's typical. Anyway, there must be better than Miss Cathcart. She giggles. All the time. Start listing names, Owain. Would-be-countesses in the Home Counties. If I have to, I'll ride out into the country to settle it."

"I know you feel strongly about your given word, but—"

"I will not break it."

Owain shook his head. He suspected that this time the Dowager Duchess of Daingerfield had won a round. Sax wouldn't find a bride in a day, or not one he wanted. He'd have to either marry poorly or admit to the duchess that he could not keep his word.

He'd never do that.

So, he was about to make a disastrous marriage.

Owain began to take the situation seriously. "Lady Mary Derby," he said, writing the name down. "Lady Caroline Northern. Lady Frances Holmes, Lady Georgina Pitt-Stanley. . . ."

A few pages later, his scrabbling memory could only come up with, "Miss Witherton?"

"Plague take it, Owain, she's forty if she's a day."

"Age doesn't matter if you just want to keep your word and thwart your grandmother. You like her company."

"If I'm going to do this, I'll have one who can at least produce a brat or two." Nims took off the cloth, and Sax rose. "I know my duty. Go over them again."

"Oh, for pity's sake!" But Owain flipped back the pages and read through his list. At the end, he closed the book. "Well?"

Sax was leaning against a wall, arms folded, parrot and dog in attendance like some strange heraldic collection. "The dragon should have called my dear uncle Grendel."

When Owain looked blank, Sax said, "Because then she'd be Grendel's mother. The monster from *Beowulf*." He shook his head. "You need to broaden your mind. And I need to marry."

He flinched at the same time as Knox shrieked, *"Marry not! Wedlock is a padlock!"*

Still he added, "Tomorrow."

The servants were all still hovering, pretending they had things to do.

"Let's test Knox's tolerance." Sax seized Babs around the waist, swung her beneath the mistletoe, and kissed her heartily.

The bird flew to a safer perch on the bed, but didn't scream one of his warnings. Instead, he said hopefully, *"Wanna nut."*

"Good idea, Knox." Babs reached beneath Sax's banjan.

With a laugh, he slapped her hand away. "Now, now. Let's not push the poor bird too far. Anyway, you're reformed."

Babs winked. "That just means I don't charge for it anymore, milord."

"The deuce! No wonder my menservants seem half asleep most of the time."

"Go on with you. It also means I can be right particular." She casually pushed Sax down onto the bed and strolled away, broad hips swaying, to stand close to Nims.

The place really was a madhouse, but Sax never seemed to care. In fact, he had created it with his careless kindness and indulgence, and his total indifference to privacy. He said servants always knew your business anyway, and that they could be useful because they knew everyone else's business, too.

Owain didn't think even the most well-informed servants could be of much help in this.

He tucked away his notebook and, with little hope, decided to try reason. "Sax, perhaps this time you should just let the old besom score a hit. She'll gloat a bit, but at least you won't be shackled for life to a woman you dislike."

Sax swung off the bed, leaving Knox there to play with the crumpled letter. Careless of the crowded room, he dropped the banjan, and pulled on the drawers and shirt Nims held out. "You didn't read the whole letter, did you?"

"Of course not."

"You're my secretary, Owain. Reading my letters is permissible."

"Not your personal ones."

"You should break this bad habit of propriety. If you'd read the whole thing, you'd know there was a second part to my promise. I was to be shackled for life by my twenty-fifth birthday, or I was to allow my grandmother to choose the leg-iron."

Owain snatched the letter from Knox's inquisitive beak. After a quick read through, he said, "What a damned fool promise to make!"

Sax was tucking in his shirt. "Oh, quite. But I gave my word and I will keep it. I will not, however, let my grandmother choose my"—he turned deliberately toward the bed—"bride."

"A bride is a bridle!"

"Quite. Therefore, I will choose my own bridle, and by tomorrow."

Owain paced the room himself. "It can't be done, Sax! Even if you decide on one of these young women, she won't consent to do it in such a scrambling way."

"You think not?"

Owain halted. "I suppose some of them would. But imagine the talk."

"To the devil with the talk."

"Then imagine putting the matter to the young lady and her family."

"That," Sax admitted, "is not a pleasant prospect. But it is immensely preferable to putting myself in the dragon's claws. The only question is, which lady receives this dubious honor?" He turned suddenly to the grinning audience of servants. "Well? I'm sure you have opinions."

"Aye, milord," said Monkey. "Choose the one wot brings the most money."

"Such a pragmatist. Do you plan to choose the woman with the most money?"

"I would if I could find one, milord, even if she 'ad a crooked back and warts."

Susie, who definitely lacked those features, kicked him in the shin. He cursed and hopped, but he was grinning at the same time.

"But, I don't need money."

"What *do* you need, then, milord?" asked Susie.

"An excellent question." He sat again so Nims could arrange his cravat. Brak contentedly flopped over his stockinged feet. "Good health. Good teeth. Moderation in her habits—I have no desire to end up trying to curb a wastrel wife."

"Trouble and strife! Trouble and strife!"

"Let's pray you're wrong, Knox. And I'm afraid you're going to have to get used to this. Discretion," Sax continued. "I don't care for the idea of fighting duels over her either. So," he said, turning slightly toward Owain, "which one fits?"

"God knows. You've surely been in a better position than I to check their teeth."

"Devil a bit. I've been avoiding intimacy with hopeful young leeches like the plague. But you can cross off Lady Frances and Lady Georgina, and Miss Stewkesly, too. I've heard rumors about all of them suggesting discretion isn't part of their character."

Owain dutifully crossed off three names. "Perhaps I should just put the rest into a hat and you can pick one." Hastily, he said, "No—"

But Sax was already saying, "Why not?"

Owain cursed his hasty tongue.

Susie spoke up. "Beggin' your pardon, milord . . ."

Both Owain and Sax looked at her in surprise, not because she'd spoken—in this household the servants seemed to feel at liberty to say whatever they pleased—but because she sounded nervous about it.

"Yes?"

The plump maid tangled her fingers in her apron. "Beggin' your pardon, milord, but if you really don't care who you m—" —she rolled her eye at the bird— "go to the altar with. . . ."

"I didn't quite say that."

"But . . ."

Sax smiled at her quite gently. "If this is a proposal, Susie, the answer is no. You wouldn't like it."

She went bright red and giggled. "Go on with you! As if I would. And anyway . . ." She flashed a coy look at Monkey, who turned as red as she. "Be that as it may," she continued rather stiffly, "I just thought you might better choose a young lady who has need of a husband."

His cravat arranged to perfection, Sax stood, easing his feet out from under the dog. "Bring a cuckoo into the nest? On no account."

"No, milord. Of course not! But a young lady who's fallen on hard times, like. You wouldn't have to beg her, then, would you? She'd be the one who'd be grateful."

"A very neat point."

Seeing his friend's interest, Owain wasn't sure whether to interfere or not. His position was a complex one—part friend, part administrator, but one of his unwritten tasks was to stop Sax following impulse into disaster.

Sax seemed in control of his intelligence, however. "I gather you have someone in mind, Susie."

"Yes, milord."

"A lady?"

"Yes, milord. At least, her father was a gentleman scholar."

Nims held out an embroidered waistcoat and Sax put his arms into it. "Certainly sounds promising. How has she come to be in straitened circumstances?"

"Her parents died, milord. Suddenly, a few months back. Turned out there wasn't much money. So there's poor Miss Gillingham with her brothers and sisters to take care of, and no money to speak of."

"A heart-wrenching tale. How do you come to know about it?" Nims was fastening the silver buttons and Knox had flown to perch on Sax's outstretched hand.

"My sister was maid there, milord. She stayed on for a while without wages, she felt so sorry for them, but in the end she had to take another post. But I'm not saying you should . . . form a union with this Miss Gillingham. I really don't know much about her. Just that there must be many others like her. Glad to go to the altar, even in a hurry, and grateful for the chance."

Knox on his hand, Sax made a contemplative circuit of the room. "She'd not expect false protestations of love," he said to Owain. "She wouldn't need to be sweet-talked into it. She'd be less likely to be extravagant or flighty. . . ."

"She could be ugly as sin."

Sax looked at Susie.

"My sister never mentioned her looks, milord."

"Where is your sister?"

"Out of town. Her family's gone to their Shropshire estate for the season."

After a moment, Sax put the parrot on his shoulder and turned to Owain, hand held out. "Coin."

Not at all happy with the situation, Owain dug out a florin and tossed it over.

Sax snared it out of the air. "Heads, it's Miss Gillingham. Tails, it's whichever of those other names I pull out of a hat."

Before Owain could protest, the coin spun glittering through the air to be caught and slapped down on the back of Sax's hand. "Heads!" he said, and flicked the two-shilling piece over to Susie. "Go and inform Miss Gillingham of the pleasures in store for her."

"Me?" Susie squeaked.

"You. And to sweeten the pot, if she goes through with it tomorrow, I'll give you and Monk enough to set up your own place."

The two servants shared a dazed look. "Really, milord?" asked the footman.

"Word of a Torrance." Sax turned to Owain. "Get me a special license—"

"But . . ."

Sax swung back to Susie. "She is of age?"

"Turned twenty-one near a year back."

"On the shelf," Owain pointed out, more uneasy about this by the moment.

"I don't give a fig. Susie, what's her first name?"

"I don't know, milord."

"Find out when you get her agreement. Owain, start on the special license. Susie, on your way and talk her into it. And look sharp. There's bound to be a bushel of paperwork to do. Where does she live?"

"Mallett Street, milord. Down south of St. James' Park. But—"

"Respectable but modest. How very auspicious." Deftly shifting Knox from hand to hand, he put his arms into the dark blue jacket Nims was patiently holding. "Find out her parish—we'll need that for the license, too, I think—and tell her the ceremony will take place there tomorrow morning at eleven."

"But, milord—"

Owain definitely felt it was time to take a hand. "Sax, wouldn't it be fair to give the lady a chance to meet you before she makes up her mind? And then you'll have a chance to meet her."

"If I buy a pig in a poke, I don't see why she shouldn't. Neither of us has time to make a rational matter out of it. It's in the hands of fate."

"This isn't a suitable matter for coin-tossing! It's for life, you know."

"Just makes the gamble more interesting."

"What are you going to do if she refuses?"

Sax put his hands on his hips and surveyed his household. "Let's establish the rules of the game. If Miss Gillingham refuses today, I'll pick one of those fashionable hopefuls out of the hat and do my best to persuade her. If she agrees, then backs out at the last minute, I'll grovel to the duchess and accept my fate. If Miss Gillingham comes up to scratch, I'll bind myself to her in holy wedlock however she turns out to be."

Knox flapped to the bed to pace a warning. *"Wedlock's a padlock! Wedlock's a padlock."*

"It's supposed to be, Knox. Bound for life, for better or worse. You're going to have to get used to it, just as I am." He took the parrot in his hand and stroked it, looking around with his charming smile, the one that could and did break hearts.

"You are all witnesses. Let fate decide!"

Chapter 3

Meg ignored the repeated rapping on the front door and went on patching the sole of Rachel's shoe with a scrap of leather. It could be Sir Arthur come back a day early, and if it wasn't, it would be a neighbor to whom they owed money. One of the most painful things about her situation was that most of her creditors were from local businesses, people she'd known all her life.

They had a right to speak with her. They had a right to fair payment for their services, too, but she'd sold everything they could do without. The house had been rented furnished, so she couldn't sell her parents' bed, or the scarce-used parlor chairs.

In Christian charity, most of their creditors seemed to be leaving them alone for the season, but once Twelfth Night passed, she knew they'd be back. It hardly mattered because before then—tomorrow in fact—she'd have to face Sir Arthur.

For the first days after wishing on the stone, she'd answered the door eagerly, expecting someone or something in answer her prayer. A distant relative come to offer them all a home. A local benefactor wanting to give them an annuity so they could struggle on. Instead, she'd been battered and bruised by the pleas and anger of people who were suffering because she could not pay her family's debts.

The knocker fell silent, and she relaxed a little, stabbing the big needle through the leather. She feared the shoe would be terribly uncomfortable, but at least it wouldn't let in rain. Then her hands fell hopelessly still. What did it matter? She'd have to beg assistance of the parish, and no matter what help they provided, it would doubtless include footwear of some kind.

She really had pinned her hopes on the stone, especially after the draining effect it had had on her. How could it have been for nothing? Now, however, panic ate at her.

Tomorrow Sir Arthur would return for his answer and—

A sharp knock on the kitchen door made her jerk in her seat. Swiveling, she saw that the impudent caller had come around to the back and was peering in the kitchen window.

Well, really!

Then the nose squashed against the grimy glass, and she saw a black patch over one eye! Gracious.

The person rapped at the glass. "Miss Gillingham?"

The grotesque face made Meg even more tempted to hide away, but she'd been caught. Praying it wasn't some bully sent to try to force money out of her, Meg cautiously opened the door.

It was no bully, but it was also no one she knew.

The plump young woman wore a respectable cloak and gown, with a black straw bonnet on her brown curls. The effect was marred by that startling black patch. Poor creature. If she was seeking charity, however, she'd certainly come to the wrong place.

The woman smiled brightly. "There you are!"

Meg stepped back, unaccustomed these days to bright smiles or enthusiasm. "Can I help you?"

"Are you Miss Gillingham?"

"Yes."

The young woman dropped a curtsy. "Then could I have a word with you, miss? I'm Susie Kegworth. My sister Mary used to work for you."

Ah. Meg saw a resemblance to the family's former maid, and remembered hearing some story of an eye injury some years ago that had ruined her sister's looks, and her chances of good employment.

Oh dear. Even though she couldn't help, she could be polite. "Come in, please. How is Mary?"

"Doing fine, miss. Very happy in her situation."

As Meg led the way to the table and indicated a chair there, she began to take mild pleasure in the unexpected visit. It had been a long time since she'd sat down to chat with a guest. What a shame the only tea leaves were days old and overused.

"How can I help you, Susie?" She quickly added, "If you've come about a place—"

"Oh no, miss. I have a good position as upstairs maid to the Earl of Saxonhurst."

"Oh yes. I remember Mary mentioning it. I gather the earl is kind—"

"That he is, miss."

"But somewhat eccentric."

"Oh, I wouldn't say that!" The maid seemed strangely alarmed by the idle comment.

Meg smiled to soothe her. "It's just that Mary mentioned that he allowes his servants great latitude." And, of course, it was extraordinary that a nobleman hire a maid with such an obvious deformity. Meg was having difficulty not staring at the patch.

"We all do our work properly, miss. But he likes to . . . or at least, he doesn't seem to mind if we take an interest, like."

"Take an interest?" Meg didn't normally gossip, but this conversation was a brief escape from grim reality.

"We always know what's going on—well, servants always do, don't they? But he don't seem to mind if we say our piece on it. Which is why I'm here," she added in a rush.

"Oh. Why are you here?"

The maid licked her lips nervously. "Well, you see, Miss Gillingham, the earl's in a bit of a pickle."

Meg stared. Had the maid come to offer *her* a position? Did the earl need a governess? With a spark of excitement, she wondered if this, at last, was the *sheelagh's* solution.

But then the spark died. How could she possibly support a family of five on a governess's salary?

"I can't imagine how I can help an earl in a pickle."

"Oh, but you can, Miss Gillingham! I swear it's true." The maid took a deep breath. "You see—and I know this'll sound peculiar—the earl promised his grandmother—a right wicked old barrel of brimstone, and that's the truth—that he'd marry by twenty-five. But he forgot about it, him being only twenty when he said it.

And on New Year's Eve—tomorrow—he turns twenty-five."

"I see." It seemed the only thing to say, but Meg didn't see. She was surprised, however, to discover that the eccentric earl was so young. She'd always supposed him to be doddering.

"Well, miss,"—the maid leaned forward over the table—"this morning the earl gets a letter from his grandmother reminding him of his promise. And that he'd said if he weren't married by his birthday, he'd let her pick his bride."

"And he intends to stand by this?"

"Oh, yes! He says a Torrance stands true to his word."

"Then we must hope his grandmother's choice of bride will suit him. I really don't see—"

The maid shook her head. "They hate one another, miss. Don't know why exactly, but that's not too strong a word. The dowager'll choose the worst possible woman in the kingdom."

"Oh, surely not," said Meg, reluctantly intrigued by the situation. It was good enough for a play.

"I suppose she'll choose one young enough to breed. Strong feelings about the succession, she has, even though it's not her title that's hanging. She's the earl's mother's mother, you see."

Head whirling, Meg tried to stick to the main point. "If the earl made such a promise, then he should have kept track of it. I don't see how I can help."

The young woman wriggled as if her stays had suddenly begun to pinch. Then she blurted out, "He wants to marry *you,* miss."

Meg was literally struck speechless, left turning the words in her head, seeking another meaning for them.

But the maid was already carrying on. "That doesn't say it right. The thing is, Miss Gillingham, he's determined to marry someone tomorrow to thwart his grandmother. He's got a list of society ladies, but there's none of them he really fancies. That's clear as crystal. So I thought . . . You're probably going to be angry about this," she admitted, face cherry red, "but I was only trying to do a kindness! I thought, if he was going to marry just anyone, why shouldn't he marry someone who really needed it? So I suggested you."

Meg slumped back in her seat. The maid was certainly flustered and embarrassed, but she didn't seem to be insane. Her employer, however . . .

Eccentric didn't begin to describe it.

"Susie, is this some sort of prank?"

"No, miss! Honest. Cross my heart and hope to die!" And the maid made a cross just above her ample left breast.

"You are seriously trying to persuade me that an earl wants to marry me—an unknown, unseen, penniless woman—tomorrow. It isn't even possible. There would have to be banns. Even a license must take time."

"A special license. Mr. Chancellor's already started on it. He's the earl secretary. Sort of. His friend, too. And adviser."

"And he advised *this*?"

Susie pulled a face. "He wasn't happy about it, and that's the truth. But he didn't have any better suggestion."

Agitation pushed Meg up from her chair to roam the kitchen. "Does the earl know me, then?"

Vague fantasies stirred of being admired from afar, but she knew the answer without waiting for it. She was not the sort of lady gentlemen developed a secret passion for. Years ago she'd come to realize that while there was nothing about her to repulse men, there was nothing to drive them distracted, either.

As expected, the maid shook her head.

"So why has he chosen me for this extraordinary role?"

"Because I suggested you, miss."

"What did you tell him of me?" The idea that this maid might have painted a fancy picture to tempt the earl appalled her.

"Just what I heard from my sister, miss. That you're a kind, steady lady who's doing her best to keep her family together despite tragedy."

"Good grief. I sound like a suffering heroine."

"Well, it can't have been easy."

"No," said Meg with a sigh. "It's not been easy."

"So you'll do it?"

"No, of course I won't! It's out of the question."

"Why?"

"Why?" Meg shrugged hopelessly. "Even if this were a real offer—"

"It *is*!"

"Even so, I couldn't possibly marry a man I've never met."

The maid fixed her with a look. "Beggin' your pardon, miss, but beggars can't be choosers." Meg started at that echo of the beadle's words, and at the memory of the alternatives.

"Marry the earl," the maid continued, "and you'll be provided for as befits your station, you and your brothers and sisters."

Meg sat down, dazed. The maid had just repeated the words of her wish. But surely the stone couldn't influence the aristocracy, or create promises made years ago?

As far as she knew, however, the stone could do anything. Her mother had said that for the stone's magic, time didn't matter. It made no sense, but then nothing about the stone did.

"Why are you so set on this?" she asked.

The young woman colored. "I'll tell the truth, miss. He's offered a reward of sorts. If you marry him tomorrow, he'll set me and Monkey up so we can marry. We've the chance to buy the inn at High Hillford, you see—"

"You want to marry a monkey?" Meg was almost relieved to realize that the maid was mad.

"No!" Susie laughed, blushing. "It's just his nickname. Monkey. The earl calls him Monk, which is kind of him because he don't much like Monkey, though it's a hard habit to get out of. His real name's Edgar. Do you think I should try to call him Edgar?"

"Yes, I suspect you should." Meg, however, was thrown back into having this be real. Into having to think it through. "There's clearly something wrong with the earl if he has to bribe you to find a bride for him. Is he mad? Deformed? Depraved?"

The maid's eyes almost bulged. "Heavens, no. Give you me word, Miss Gillingham. If he were to stand in

Hyde Park tomorrow and offer himself up as husband, there'd be ladies killed in the rush."

"Then, *why*?"

The maid heaved a hugh sigh and held up a plump hand. "One," she said, counting on her fingers, "he's met the likely ones and not fallen in love with any of them. Two, it would be an awkward business trying to explain to them and their families why he has to marry in such a hurry. They'd do it, but he doesn't like starting out that way."

"But he wouldn't mind starting out that way with me?"

"The obligations would be mutual, miss, if you see what I mean."

"Ah," Meg said. "Pride."

She understood pride. She had plenty of it herself, which was why she was trying desperately to keep her family together against all odds.

Susie nodded. "He has his pride, that's for sure. Haughty as the devil, some say. But I don't see him that way," she added quickly.

"If he discusses these matters with the servants and takes their suggestions, I don't suppose you do." Meg was trying to think coherently about all this, trying to take it seriously, but she couldn't. "It really doesn't make sense, you know."

"It does if you know him. You see"—Susie leaned forward again—"he likes to take chances, Sax does." Doubtless because of Meg's surprise at the name, she added, "Everyone calls him Sax, though us servants don't to his face, of course."

"I don't see that there's any 'of course' about this extraordinary situation."

"You'll see." Before Meg could protest that, Susie added, "He treats life like an endless game. Not that he neglects his responsibilities, but he doesn't like to always do the expected. He makes decisions by tossing a coin or rolling dice. He doesn't gamble for high stakes, but he'll use cards and dice to risk other things."

"Are you certain he shouldn't be in an asylum?"

Susie giggled. "Oh, miss!" But then she sobered. "It's

a true offer, though, and you'd be a fool to turn it down."

"A fool? To turn down the offer to marry an eccentric, possibly a lunatic, sight unseen?"

"A very rich eccentric."

Money. The root of all evil, but so very important when one didn't have any. The maid was right. Here was the chance to save her family from disaster—the chance, surely, she had asked for. How silly to sit here quibbling. After all, she had been willing to become Sir Arthur Jakes's mistress to save them all. Could this be any worse? At least she was offered marriage.

She stood. "I will come with you now to meet the earl."

The maid, however, stayed in her chair. "I'm sorry, miss, but he says not. If you want to do it, you're to turn up at the church tomorrow at eleven o'clock."

"What church?"

"Whatever your parish church is. I'm to find out."

"This *is* insane! What possible reason can there be for us not to meet? Unless there is something about him that will repulse me. But then," she added thoughtfully, "I could refuse to go through with the ceremony. . . ."

"Exactly. I don't know his reasons, miss, except that it's the way he is. He flipped a coin, and it pointed to you. If you don't agree, he'll pick a name of one of the society ladies out of a hat. But if you say you will, then don't go through with it, he'll let his grandmother have her way."

"Flipped a coin!" But then, was that any worse than making a wish on a risqué statue? "Describe the earl to me."

"Oh, he's a handsome man, miss. Tall, well built."

A *strong* maniac.

"And his nature?"

"He's a pleasant enough gentleman. Right charming to the ladies when he's of a mind to be."

And when he's not? Meg wondered, a little shiver running down her back. "You say he's handsome. Is he dark, pale . . . ?"

The maid wrinkled her brow. "Well, he's sort of yellow, miss."

"Yellow? You mean blond?"

"Sort of. His skin's darker than most gentlemen's because he loves to sail in the summer and don't have a care to wearing hats. His hair's a darkish kind of blond—from the sun, see—and his eyes are kind of yellow, too. Yellowish brown."

"Are his teeth yellow, too?" Meg was beginning to think she knew why the earl had trouble finding a bride. This story was perhaps largely a face-saving exercise.

Susie giggled. "No, miss! White and strong and healthy. Are yours? It was one of his things he had to have."

Meg stared. "Are you supposed to inspect them?"

Susie actually leaned away. "Er . . . no, miss. It was just a comment. He didn't say anything about *your* teeth."

"So I should hope! He is undoubtedly mad. Tell me the truth. Will I and my family be safe with him?"

"Safe?" The maid's astonishment was reassuring. "Of course you will, miss! Even in his tempers he never touches *people*."

"His tempers?"

The maid looked as if she wished she'd held her tongue. "Oh, he just flies off the handle now and then and smashes things. But only things."

Meg sank back into her chair. In a strange way these problems comforted her. If the Earl of Saxonhurst had been a normal gentleman, she would have been more suspicious. Now, despite the maid's attempts to paint a good picture, it was clear that he was a gentleman who had his problems. She could put up with his foibles and thus earn his support of her family.

"I have one condition."

"A condition, miss?"

Meg knew she was in no position to bargain, but the earl did seem to be in a predicament. "I want Lord Saxonhurst's word that my brothers and sisters will live with me under his roof, and be assisted by him to make their way in life."

"Oh, I'm sure he would—"

"I'll have it in writing. Wait here."

Meg went to her father's study—an empty shell now,

stripped of the pictures and books, all sold for what they could raise. His engraved stationery remained, however, for that would bring little. She pulled out a sheet, then realized that the silver standish had gone, and the ink with it. She dug out the stub of a pencil.

She had to sharpen it, and almost cut herself, her hand shook so much. She was mad to consider this; mad not to grab it.

When she sat to write, she had to wait for her nerves to steady. Her writing must look clear and determined.

> *To the Earl of Saxonhurst,*
> *My lord, I am surprised and honored by your offer of marriage and find that my situation obliges me to give it serious consideration. Before I can come to a final decision, however, I must have your assurance that my two brothers and two sisters will live with us after marriage, that they will be educated as befits their station as ladies and gentlemen, and be provided with modest sums to enable them to proceed in life.*

Meg hesitated here, chewing the end of the pencil. She knew what she had to write, but feared to commit herself. With a steadying breath, she continued:

> *If you can give me that assurance, my lord, I will be at St. Margaret's church at eleven tomorrow and will marry you.*

She looked it over, tempted to tear it up. But then she remembered Sir Arthur's designs on Laura.

She had no choice.

On the whole, she told herself, she had escaped quite lightly. The sting in the *sheelagh's* magical solution seemed likely to be bearable. Of course, she still knew little of her future husband, but the maid—Susie— seemed honest, and her sister had been a good person.

They were only servants, however, with no power over a lord.

Her mind was swinging backward and forward like an off-balance pendulum and quite predictably, giving her a headache. She wished desperately that her parents were here to advise her.

But if they were, none of this would be happening.

Laura, she reminded herself.

That was the simple, conclusive reason to go through with this.

And she herself would have a home and family. Since men didn't pursue her, she'd pretended not to care, but she had always wanted marriage and children. An eccentric, rather ugly earl was a small price to pay.

Moreover, she reminded herself, if he turned out to be worse than that—foul, drooling, clearly insane—she simply wouldn't say her vows.

Suddenly worried about the legalities of written promises, she picked up her pencil and added, *if we find each other congenial.*

There. After another teetering hesitation, she folded the paper, took it downstairs, and gave to the maid.

"He might not reply, miss. He's a devil for keeping to his arrangements."

It was tempting to back down, but if the earl wasn't going to support and house her siblings, there was no point to this. "If he doesn't reply as I wish, he will have to draw his bride by lot and hope he can persuade her to the altar."

The maid chuckled. "You are a one. I think you'll do." She tucked the note in a pocket. "I need your full name, miss. For the license."

"But I haven't committed myself yet."

"Just because you have a license doesn't mean you have to use it, and apparently things like that take time."

Meg was as much reluctant to tell her flowery baptismal names as she was to commit herself. But it couldn't be helped. "Minerva Eithne Gillingham," she admitted.

"Pretty," said the beaming maid, and hurried out.

Meg collapsed back into her chair, wondering what on earth she had done.

When Laura and the twins burst in, mid-argument, it was a welcome relief.

"Sit!" Meg shouted. Richard and Rachel fell into chairs at the table, two grubby urchins ready to be fed.

Meg was beginning to think of them as like baby birds, mouths always open.

She cut thick slices of bread, spread them with dripping, then poured boiling water over the old tea leaves and served the weak brew. They ate and drank without complaint, but she knew they couldn't go on like this. And tomorrow Sir Arthur would be back.

With a shiver, she knew she was going to have to marry the eccentric Earl of Saxonhurst, even if he was foul and drooling.

She heaved their iron pot onto the stove, and set the twins to building up the fire with the scrap wood they'd found on their walk. That was the real purpose of their walks these days—foraging. London wasn't like the country, though. Little went to waste, and hundreds sought it. The twins had grown quite clever at finding bits of wood for the daily cooking fire and took pride in it, but they shouldn't have to be thinking of such things at their age.

It was soup for dinner. She'd bought some vegetables—mostly potatoes and cabbage—and the butcher had given her a shinbone. Charity, but she was beyond pride. It would give a little substance to the meal, and the pot would probably stretch until tomorrow, when one way or another, their fate would be sealed.

Bread she always had because her earlier stone-brought suitor now ran his father's bakery. He was married, and to a very pleasant young woman, but perhaps some trace of the magic lingered. Whenever Meg went into the shop, he always had old loaves he needed to get rid of cheap. They always seemed to be remarkably fresh, too.

Even so, Sir Arthur aside, her family couldn't go on like this. They were all thinner, and that couldn't be good for growing children.

The knock on the back door froze her to the spot.

What if *he'd* come in response to her note?

What if he saw her like this and instantly changed his mind? She pushed uselessly at the tendrils of hair straggling over her hot face.

What if he was a monster she simply couldn't endure? While she hesitated, Richard ran carelessly to open the door. Susie stepped in, brightly smiling. "All's set!" she announced, pulling out a different piece of paper.

Aware of her fascinated siblings, Meg took it with unsteady hands and broke the crested seal. Smoothing out the sheet she saw the same crest embossed into the heavy paper. The handwriting was a little careless, sloping to the right and with vigorous loops. There was nothing palsied about it, however, or suggestive of a disordered mind. Of course, he had a secretary who might write for him.

She looked at the signature, a boldly scrawled Saxonhurst. Though even more careless, as signatures often were, it was in the same hand as the rest.

> *My dear Miss Gillingham,*
> *I am delighted that you are inclined to accept my offer of marriage, and happy to assure you that your brothers and sisters will instantly become as my own, to be raised and educated with the same care, and suitably provided for.*
>
> À demain,
> *Saxonhurst.*

Meg read it through again, though it was direct enough. It even included a clear recognition of his offer of marriage that she could take to a court of law and use to claim damages. Susie was right. He was a rash man.

But the handwriting soothed her. It had been her observation that handwriting indicated personality, and the earl's showed nothing too terrible. She could handle a rash, impetuous man with eccentric ways. And if he was physically unattractive, she certainly had no right to balk at that.

"Very well," she said to the maid. "Tomorrow at eleven."

Susie's smile was blinding. "You won't regret it, Miss Gillingham! You'll have all the servants on your side if he gives you any trouble."

As the door banged shut, Meg sank into a chair. *Gives me any trouble?* Oh dear . . .

"What's happening at eleven o'clock tomorrow?" Rachel demanded rather shrilly.

How scared the twins were. She'd thought she was doing a better job of hiding the seriousness of the situation.

She called up a bright smile. "I'm getting married."

They all just stared at her and she laughed, a genuine laugh of relief. Whatever the consequences, they were surely better than the worst. "I'm not mad, sweethearts! I'm getting married. We'll move to a big house. There'll be no more scrimping and saving, and you'll have good food to eat."

The twins still looked doubtful. "Truly?"

"Truly!"

"But who?" asked Laura, rather pale. "Not . . . not Sir Arthur."

Meg leaped up to hug her fiercely, thanking heaven for their escape. "Not Sir Arthur. The Earl of Saxonhurst."

"An *earl*?"

Meg looked her in the eyes, knowing that none of them, but especially Laura, must suspect that she was doing this for them. "Do you not think me worthy of an earl?"

Laura flushed. "Of course. You're worthy of a prince! I just didn't know you knew any noblemen."

Meg hastily assembled a story. "We met at the Ramillys'."

"But why tomorrow? There's no time for any preparations!"

"When you know the earl, you'll know he acts on impulse. Our situation is dire, so why wait? Which reminds me," she said, turning back to the chopping block, "we still have to eat today."

Laura started to cut onions, but said, "Aren't you going to describe him to us?"

"No." Meg set the bone to simmer. "You can wait and see."

When Jeremy returned home, however, it wasn't so easy. A stocky seventeen, he was very like Meg in looks, with their mother's soft brown hair and their father's square chin. He was far cleverer, however, and loved to study. Walter Gillingham had predicted that his elder son would far outstrip him in scholarship.

That was back in the good days, when it had been assumed that Jeremy would follow his father to Cambridge. Recently, he'd talked of finding employment as a clerk. He couldn't even have continued with his studies if Dr. Pierce hadn't insisted on carrying on without pay.

New joy brought the sting of tears to her eyes. She was going to give him back his dreams, his destiny. What he deserved. He must never, however, know the truth. He was as stubborn and resolute as she, and would never let her sacrifice herself.

He didn't accept the story as easily as the others, but after a few searching questions, he gave up. She knew she'd have to deal with him later.

Though clearly concerned, Jeremy and Laura followed her lead and scarcely mentioned plans for the next day, but the twins were not so easily suppressed. When Meg laughingly refused to answer questions, saying it was all to be a surprise, they settled into wild speculation, ending up with an idyll full of cakes and ices, gold plates and jewels, and fiery horses, half a dozen for each of them.

When they'd finally been settled in bed, Meg rubbed her aching head and hoped they'd not be too disappointed by reality. She supposed they'd at least get the cakes and ices on special occasions.

And now she had to deal with Jeremy.

He drew her into the chilly privacy of the parlor, leaving Laura darning in the meager light of a tallow candle. They couldn't go to the church with holes in their stockings.

Meg repeated the story she'd thrown together. She'd met the earl at the Ramillys', he'd offered for her when he learned of her situation, and she was delighted to have the chance to marry so well.

"But why in such a rush, Meg?" he asked, managing to look astonishingly like their father in a stern mood.

Good heavens. She'd never imagined that anyone might think she *had* to marry! Already hot-cheeked, Meg told him about the earl's grandmother.

"Good lord, Meg. He does sound ramshackle to be forgetting such a thing, then insisting on going through with it."

"It's not ramshackle to keep his word."

"I suppose not, but even so . . ."

"Even so, I'm going to do it."

"You admit you don't know him all that well. I don't think this is very wise."

She reminded herself that he didn't know about the awful alternative.

"It is a gamble of sorts, Jeremy, but the chances of winning are high. And if at the last moment I change my mind, I can refuse to go through with the ceremony."

"I'm coming with you." His jaw set in a very resolute way.

"Of course, you are! Would I get married without my family?"

That seemed to calm him, but as he went off to his books, he muttered, "It all sounds pretty rum to me."

Meg had to admit that it did. That it was. She pushed anxious questions out of her mind, however, and went to help Laura with the darning. She still had her pride and didn't want them to look like the paupers they were. By the time everything was as neat as possible, her back ached and her eyes stung from straining in the poor light.

Wax candles. Surely an earl would have wax candles. She prayed an earl would be willing to replace worn-out stockings.

Laura rubbed her back, too, then packed needles and thread in their mother's inlaid wooden sewing box. Meg had kept it till last, but it would have been the next thing to go. She'd already inquired of a dealer how much he would give for it. She touched it tenderly. Another blessing . . .

"Now you!"

"What?" Meg looked up at her sister, trying to disguise her weariness.

"What are *you* going to wear for your wedding?"

"It doesn't matter."

"Not matter! Nonsense. Let's check your wardrobe!"

"Rachel's asleep." They'd taken to sleeping two and three to a bed for warmth.

"We'll be quiet."

"I don't expect that a suitable gown will appear by magic. Everything I have was chosen for a governess in a sober household."

"There has to be something. Come on!"

A few moments later, Laura was easing open drawers in Meg's armoire, frowning at the dull gowns within. "You could always ask that stone thing," she whispered.

"What?"

At Meg's tone, Laura looked over. "The sheelagh-maging."

"Sheelagh-ma-gig." Meg drew her sister out into the corridor. "I wasn't sure you knew about it."

"Mother showed me." Laura shrugged. "She assured me it had these powers, but I wished and wished for a pianoforte and it never appeared. She said it worked for you, though. So you could—"

"No! It's dangerous, Laura. Definitely not to be used for trivial things."

"A wedding dress isn't trivial!"

Meg hid a smile at this evidence of how young her sister was, of how right her decision was. "There's a cost to the *sheelagh,* Laura. Too high a cost for vanity. You do know never to speak of it."

"Oh yes." She looked as if she would say more, but returned to the room to dig through the drawers. "Everything is awfully dull."

"Suitable for a governess. And very practical."

She pulled out a gown in light blue. "It'll have to be this."

"Good," Meg said, glad to have it settled. The gown was her Sunday best—a serge walking dress with dark blue trimming.

"It's awfully plain for a countess, though," Laura whispered, draping it over a chair. "We could retrim it—"

"No." Meg was shocked—almost appalled—by the idea of being a countess. "I'm sure the earl will be pleased to buy me new garments more suited to my station."

"But—"

"No. Get to bed."

As they helped each other undress, Meg sighed at the thought of being a countess. She was ready to marry an eccentric earl, but had not thought it through. Why it should seem so terrible to be a countess she couldn't say, except that she was a very unlikely person for the part.

As she plaited her hair, she studied herself. Shouldn't a countess have a chiseled nose and a long swanlike neck? She shrugged. She would be a dutiful wife to an earl. That was the best she could offer.

Laura's fussing about clothes had raised another problem. As she settled into bed, Meg thought about her underwear.

In her years with the Ramilly family, there had been many quiet evenings. She supposed some people might have thought of them as lonely, but she had found them peaceful. The main reason she'd sought employment, after all, was to escape the ramshackle chaos of her home. She loved her family dearly, but the constant disorganization, and her parents' blithe dismissal of all concerns, had driven her distracted.

The Ramilly household had been extremely well-organized. The family were sober and kind, the children well-behaved, the servants meticulous. Once her charges had been in bed, her evenings had mostly been her own, spent in her own private room, amid peace and quiet. Often she read, or wrote letters home. But she also spent much time in embroidery and lace-making, tranquil, delicate arts that gave her great joy.

At some point she had tired of trimming handkerchiefs and making sober bands for severe gowns. She had begun decorating her plain, functional underwear. It had started mildly with a few sprigs of flowers on shifts and nightgowns. Then she'd settled to a narrow trim of Renaissance lace on a petticoat, which had certainly taken a nice long time.

When that was finished, however, she couldn't stop. Openwork and cutwork, drawn thread and counted thread, satin stitch and hardanger, her plain cotton garments had become canvasses for her imagination. She kept the colors subdued, for the laundry woman had to see everything, and most of it ended up blowing on the line to dry, but the designs were complex and satisfying to work.

It had taken her some time to realize that she had two sorts of garments which no one but she ever saw—

her corsets, and her drawers. Her corsets could not be washed, and her scandalous drawers she laundered for herself.

On her corsets and drawers, therefore, Meg had let her wildest fancies break free. These clothes were her guilty secret, ridiculous for a plain young lady of a serious turn of mind, but so very precious. It had been easy to keep them from others. What of a husband, though?

It shouldn't be a problem. He would come to her when she was in her bed, wouldn't he, and her nightgowns were very plain. What, however, if he intruded when she was in her underlayers?

She turned over, begging sleep to come. She'd buy new, that's what she'd do. She'd claim her old clothes were all worn out and buy new. Giving up the others would be a sacrifice, however, a sacrifice of a special part of herself.

Sleep eluded her.

This was apparently her last night as a single woman.

Untouched.

A virgin.

She could hardly bear to think that tomorrow she would have to let a total stranger have access to the most private parts of her body.

Beneath these worries ground another fear.

The *sheelagh's* gift was too much. An earl, even a rather peculiar one, would never, of his own will, marry Meg Gillingham.

What price would she have to pay for that?

And worse, she had stolen his free will. She'd felt guilty enough over summoning the baker's son with a cake. Now she'd trapped someone for life!

It had to be a sin.

She'd always suspected that the *sheelagh* was evil, and now she knew it was true.

But she had no choice. She'd give even her soul to save her sister.

Chapter 4

Owain still wasn't sure whether his friend's course was wise or not, but he knew he had no chance of changing it now. So, he thought, as they returned to the house from White's in the early hours of the last day of the year, he'd better smooth the way.

Despite the freezing temperature and a bitter wind, they were walking. Sax always needed to burn off energy after sitting around for hours, and for once he had been sitting. Most of the time had been spent in casual gaming for idle stakes, but he'd also made up doggerel with Vane and Petersham, and then indulged a homesick Scot who needed to talk of Hogmanay. Poor McCallum had invited Sax to his rooms the next night for a proper greeting of the New Year, but Sax had told him he was already engaged. Only a slight twitch of the lips had registered the pun.

It was generally best to be blunt with Sax, so as they turned into the quiet square, Owain said, "Don't you think you should make some preparation for your bride?"

"Devil take it, why didn't you say something earlier? She'll need a bed at least."

"At least. And don't forget her brothers and sisters."

"Aren't you supposed to look after these details for me?"

"Only when given instructions."

"Doesn't usually deter you." Sax ran up the stairs to ply the knocker. He never carried keys, so a servant was always available when he was out. Tonight, it was Stephen, the running footman when required, who'd developed his speed fleeing honest citizens after filching their handkerchiefs. He took their hats and canes, smothering a yawn.

Brak leaped up from his patient vigil by the door to fawn around and be greeted. Once the dog was appeased, Sax grabbed a lit candle from the hall table and headed straight for the stairs, dog at his side, flame flowing behind like a banner. Owain followed, hoping the whole house wasn't about to be roused. It had happened before.

Owain knew Sax was right, though. He should have taken care of matters himself. He suspected he'd been trying to wash his hands of the whole business.

Sax went into the room next to his own bedroom, his breath puffing in the unheated air. "The countess's." He put down the candle and flung back the curtains as if daylight would magically appear. "More candles!"

Owain had already gone into the other bedroom and returned with a branch of them. In moments, Stephen ran up with another candelabra.

In the shimmering light, Sax looked around at dark wood and olive-green hangings. "Dull, thirty years out of date, but good enough for the moment. Tell someone to light a big fire and get this bed aired."

"It's two in the morning."

"In the morning," Sax added, as if he'd always intended to say it. And perhaps he had.

He'd stopped in front of a small painting of a simple, white-capped woman cutting a yellow cheese. "Dammit, it's that Dutch artist." He snapped his fingers. "Vermeer. Lovely, isn't it?"

Owain could never tell if Sax was joking about art or not. He himself liked the quiet simplicity of the picture, but could it really appeal to his friend, who seemed to have different tastes? Sax had purchased quite a number of works by Fuseli, who was inclined to put fruit and animal faces on his subjects, and Turner, who reduced everything to a wash of color.

Sax touched the plain frame. "I wondered where this went after I bought it. I'll have it in my own room. Stephen—"

Before the footman could move, Owain said, "Better not."

Sax's brows rose. "Do you think I'll smash it? I am, like Hamlet, only mad north-northwest. When the wind is southerly, I know a Vermeer from a gloomy monk."

"It'll give you a reason to visit your wife."

Sax put his hands on his hips. "You're in a damn funny mood."

"This is a damn funny business." With a jerk of his head, Owain sent Stephen on his way.

"Am I about to suffer a lecture?" Sax opened empty drawers and cupboards. "I won't mistreat her, you know."

"I know. But you're a lusty man."

"Isn't that what a wife is for?"

"You don't know how she'll feel about it. She'll do her duty, I'm sure."

"Duty." Sax curled his lip. "It's time you found the joy in it, my friend."

"I'm not without experience. I'm just more . . ."

"Discriminating? My dear fellow, I'm excessively discriminating. Only the best."

Owain just said what he needed to say. "You can't keep bringing your women here."

Sax closed the door of a walnut armoire with a sharp click, and turned. "You know what you're telling me, don't you?"

"Do I?"

"That the Daingerfield Dragon has won. She's finally managed to steal some of my freedom."

"Make a happy marriage of it and you can thwart her."

"Now there's a thought! We'll just have to hope that my bride has as brisk an appetite for sex as I do. In fact, I suppose it's my husbandly duty to stimulate it. Could be fun. Children," he said abruptly. "Rooms for."

"Not for a while."

"Ah-ha!" Sax's grin flashed charmingly brilliant. "I have you flustered, my efficient friend. You've forgotten my bride's siblings."

"Damnation."

"How many?" Sax swept up a candelabra and headed for the next floor.

Owain hurried after. "I'm not sure."

"Ages?"

"I don't know."

Sax turned at the head of the stairs to laugh, a magical chiaroscuro in the candlelight. "Poor Owain, caught out again. Never mind." He walked on to fling open a door. "I don't suppose there are babies."

"This is the nursery?" Owain had never had reason to come up here, but his efficient soul was pleased to see that the room was clean and cared for. It also appeared unchanged since last use. When? "Were you a baby here?"

"My father didn't come into the title until I was eight, and even then we didn't come to London much. But I remember this." Sax ran a hand along the iron rail around a small bed. "My sister was using it."

He broke off. "Our nurse was Nanny Bullock. She died when I was twelve." His hand lingered on the cold metal a moment longer, and then he walked briskly into the corridor to open the next door.

"This was my bedroom."

Brak set off on an interested sniffing exploration of the icy room. Owain was beginning to shiver.

"Three?" Owain asked, indicating the three narrow beds lined along one wall.

"Left over from my father's time. He had two brothers. We're great ones for tradition, we Torrances. This is the boys' room, and this," he said, flinging open the door to a room across the corridor, "is the girls'. Just two beds, for my two aunts. No mattresses."

"So I would hope. And no, I don't think we can get some before tomorrow night."

"With money, anything is possible."

Owain wrote a note in his book, knowing what Sax said was true. "The Gillinghams probably have their own and could bring them."

"Buy them new." Sax was into another room—the schoolroom, containing a long table with six chairs around it.

Originally, Owain supposed, half a century or more ago, the seating had been for five students and a governess or tutor. There was no sign of how Sax and his teacher had fit into this room, though the fading map on the wall surely went back fifteen years, not fifty.

He found these rooms eerie, as if generations of children had wandered away, leaving shadows. Two ancient embroidered samplers hung beside the more recent map. A wooden globe sat beneath the window with pins stuck into various spots. Six battered tin inkpots were lined up on an open shelf. A few faded volumes tilted on bookshelves.

But it had been just two children who'd left—fifteen years ago. The three-year-old girl had died with her parents in that carriage accident, and the boy, at ten, had been taken away to be raised by his maternal grandmother, the Duchess of Daingerfield.

For the first time, Owain truly sensed the devastation of that event. The duchess had even dismissed the nurse who'd been with Sax since birth—Nanny Bullock.

Sax was running his fingers down the battered spines of the books. "I didn't know these were still here. I have new and better copies downstairs."

Owain doubted that better was true in any sense that mattered.

"I suppose we'll have to hire a governess, or perhaps a tutor." Sax turned to survey the room. "That's not urgent. Do you think this will do when warm and freshened up a bit?"

The slight hint of uncertainty was almost heartbreaking. Sax could take on an unknown wife sure that he could handle her, but children were another matter. He was carelessly fond of youngsters, but his own true childhood had been cut cruelly short.

Owain began to worry about the new countess's brothers and sisters as well as about her. Sax was generous, but so unpredictable. "The young ones could perhaps be given some say in the refurbishing of this area."

"Good idea."

With the Torrance traditions in mind, Owain asked, "Will they be allowed to do as they wish?"

"Within reason. Why not?" There was one more door off the corridor, and Sax glanced in. "Thought so. Room for the schoolroom maids. I assume my impoverished bride isn't bringing any. See if any of the staff want the job."

"Pick the ones you want to do it."

"Volunteers are always better. And the boys would probably like a manservant. But we'll observe the proprieties and have him sleep elsewhere." He then retraced his steps, gently closing each door on the past.

He ran back downstairs with his usual energy, candle flames streaming. He paused at his bedroom door. "Shame, really."

"What?"

"To be so celibate on my last night of freedom. But I suppose it'll be good practice."

"For marriage? Hardly."

"Ah, but your doubts have infected me." He blew out one of the three candles. "My bride will shrink away, which will shrink me." He blew out the second. "It's going to be a labor of Hercules to fill those seven beds with offspring of my own." He opened his door, and Owain saw Nims there, patiently waiting.

"But I will strive," declared Sax, puffing out the last flame, "and Nims will stand as my trusty squire, to ready me for the fight."

He put the candleholder in Owain's hand, said a fond good night to Brak, and gently closed the door between them.

Through the wood Owain heard him declare, "I will stand proud and valiant, and will have the endurance of ten men and the patience of Job. Just pray that I don't get his boils. Sweet dreams, Owain."

Owain went off to his study, laughing, and wrote a long list of instructions for the staff. When he sought his own bed, however, he was plagued with anxieties on behalf of Miss Gillingham and her needy brothers and sisters.

Sax was so damned unpredictable.

Though Meg had been exhausted, she hadn't found much sleep. She'd lain awake most of the night, imagining the worst possible consequences of her action. Always, however, the image of Sir Arthur returned to remind her of the very worst.

At the first morning light, she eased out of bed and broke the thin layer of ice on her washing water. A brisk scrub of her face brought up a bit of color. Then she brushed her hair until it crackled.

She still didn't look like a countess.

However, with her week's grace gone, Meg's greatest fear was that she was the victim of some malicious trick. Today, Sir Arthur would come for his answer, and when she refused to let him have her sister, they'd be out on the street. A glance through the frost-laced window showed a scattering of snow on the dormant garden, and the trees whipping in the wind. They could freeze to death out there.

And there was worse to fear.

If this marriage didn't happen, Laura was quite capable of sacrificing herself.

Impossible.

But horribly possible if Laura ever suspected Sir Arthur's plan. And he'd tell her.

No, the *sheelagh* had found a solution. As usual, it came with a sting—that Meg must marry a deranged and possibly deformed stranger. But it provided for all their needs.

As she woke her sisters, therefore, she prayed most earnestly that it not be a trick.

She picked up the earl's letter and re-read it. It seemed clear, and why should such a man take it into his mind to trick poor Meg Gillingham?

Why should such a man take it into his mind to *marry* poor Meg Gillingham?

Putting the letter aside, she helped the others to dress, fingers clumsy with cold, nerves, and guilt. After all, if the earl did turn up at the church, he would have no more idea why than the baker's son.

It was wrong, but she couldn't let that sway her.

Whatever the cost to her or him, her siblings must have security and hope for the future. Laura must be saved.

Weaving Rachel's fine hair into a plait, Meg told herself that Lord Saxonhurst was getting exactly what he'd bargained for. A hardworking, honest, dutiful wife.

Her sister was one long wriggle. "Is it true that you'll be a countess, Meg?"

"I suppose so. Sit still."

"I wish I were going to be a countess. Will you go to Court?"

"I have no idea." Pushing aside that terrifying thought, Meg tied a tight ribbon around the end. "There. You'll do. Go start the fire."

Laura was nearly as bad. "You'll have robes, won't you? And have to take part in state occasions."

"I dearly hope not. Let me fasten your buttons."

Laura stood with her back to Meg. She'd chosen a pretty dress far too flimsy for such a day, but Meg hadn't the heart to make her change. She'd be warm enough with her woolen cloak over.

"What if the king dies? He could, couldn't he? Then there'd be a coronation, and you'd be there!"

"Laura, you can't wish for the poor man's death!"

"I'm not. I'm just thinking."

Meg's sensible gown buttoned at the front, so she fastened it herself. "Can you see me in velvet and ermine? I'll be the sort of countess who runs an economical household and rears happy, healthy children. Come on. Let's get breakfast."

As she stirred the porridge, Meg held the vision of happy, healthy children in her mind as a shield against the terrifying vision of robes and state occasions.

They ate the porridge with salt and heavily watered milk. She was sure an earl's household had cream and sugar in abundance, and that was what she was paying for with her freedom.

When they'd finished and washed the bowls, she made sure everyone was neat and warmly dressed, and led them to St. Margaret's Church.

She thought she had herself completely in hand, but at the sight of the church—where she went every Sunday for service—her feet froze to the ground.

Marriage.

She was about to give not just her body but her life into a stranger's hands. She would no longer have privacy, or be free to come and go as she pleased. She would be giving him power over her family. . . .

"What's the matter?" Laura asked.

"There's no carriage. What if there's no one there?"
The outer doors stood open, but there was no hint of
anyone being around.

"No one there? Why wouldn't he be there? He asked
you to marry him, didn't he?" A hint of suspicion rang
in her voice.

"Yes, of course."

Jeremy said, "They couldn't keep horses standing in
this weather, Meg."

"I'll go peep—" Meg seized Richard's coat before he
could run across the road.

"No, love. It's just silly bridal nerves. Jeremy's right.
I'm sure he's there waiting."

What folly to hesitate. How private or free would any
of them be as paupers on the streets, or residents of
the workhouse?

And she mustn't forget Sir Arthur's vile plans for
Laura.

She forced a smile. "After all, I don't expect to be a
bride again, and I intend to enjoy all the stages, including nerves and watery tears!"

"Silly," Laura said, but with a relieved laugh. "You
never cry!"

"I've never been married before." It came out more
grimly than she wanted, so she grinned at her brothers.
"Gentlemen, prepare to catch me when I faint!"

Resolutely smiling, she led them up the stone steps
into the church vestibule, into the familiar smell of
musty hymn books and remembered incense. Another
set of doors stood between her and the nave, concealing
her future. With only the slightest hesitation, she opened
one and walked through.

For a moment the contrast between daylight and
gloom blinded her. Then, in the weak winter light shoot-
ing through stained-glass windows, she saw people standing near the altar. The church clock began to sound
eleven and they all turned.

Six men, two women.

She couldn't make out details.

She had frozen in the doorway, and Laura pushed her

gently forward out of the way. "Which one is he?" she whispered, nothing but excitement in her voice.

Meg walked forward, walking as slowly as she dared down the long aisle. Which one was he? As her eyes adjusted and her nerves steadied, she eliminated Reverend Bilston and a few other men who were clearly servants.

That left two gentlemen, one brown haired and one blond.

Dirty yellow! What a way to describe that elegant arrangement of dusky gold curls. She wasn't close enough to see his eyes. She was quite close enough, however, to see that he was tall, handsome, elegant, and terrifyingly everything one would expect a young earl to be.

He was no desperate charity case! How had the *sheelagh* managed this?

He was looking back at her, assessing her in a quick, intelligent way. She searched his features for any sign of shock or disappointment. All she saw was a sort of interest marked by a sudden, charming smile.

He was clearly slave to the magic.

She stopped as if a wall had sprung up in front of her. It wasn't right.

No matter what her need, it wasn't *right* to bewitch someone like this. No good could come of it.

"I'm sorry." She turned and pushed past her startled family, hurrying back down the aisle.

Someone had closed the door. In her panic, her cold fingers fumbled the latch. Then a hand appeared, pressed firmly against the dark wood, preventing her from opening it.

"Miss Gillingham, please don't run away."

He must have run to stop her, but his voice was beautifully modulated, and used—consciously she was sure—to soothe. It didn't help. Susie had said the earl could easily find a bride, and it was clearly true.

It was all magic, evil magic.

"Please, my lord . . ."

His hand did not move. It was beautifully made, with long, elegant fingers and buffed nails. An earl's hand.

His large body loomed behind her, placing her in

shadow. Without looking, she knew he must be close to a foot taller than she.

Lacking any choice, she turned against the oaken door to look up at him, grateful for the shadows. She couldn't tell the truth—she could never speak of the *sheelagh*. "It is just so ridiculous, my lord. I thought I could. But now . . ."

"But now you need a moment to collect yourself." He moved back slightly, and smiled again, that charming, practiced smile. "Come, sit in this pew with me, Miss Gillingham, and we will discuss it."

He took her gloved hand and led her to the nearest row of seats. She couldn't think of a reason to object. As she sat down she saw Jeremy, Laura, Richard, and Rachel watching wide-eyed. With a jolt, she remembered why she had to do this.

The twins looked frightened, and Laura looked bewildered. Jeremy, however, was beginning to look pugnacious. She found a smile to reassure them all, but feared it was all wobbly.

"Miss Gillingham," the earl said, sitting beside her on the polished seat, "I assure you I am not so terrifying."

His eyes *were* yellow, or at least a strange pale hazel ringed around the iris with dark brown. More to the point, they were powerful. She didn't know what made eyes powerful, but they were. Even with light brown brows and lashes, they shone intensely and sparkled with energy.

She looked away, away at a memorial plaque on the wall—to the Merryam family, one of whom had been Lord Mayor in the last century—trying desperately to sort through her thoughts. "You're not terrifying, my lord. Far from it. That is why I wonder at your wanting to marry me."

"Susie explained my predicament."

She had to look at him. Unfortunately, he was just as handsome as before. "It seems a foolish reason to tie yourself to me for life."

"You think my word of honor a foolish thing?"

She felt herself color. "No, my lord. But is it so impossible to admit to your grandmother that you have been unable to keep your promise?"

"Yes. Completely. Come now, Miss Gillingham, let me turn the tables. What possible objection can you have to me?"

His easy self-confidence made her want to roll her eyes, but he was right. She had no rational objection. How could she say she didn't want to marry him because he was victim of a magic spell? Or that she was dismayed because the bargain would be so unequal? That she wished he were grotesque and drooling.

"You are very tall," she said weakly.

"Not *very*. And sitting down, the difference in our heights is not so obvious. I will try to sit a lot." Then he challenged her. "I thought we had an agreement, Miss Gillingham. A promise."

"I did add that we would have to find each other congenial, my lord."

"I find you congenial."

"How can you? You do not know me."

"I like the fact that you have these nervous doubts."

"What?"

"If you'd marched in here and said your vows without a flutter, Miss Gillingham, I would have been concerned. After all, *I* am somewhat nervous. But it won't be hard for two reasonable people to rub along together, especially when cushioned by wealth. And, of course, I will take care of your siblings."

It was a trump card and he played it without flourish, but she knew he had played it deliberately.

"Won't you introduce them to me?"

There was no way to refuse, and so Meg gestured them over.

The twins were wary, but in a few moments of casual conversation became adoring.

Laura was awkward, but he soon had her blushing.

Meg watched these easy conquests with misgiving, and was pleased that Jeremy remained stiff. "My lord," he said, "Meg doesn't have to marry you if she doesn't wish to. We can make do."

"I'm sure you can. You all look like capable, hard-working people. But all our lives will be made more comfortable by this arrangement, and I will be eternally grateful."

He then began to converse with them, asking about their schooling and interests. Under this skillful handling, soon even Jeremy had relaxed, seduced by casual references to the earl's own time at King's College, Cambridge.

Meg should have been glad that her family was shedding their anxieties, and in most ways she was, but she also felt threatened. The Earl of Saxonhurst had the confidence of a man who'd never been crossed since the day he was born. He was wickedly charming, and he knew it. Knew how to use it. She'd felt the effects when he'd talked with her so briefly—almost a warmth melting her fears and doubts.

It was unreasonable to object and yet she did. She felt as if *she* were being *spellbound.*

So! She almost gasped aloud.

That certainly served her right. He was spellbound by the *sheelagh,* and she was in danger of being spellbound by him.

Watching him, she could almost see his charm like a halo . . .

Then she shook her head at the fancy. It was just a shaft of sun through one of the church's colored windows. But no. That was not all it was. She couldn't deny his effect, or the panic it stirred in her.

He was too much, too much man for mousy Meg Gillingham.

But she had no choice.

Chapter 5

He turned to her at last, assessing her. Clearly he decided she'd had time to settle her nerves, for he raised her to her feet. He believed that she wouldn't resist anymore, and he was right. It was simply a matter of need, however, not inclination. Her family desperately needed his help.

She truly did wish he'd turned out to be an ugly eccentric. She'd be much happier with her fate.

In moments, they were standing in front of the vicar.

Thin, white-haired Reverend Bilston looked at her with concern. He had known her most of her life and buried her parents only three months before. "Are you quite recovered, Meg? There is no need to rush, you know. The license will be valid tomorrow or next week. If you are at all uncertain . . ."

She glanced at the earl again and saw that he would not pressure her anymore. He had rolled the dice and now merely watched to see how they would lie.

Laura, Laura, Laura.

Having fortified herself with that incantation, Meg smiled at the vicar. "It was just an attack of nerves, Reverend. I am quite ready now."

After a slight, concerned pause, Reverend Bilston began to recite the service. For Meg, the time for questions was over, and she made all the appropriate responses, letting herself be carried along the course she had decided on. Nothing had changed, after all, except that the earl was not an object of pity, and it would be strange indeed to regret that. . . .

Then he was turning her toward him.

They were man and wife!

"Now, now," he said calmly, clearly seeing her flare

of panic. "The worst is over. Thank you, Lady Saxon-hurst." And he kissed her hand close by the ring he'd placed there.

She was suddenly, blindingly grateful that he had not kissed her lips. But, heaven help her, if she wasn't ready to be kissed, how could she face the coming night?

He studied her a moment, then smiled. "I'm sure these doubts and fears are quite normal, but do try not to let your imagination run away with you, my dear. Now, let us sign the register and have this done."

As soon as the formalities were complete, the earl turned to her family. "Welcome! I have no brothers and sisters, you know, so I am delighted by an instant family."

"Wait until you get to know them, my lord," Meg said.

At her mild joke, he flashed her a look of surprised approval. It felt strangely like the lick of a flame.

Warming, but dangerous.

She hastily turned to accept the good wishes of all around.

Jeremy was still watchful, but a glowing Laura ran over to hug Meg. "I think this is all *wonderful*!"

The earl claimed a kiss on the cheek, then gave her into the care of his secretary. "Owain, take especial care of my new sister."

Owain Chancellor, with his brown hair and square face, was such a pleasant-looking, *ordinary*-looking gentleman. Meg wished she was in his care, not that of her handsome husband.

Then she noticed that the twins were looking up at the earl with their curious look. Oh dear.

"Do you have robes?" Rachel asked.

"My earl's robes? Yes. And a coronet. Your sister will have them, too."

Richard demanded, "Will I?"

"Not unless you earn them for yourself. Which is more than I did."

"Have you met the king?" Rachel asked.

"Not recently. He's too unwell for visitors."

"But you must have met the prince," Richard said. "Is he really, really fat?"

"Very. Now, let's be on our way. A luncheon awaits."

"What's to eat?" The twins said it in unison, with the true fervor of ten-year-olds who'd been on short rations.

"Wait and see." The earl tucked Meg's hand into the crook of his arm and led her toward the door. The twins instantly bracketed them—Richard at the earl's side, Rachel at Meg's, like sheep dogs making sure that their charges wouldn't stray.

Meg fought tears. How frightened they must have been since losing their parents! Surely this must all turn out to be an improvement.

The twins were never easily silenced. "Will there be ham, sir?"

"Goose?"

"Cake?"

"Mince pies?"

"Nuts?"

"Oranges?"

"Missed your Christmas dinner, did you?" the earl asked indulgently. "There'll be whatever you want that we can find. We can't do magic, however, so the goose will have to wait."

"Ices?" both twins said at once.

The earl halted to turn back to the servants. "I assume we can produce ices?"

"Gunter's may have some, milord, though it's not the time of year for them."

"Find out." And he continued out into the sunshine.

"There's no need," Meg protested. "It's winter!"

"But no need not to, winter or no. This is our wedding celebration, and my birthday, and I like ices, too."

"You'll spoil them."

He smiled down at her. "I'm sure you'll prevent me."

That was all very well, but Meg feared that preventing the Earl of Saxonhurst from doing anything would be like preventing the Thames from flowing to the sea.

Three elegant carriages had appeared, drawn by fine, steaming horses. Each horse was protected by a heavy, emblazoned cloth in the same blue and gold worn by the liveried servants letting down the steps. Each carriage bore a gilded crest on the door.

He really was an earl! Meg hadn't exactly doubted it, but she'd not quite believed it either.

In moments, he was handing her into one and settling beside her on the deeply padded, blue brocade seat. When Richard and Rachel didn't follow, however, she snapped out of the enchantment and looked out of the window.

The earl tugged her back. "Owain will take care of them all. What do you think we're up to? The slave trade?"

"Of course not."

"So, relax and enjoy your wedding day. I hope neither of us have another."

That startled her. Thus far, she'd only thought of the immediate, of getting this done so that Laura would be safe, so they would all have the means of decent survival. But marriage was for all eternity.

Oh dear.

She made herself meet his eyes. "I'll try, my lord."

"Good." But then, as the carriage moved off, he drew her close, his intention clear.

Meg instinctively braced her arms to hold him off.

His brows rose. "You object to kisses?"

"Anyone could be watching!"

"We're in a closed carriage on an empty street, but I'll draw the blinds if you wish."

He had every right to kiss her, but . . . She tried for an honest explanation. "It's all so sudden, my lord. We may be man and wife, but you are still a stranger."

"We certainly *are* man and wife, but I understand." He moved back, leaning in his corner, legs stretched out. "Am I to assume that you won't feel ready for more intimate attentions by tonight?"

Meg looked away, her cheeks burning. "I will do my duty, my lord."

"To the devil with duty. We're wed till death us do part, so I'm sure consummation can wait a night or two."

Hearing neither disgust nor annoyance, Meg glanced back. She understood men to be somewhat greedy in their appetites. But then, of course, he didn't feel that way about her.

Why should he?

Any more than she felt that way about him.

Though she did feel something, she had to admit. Whatever it was, it was not at all comfortable.

"You look so very agitated," he said with that devastating twinkle in his eye. "I should warn you that maidenly flusters are often quite stimulating to men. The wide eyes, the heated cheek . . ."

His indulgent tone put her on her mettle. "Men suffer from a hunting instinct, I see."

His brows rose. "Hunting?"

"Blushes and big eyes being like the smell of the prey to them."

He laughed. "A novel notion, but likely true. Men can be very predatory."

She suspected his flash of strong, white teeth was deliberate and wanted, so desperately, to dent his confidence. "Predators are not very discriminating, though, are they, my lord? Any prey will do."

"Not at all. The hawk in search of rabbits doesn't snatch a hedgehog."

"Am I rabbit, then?"

"I am very much coming to doubt it."

She felt an absurd warmth. "Good. I can be quite prickly."

"So I see." Still at his ease, his lids lowered in a way that started a beat of panic in her chest. "I should warn you, my dear countess, that danger intrigues me, and I enjoy a good hunt."

"Pity the poor hedgehog, then, who won't."

After a moment, he said, "I am pondering the image of a hedgehog hunt. . . ."

And she couldn't help but laugh with him at the absurdity. At that moment, she felt comfort ease into her, pushing away panic. She could talk to this man. Match wits with him. That was something. That was a great deal.

Then she realized some of the comfort might be physical. "This coach is very warm."

He bent to move the carpet on the floor, showing tiles. "They're kept heated and put in place before we use it."

Meg couldn't think of what to say about such an extraordinary indulgence, but she had to unclasp her cloak and push it off her shoulders.

He smiled. "A hedgehog hunt would be a slow hunt, but there is nothing wrong with that."

"It would be no hunt at all, and you know it."

"But think of the spines. The hunter would want the creature to unroll, to cease being wary. Perhaps it is the hunter's skill to make that happen." He reached out, and soft as a feather, stroked her cheek. "To make the quarry welcome its own end. . . ."

Meg couldn't help inching away. "This is not truly a hunt."

"But you have turned it into one." His finger touched her ear, tracing the sensitive edge, the faint rasping sound so loud it made her shiver. She was pressed back against the corner squabs now, with nowhere else to go.

"I desire you, my wife."

"You can't possibly—"

"But you refuse me. Therefore I must hunt. Which means, I must seduce you."

"Seduce!" She found an extra inch to retreat.

He caught her earlobe between two fingers and tugged. "Seduction is sanctioned within marriage, you know."

She couldn't help it. She twitched sideways, away from his devastating touch. "You agreed to wait!"

He let his hand drop, relaxed again, but not a mite less dangerous. "Of course. Word of a Torrance. Until you unroll from your spiny ball and present your soft vulnerability. Willingly. Eagerly—"

"Eagerly?" It came out on a breath, a whisper. With just his eyes, his remarkable eyes and his big body, his long legs dominating the space, his wide shoulders filling her vision, with just these things, without touching her, she knew that he was halfway to the kill.

There was one way to cut this short, but she had to look away to say the words. "I think it would be better if we consummated the marriage tonight, my lord."

Silence stretched. "You think that the safer option?" She didn't have to look to know that his eyes were dancing with humor. "If I come to your bed tonight," he said, very softly, but every word clear, "it will be no simple matter. I will seduce you, Lady Saxonhurst. Seduce in every meaning of the word."

She shivered again. She'd thought it would be simple. They would go to bed together, both in their nightgowns. He would do the necessary, then turn over and go to sleep, suitably appreciative of her calm acceptance of her unpleasant duty.

The kisses involved would be light and respectful, and there would not be any touching of ears or necks, or any sense of danger, of something stealing the air all around and making her dizzy.

His hands touched her shoulders, sending a jolt right through her. He turned her to face him. "If we are to be intimate so soon, we really must begin. A proper consummation takes time. A great deal of time. Prepare yourself, Lady Saxonhurst, to be kissed."

She expected to be seized, assaulted even, but he used only a finger to raise her face to his. His lips only brushed gently over hers. The aura, however, the greater reality he seemed able to summon, fell over her like a heavy mist, making her breath falter.

How could he do this to her with just a light kiss?

She would have broken away and protested, but pride would not let her. This was her idea—wasn't it?—to cut short his tormenting pursuit by immediate, coldblooded surrender.

Her blood was definitely not running cold.

He used his lips to tease at hers, making them tingle almost unbearably. She parted them without thinking and felt his tongue against hers.

She flinched, but would not retreat. That would be to admit his conquest. She opened her eyes—when had she closed them?—and stared at him.

She saw the smile, felt it in his mouth, heard it in his voice. "You are delightful, Lady Saxonhurst. You are going to give me so much pleasure."

"In the hunt?"

"And the capture. You are no shy hedgehog, are you?"

"At the least, I insist on being a cunning fox."

"Vixen, my dear. Vixen." His fingers teased at the

edge of her hair, at her ears, her neck, his mouth still close so their breath mingled.

She would not back down. "Fox or vixen, they find no pleasure in the chase."

"They can, in this hunt. Pleasure such as you have never imagined. Trust me on that."

He slid his hand behind her neck and kissed her suddenly, deeply, shocking a half-cry from her, almost bruising her lips. It was a warning kiss. A huntsman's horn of a kiss. Meg truly felt like a vixen then, huddling in a covert, hoping the hounds wouldn't sniff her out, but knowing they were already on her trail.

Well on the trail. Her breathing was unsteady and her whole body felt strange, almost fevered.

With shock, she recognized sensations similar to those from the *sheelagh-ma-gig*—that sickening, dizzying wave that went on and on, almost longer than a body could bear.

No wonder her mother had been reluctant to discuss it!

Could marital consummation be like that—powerful, overwhelming, terrifyingly close to death?

With a jolt of relief, she realized she was safe. Clearly many women found a husband's attentions pleasant. Her mother had said that she did. But Meg had experienced it through the *sheelagh* and had not liked it at all.

Despite his many charms, the Earl of Saxonhurst's hunt would fail. He would not be able to make her want or enjoy his ultimate attentions. It might be a case of cutting off her nose to spite her face, but she was glad of it. Glad he was not going to be able to provide pleasure such as she had never imagined.

He was just too glossily confident to be borne.

He drew back, studying her, and she thought he already looked a little puzzled. She willed her eyes to be steady. Yes, it wouldn't be pleasant to have to be intimate with him tonight, but she was looking forward to seeing him thwarted.

After a moment, he pulled a cord to attract the attention of the coachman. The trap opened in the roof. "Milord?"

"Pause at Mrs. Ribbleside's in Crane Street."

"Yes, milord."

"Why?" Meg demanded, sure he had thought of another twist on the hunt.

"You have to permit me *some* pleasure," he said, looking both amused and mischievous.

It was very hard to imagine someone so lighthearted as wicked, but what amused this man might well be very wicked indeed. Meg had heard stories about houses of sinful purpose, and at the moment, she couldn't be sure anything was impossible. She shouldn't have been afraid for her siblings, but for herself!

The carriage halted and she looked out, expecting something terrible. She only saw a respectable street of tall houses and occasional shops. She saw a haberdashery and a millinery. . . .

A footman opened the door and the earl leaped out, virtually dragging Meg with him. "My lord!"

"Come along, or the others will think I've abducted you."

"What *are* you doing?" she demanded as she was hustled through a door. A moment later she realized a sensible woman would have screamed.

But this was her husband, God help her.

He whipped off her bonnet. Even as she protested, she realized they were in the millinery establishment.

"My lord?" The plump young woman was clearly startled, but not at all unhappy to be invaded in this way.

"A bonnet, Mrs. Ribbleside. Not your most fanciful creation. It must match this gown. But something a little more enlivening than brown straw."

"Of course—"

"And in a hurry, please. Oh, and this is my countess. She'll doubtless become a very good customer."

The woman gaped for a moment, then put on a brilliant smile. "Your ladyship! What an honor! Please, be seated—"

"No time for that. Just pick one. Your taste is excellent."

As a gesture of rebellion, Meg sat firmly on the chair the milliner had indicated. "Perhaps I don't want a new bonnet."

"Don't be foolish. Women always want new bonnets."

She gritted her teeth. "If I am to have new clothes—and I'm sure you will insist on it, my lord—I will buy new bonnets then!"

"We'll have a special outfit made to go with your wedding bonnet." He tossed her poor straw into a corner. "That thing depresses me."

Before she could protest, he gave her a shining smile. "Humor me, my dear."

Despite her best efforts, Meg's anger and resistance thawed. Then the milliner hurried over with a handful of honey-brown velvet trimmed with blue braid.

"The latest thing, milady. A Portuguese cap. It'll suit your face and not look too fancy." She settled it firmly on Meg's head and directed her to look in the mirror.

"There, see," the earl said. "I knew Mrs. Ribbleside could do it. I'm not sure heavy brims suit you. That cap, with just your curls around your face, is very fetching."

Meg couldn't disagree. It did look well. She'd thought they'd force her into some ridiculous confection of white straw and feathers. The cap, however, covered all her hair except the curls at the front, and the warm color suited her, as well as working with her plain dress.

To object would be churlish and she had enough battles to fight without that. She stood and smiled. "Thank you, Mrs. Ribbleside. Now, my lord, may we go? My family will be worrying."

With bright thanks to the milliner, he swept her out to the carriage and ordered the coachman to make more speed. As they sped off, Meg noted that price or payment had never been mentioned. There was a sinful pleasure in that, in not needing to worry about the cost.

The fast-moving carriage swung around a corner, and she fell against him.

He sat her straight. "We're entering the square and I'll go odds we're hardly late at all."

Meg laughed, feeling caught up in a whirlwind, but a rather pleasant one. She looked from his sparkling eyes to the handsome square. "This is where your house is?"

"My London house, yes. Marlborough Square."

She saw a large, well-maintained garden in the center of the square. It even had a small duckpond, and some children were playing there, watched by nursemaids. The square itself contained grand row houses and a few detached mansions.

"It's lovely."

"I find it so. My main seat in the country is Haverhall in Sussex. I hope you don't mind the country."

The carriage was drawing to a halt and waiting servants sprang to open the door and let down the steps.

"I spent the past four years in the country as a governess, my lord. I liked it well enough." What a hasty shopping stop that had been. The carriage carrying her siblings had only just arrived. The earl seemed to do everything in a rush.

Except, apparently, make love to his wife.

Oh dear. Somewhere in this house there was a bed, and the night loomed. . . .

He jumped down and turned to hand her out. "You're going to have to call me something other than *my lord,* you know."

"Am I?"

"But of course. My friends call me Sax. You wouldn't like that."

Meg almost disagreed, but then guessed that was his plan. "It doesn't seem appropriate." She let him tuck her hand in his arm.

"My given names are Frederick George. I do not like to be called Frederick."

"Then perhaps I should call you Freddy."

"Do you really think so?"

She knew she could not. A less Freddy-like person was hard to imagine. Then she realized she was smiling at the thought.

"That's better. We're not opponents, my dear, even though I can be an irritating fellow. You and Owain can weep into your teacups over me. But for now, why not settle for Saxonhurst? It's better than 'my lord,' and may in time slide into the friendly Sax."

Meg accepted the olive branch with gratitude. "Very well, Saxonhurst. And what are you going to call me? You can't call me 'my dear' all the time."

As an attack, it was daunting as a feather. "I will be happy to call you 'my dear' all the time if you wish.

However, I would prefer to use your given name. Minerva, is it not? The goddess of wisdom."

Meg was about to correct him, but bit it back. Minerva was her real name, and it would keep a sense of formality between them. At the moment, the more formal the better.

Anyway, how much more elegant, how much more "countessy" it sounded. "Minerva Saxonhurst," she said, almost to herself, for she knew that a countess used her husband's title rather than his family name.

"Delightful." He gestured. "Pray, Minerva Saxonhurst, step into your home."

Aware of smiling, indulgent servants, who clearly thought their flamboyant employer top-of-the-trees, Meg obeyed.

Chapter 6

The house was a tall, double-fronted town house of gray stone, and in the spacious, tiled hall, a small army of servants stood ready to greet her. Every one was neatly turned out and bright eyed with curiosity.

Meg put aside another preconception. She wasn't needed to rescue the deranged earl from disorganization and chaos. She wasn't entirely sure he wasn't deranged, but not in any way that good housekeeping and tender nursing would mend.

Perhaps all she was needed for was the threatening bed.

Ah well, she intended to fit the role of wife in whatever way he wished. In fact, her rebellious banter in the coach could have been unruly. She glanced at him. He clearly hadn't minded. The idea of having someone to fence words with, someone who didn't mind her frankness and could give as good as he got, was rather exciting.

She'd certainly not expected it in a husband.

She spotted one liveried footman and just knew from his lively face and small stature that he was Susie's Monkey. He winked at her, grinning. Not surprising that he was happy when she'd just provided him with the means to start up in business.

A stately, gray-haired gentleman, doubtless the butler, came toward the earl, but before he could speak, one of the servants who'd been at the church cried, "Lord and Lady Saxonhurst. Hip-hip-hooray!"

And the hall rang with cheers.

In the following moment of silence, a voice said, "What folly have you fallen into now, Frederick?"

Meg felt the earl's arm turn to iron beneath her hand.

He whipped to face the side of the hall, where a silver-haired lady sat in an ornate, old-fashioned sedan chair, two chairmen liveried in crimson and silver standing like statues between the shafts.

The chair door stood open so Meg could see that the woman was dressed entirely in black, but of rich silk encrusted with jet. Her silver hair curled out from under the brim of a ruched, black silk bonnet. Her eyes had a familiar yellowish glint, and in the lined face those eyes looked hawkish.

"Your Grace, what a surprise." Meg had never before heard a voice convey bitter acid.

The old woman didn't flinch. She turned her hawk's gaze on Meg. "My poor child. This really wasn't wise, no matter how urgent your need—"

Before Meg could force any response out of her paper-dry mouth, the earl said, "Minerva is a respectable lady and now my countess, Your Grace. I must insist on complete courtesy."

The butler cleared his throat. "The dowager duchess brought baggage, my lord." He indicated a huge pile of valises and bandboxes tucked away in a corner.

"Will you throw me out into the street, Frederick?"

"I wouldn't dream of it."

Meg was pleased that at least the earl didn't intend to deny his grandmother a bed for the night.

Then he continued. "I will have you and your possessions most *carefully* removed and conveyed to Quiller's."

A hotel? "My lord—" Meg protested.

"Don't." His voice was quiet, meant only for her, and his eyes never left the woman in the chair. He seemed strangely like an animal at bay, eyeing growling hounds.

The duchess did not seem worthy of such rage. After all, this marriage *was* folly, and Meg would not have agreed to it if her need hadn't been truly urgent.

Suddenly, he produced a quizzing glass and raised it. "Cousin Daphne! Imagine you being here."

Meg hadn't noticed the young woman standing beside the old woman's chair, even though she was dressed in an expensive-looking, full-length spencer trimmed with fur, and a large bonnet frothed with plumes. The clothes overwhelmed her thin, pale form. If the earl seemed to be always taking up all the available space, this Cousin Daphne took up far less than her share.

Why, then, did the earl's voice have such a caustic edge?

The woman raised her chin, pale mouth trembling. "Why shouldn't I be here?" She pulled her left hand out of her enormous fur muff to reveal an old-fashioned ring bearing a large emerald. "I wear the Torrance betrothal ring."

Meg gasped, but her husband said, "I am not and have never been betrothed to marry her."

"We were to marry today!" Cousin Daphne declared.

"You are mistaken."

"It's been understood forever. The duchess said—"

"Occasionally, even the Dowager Duchess of Daingerfield makes a mistake. Pringle—"

"Philanderer!" snapped the duchess. "You played with Daphne in the cradle."

"If I did anything improper, it was my nursemaid's fault. Pringle—"

"*Saxonhurst!*" Daphne shrieked, crimson splotching her cheeks. "You disgusting man."

"My goodness, Daphne"—he stared at her again through the quizzing glass—"you've turned quite red. What *did* I do to you in the cradle? I must say, it's rather a feather in my cap to have been so precocious."

"You vile cad!"

Meg, horrified, silently echoed that. "My lord . . . !"

"Be quiet," he snapped. "Pringle, I am not accustomed to being ignored."

"My lord!" The butler almost snapped to attention. "You wish the duchess removed?"

"I thought I made that clear some time ago."

The duchess stared at him as fixedly as he stared back. "I defy you to throw me from the house, Frederick."

"She dismissed her carriages, my lord."

"Then use mine."

"I will not be moved. Stand your ground!" the duchess ordered her chairmen.

"Use all my carriages if you have to," the earl ordered. "Get the baggage out of here, and that includes the duchess and Lady Daphne."

"Saxonhurst!" exclaimed Lady Daphne. "Even you cannot—"

"Watch me."

"My lord," Meg protested. "It's the Christmas season—"

"Hold your tongue."

Horrified, Meg dashed over to put her arms around the twins. What had she done to bring her family here?

The servants sprang into action, positively sweeping the pile of baggage out of the hall. When the staff seemed likely to sweep out the sedan chair, too, the duchess slammed the door and ordered the men to move. Her hand made a claw on the edge of the lowered window. Stiff-necked, Cousin Daphne stalked alongside.

As the chair passed close, she glared at the earl. "You are beneath contempt, Saxonhurst."

"Then why the devil do you want to marry me?"

"Only for the duchess's sake. You pain her most terribly."

"You mean you don't lust for my body? Not even after all our merry cradle games?"

"You disgust me!"

"I think it's rather unfair to hold my infant technique against me. I assure you that now—"

"I will never darken your door again!" She would have stormed forward, but the earl put a hand out to stop her, and stepped closer to the sedan chair.

"May I hope that goes for you, too, Your Grace?"

The dowager looked up with the expression of an early martyr—of the sterner sort. "You are my sacred trust, Frederick. I will never wash my hands of you."

Saxonhurst suddenly looked around, seized Meg's hand, and dragged her to his side. "You were never properly introduced, were you? Minerva, Lady Saxonhurst, make the acquaintance of my mother's mother, the Dowager Duchess of Daingerfield, and my cousin, Lady Daphne Grigg."

The duchess looked up at Meg and truly did seem long-suffering. Meg could understand. The earl's behavior was completely beyond the line. Though not deranged, he was distinctly unbalanced and intolerably rude.

"I cannot in honesty welcome you to the family." The duchess's hawk's eyes swept over Meg's clothes, assessing and dismissing. "You are clearly unsuited for such high station and unlikely to bring Saxonhurst to any sense of his failings. But I cannot abandon my family. When you need advice, come to me. I will stay in town until Twelfth Night, apparently at Quiller's Hotel. Now, Frederick, if you will permit it, we will do as you wish and leave your disorderly house."

The earl stepped back sharply. The chair—which Meg now saw had a ducal coronet on the roof and a rampant lion on the door—was raised again by its attendants and carried out of the door.

The lion and the unicorn, fighting for the crown.
Upstairs and downstairs, and all around the town. . . .

She certainly felt as if she had tumbled into a war between mighty predators. What on earth was going on?

Daphne was no bride for the earl, and the duchess must know it. Susie had been right to suggest that the earl's grandmother would find him an unsuitable wife. It was especially horrid that the woman had seen him as a case to be reformed.

But then, he clearly was. No matter what lay between them, it was wrong to refuse hospitality to relatives, especially at this time of year. With a chill, Meg realized he had never once addressed the duchess as grandmother.

"She's upset you."

She searched him for signs of madness and saw only suave gloss. "I *am* unsuited to be an earl's bride."

He tucked away his quizzing glass. "What you need to know you can learn." With the closing of the door on the departing women, the angry, vicious man had faded like hoarfrost under the sun. "The staff here, though rascals one and all, know their business and will take care of you."

"But—"

"Don't pay the duchess any heed. In particular, don't scurry off to Quiller's asking for advice. That, I absolutely forbid."

And he meant that word, she saw.

"Now," he said, smile flashing, eyes brightening, "let's eat our luncheon before the twins starve to death!"

Servants came forward to ease them out of their outdoor clothing and carry it away as if every item was of silk and velvet.

"Where's Brak?" he suddenly demanded, making Meg tense, wondering what might appear next.

"We removed him in case of unpleasantness, milord," the butler said, and the next moment a huge, snarling beast raced into the hall.

"Sit!" the earl said sharply, and the dog skidded to a halt and onto its haunches. It still snarled, however, as if it, too, was starving to death, and it was the ugliest dog Meg had ever seen. Shaggy and a mottled gray-brown.

To her surprise, the earl went forward to hunker down before the beast and fondle it. Then she noticed how the dog's tail thumped the floor as if it wanted to shatter the tiles.

What a very strange pet for a nobleman. Coming on top of the horrible scene with his grandmother, she had to seriously doubt his mental balance.

He rose, saying to his dog, "Come and greet the new members of the family. They won't hurt you."

They won't hurt *you*!

He brought the dog over to Meg. "This is my countess. Greet her like a gentleman, Brak."

Though the tail had stopped wagging, the dog sat and presented a paw.

Meg made herself take it. "Good morning, Brak."

It still snarled.

"His mouth is misshapen," the earl said. "Ignore his teeth. He's a terrible coward and would never attack anyone."

The earl then introduced the dog to Meg's family, and it was clear his intent was to soothe the animal, not the children. In fact, he said to the twins, "I'm sure he'll enjoy your company, but you are not to tease him. And don't ever think he'll defend you, for he won't."

Meg longed to ask why he kept such a useless burden of a dog, but held her tongue. It could be a form of insanity, but it offered hope for another useless set of burdens he'd taken on.

Now that the dog was apparently happy, the earl swept Meg toward a room, but halted as a footman hurried forward and whispered something in his ear.

What now? Meg turned to make sure her brothers and sisters weren't upset by this mayhem. Laura rolled her eyes, but with a grin. The twins were somewhat nervously attempting a friendship with the snarling dog. Jeremy was studying a Greek statue in an alcove. None of them seemed as disturbed as she.

Of course, none of them would be sharing a bed with this strange man tonight. Why, oh why, had she not left him to hunt as he pleased? She could probably have avoided the trap for weeks, perhaps months!

He gave some instruction to the servant, then shepherded them all into a moderately sized dining room. Meg was pleased to see the dog stay outside. She supposed it was to the earl's credit that the creature was well trained.

A gleaming table set for seven was laden with dishes. She heard Rachel whisper to Richard, "Look. Gold!"

And there were indeed two gold platters in the center holding fruit and nuts. It was all going to be too much.

She glanced at the excited twins. "Richard and Rachel don't usually . . ."

"Eat with the adults? But this is a special day. Sit, everyone!"

Meg took a seat at his right-hand side, but kept a nervous eye on the young pair. They were eyeing the extravagant display of food as if it might disappear if they blinked. They'd end up sick, she was sure of it.

Then servants entered and put dishes of ice cream in front of everyone.

"My lord, we can't eat this first!"

"Why not?" He picked up his spoon and dug in. "They didn't have much ice left to pack it in, and we were delayed. It will melt."

"It's cold enough outside to hold it."

"Birds will eat it."

"My lord—"

He raised his spoon to her lips. "Come, Minerva. Live decadently for once."

Commanded by his vivid eyes, she closed her lips around the spoon. At the delicious burst of sweetness and vanilla, she knew she'd taken the first step on a very slippery slope.

With a smile, he gave her the spoon and took hers, then proceeded to eat his ice cream with relish. Meg had to admit to enjoying hers, too, even though it seemed thoroughly wicked to eat such luxury before the nourishing food.

It wasn't wicked though, just a minor folly. She watched her siblings enjoy the treat and relaxed. This was part of what she wanted for them, wasn't it? Good food with occasional luxuries.

The room was still decorated for Christmas, with evergreens, bright ribbons, gilded nuts, and kissing boughs—all the things the twins had missed. This wasn't a Christmas dinner, but it was close enough. There was ham on the table, and nuts and oranges in bowls. There were still six days of Christmas left, and her family wouldn't miss all of it, thanks to this man.

Once the ices were finished, servants brought hot dishes, and served wine to the adults, lemonade to the younger ones.

Owain stood and raised his glass. "To Lady Saxonhurst, the gracious lady who has made us all so very happy."

Meg blushed as everyone said, "Hear, hear!", the twins particularly loudly. Then Richard and Rachel gulped their lemonade as if they lived in a desert.

The earl rose. "On behalf of my wife, I thank you, and I thank her, too, for the charming family she brings as dowry. To Minerva." He raised his wineglass to Meg, and looked at her as he drank.

For a moment, she felt quite dizzy. Despite everything, the look in his eyes seemed sincerely affectionate and appreciative, making her feel that the air was suddenly thin. It was hard to remember the cold man of the confrontation. Instead, she was almost engulfed in charm.

But then she remembered the hunt.

It had seemed so clever at the time—to prevent seduction by getting through the business more brusquely. Now, however, her bold words sounded as clever as a rabbit leaping into the fox's jaws to avoid being chased!

"I'm studying your tastes."

The earl's voice made Meg aware that she'd been so busy eating and keeping an eye on the twins that she'd neglected conversation. "My tastes, my lord?"

"Saxonhurst," he reminded her.

"Yes, Saxonhurst. Why are you studying my tastes?"

"So I will know how to please you."

"I am not hard to please." But then her mouth dried and she took a gulp of wine to ease it. "You mean, you are studying how best to hunt me."

"Didn't you promised to come gently into my snare? Tonight."

Now might be a good time to announce a change of plans, but she hated to back down. Anyway, she could hardly get into such a matter at the table. She realized that after the ice, the earl had eaten lightly. He wasn't eating now, but just sipping from his wine, relaxed back in his chair.

She, on the other hand, had been as gluttonous as the twins. Embarrassed, she put down her knife and fork, even though that left half a shrimp tart uneaten.

He raised a finger and a footman hurried forward to refill her wineglass. Meg wasn't sure it was wise to drink more, but it was a very fine wine, and she needed something to do with her hands.

"I am studying your tastes," he said again. "You like shrimp, but you do not seem to care for whiting. You chose artichokes, but not parsnip."

"Perhaps there is just too much choice. I am used to living simply."

"But you have left part of your shrimp tart. That puzzles me, since it is your second. Is something wrong with it?"

She blushed. "Truth to tell, I was merely trying to be genteel. To eat as little as you." She picked up her knife and fork. "I can't let it go to waste, though."

He laughed, and the effect was enough to deprive her

of her wits entirely. She concentrated on the puff pastry and shrimp.

"I have a very healthy appetite, I assure you. Very healthy." He let that wind around her for a moment, then added, "But I ate a large breakfast. I'm sure I'll be hungry. Later."

Oh dear.

"What would please you this evening?"

Meg almost choked.

"In the way of entertainment."

She stared at him.

"Family entertainment," he added, a distinct twinkle in his eye. The wretch.

"We normally read, my lord, if there's light enough. Or do needlework." Trying to cover embarrassment, Meg gabbled on. "Play games, perhaps. Usually, we go early to bed. . . ."

No, no. That wasn't wise.

"How delightful." Eyes positively glittering with wicked amusement, he sipped his wine again. It seemed to focus her attention on his lips. They were very well-shaped, neither too thin nor too plump. Perfect, in fact, and she could remember how they had felt against hers—

"But tonight, perhaps we could be a little more adventurous. More daring? For my birthday."

She stared, feeling very like a rabbit waiting for the snap of the fox's jaws.

"It is New Year's Eve, too, and the theaters are presenting special fare."

Meg broke the spell of his eyes and sipped her own wine. "In truth, my lord, we would probably enjoy Astley's, if they still do their equestrian shows. My parents took us years ago, but the twins were too young."

Little pitchers have big ears. "Astley's?" Richard exclaimed, deplorably around a mouthful of food.

"Really?" Rachel asked.

The earl laughed. "Astley's it is. Owain?"

The secretary turned to the hovering Monkey, who hurried out.

Meg must have looked puzzled, for the earl said, "I let Owain make all these arrangements. He can keep track of them so much better than I. Besides, he needs employment. The devil finds work for idle hands." Mr. Chancellor snorted. "Monk will buy us good tickets—footmen know about that sort of thing. You must feel free to ask Owain whenever you need things arranged."

"I do have business matters to discuss. With you, my lord." Meg hated to raise money matters so soon, but her debts hung over her like a sodden, dark cloth likely at any moment to smother her.

"Then we will attend to them after the meal. Another cream or jelly?"

"No, thank you. I have already eaten far too much."

"I think you all need filling out. Anyone else?"

Laura and Jeremy declined, but Meg saw temptation in the twins' eyes, even though they must be stuffed. "No more," she said to them firmly. "You can have something later if you find yourselves hungry."

She knew it would take a little time for them to grow confident that good food would appear at regular intervals. Just as it would take time for her to accept that they had all more or less fallen on their feet.

And they had, despite the earl's erratic behavior, and the rapidly approaching marriage bed. Everything, it appeared, was now theirs at the snap of the fingers.

They all left the table, and on the earl's suggestion, Mr. Chancellor took her siblings to inspect the rooms set aside for them. He called after them, "Be sure to ask for any changes you want!"

Then he escorted Meg to another room, and the dog rose to accompany them.

Meg was relieved to find herself in a kind of study with a large desk and bookcases. A safe sort of room. And cozy. The dog settled itself in front of the glowing fire.

Meg realized that every room here seemed to have an extravagant fire. Even the hall had been tolerably warm. Perhaps some of her heat at the moment, however, was from awkwardness and embarrassment, not just coals. She was truly alone with her husband for the first time, and was going to have to discuss money.

Saxonhurst directed her to the sofa which sat near the fireplace. She looked longingly at the two chairs, a decorous yard or two apart, but she perched at one end of the sofa. "This is where you conduct business, my lord?"

"Owain does everything—he has his own rooms—so I lounge around here in idleness just to keep up appearances." He suited action to the words by lounging at the other end of the sofa, arms draped along back and side. The Earl of Saxonhurst had an irritating way of taking up all the available space. "Now, what business matters do you wish to discuss?"

"Perhaps Mr. Chancellor should be present." She was genuinely curious about how he arranged his life, but much more anxious for a chaperon. His arm along the carved top of the sofa placed his hand perilously close to her shoulder.

"I'll give him the work to do, but your personal affairs are best discussed in private."

He was right about that. Meg had become so used to struggling alone that it was difficult to lay her problems before even one other, even if he was her husband. She particularly hated the fact that she was going to have to ask for money.

"So," he prompted, "what concerns you?"

"I have debts," she said bluntly, looking down at her hands in her lap. "I know this wasn't mentioned, and I'm sure you are not obliged to pay them—"

"There you are wrong, my dear. A husband assumes his wife's debts."

"Oh." She frowned at him. "Weren't you a little foolish not to ask about them, then, my lord?"

"Minerva, I would be astonished—more than that, even—if you have liabilities that can make even a dent in my fortune. I needed to marry and was willing to pay the costs. So, what debts?"

When she continued to frown at him, trying to phrase a suggestion that he be more cautious, he added, "Don't. Stronger arms than yours have tried to change me. What debts, Minerva?"

She surrendered, for the moment. Despite his words, however, she resolved to try to eventually teach him to be more sensible.

"The local tradespeople have been kind in extending

our credit. I've paid what I can, but much is still outstanding. I would like to see them get their money, for they are all hardworking people. . . ." Oh, she hated this. "If you planned to give me any kind of pin money, my lord—"

His firm grip on her shoulder silenced her. She'd been staring into space, she realized, desperately embarrassed.

"Minerva, there's no reason to sound as if you are confessing to sins. Of course, you have bills you have not been able to pay. And of course, I will pay them. I certainly won't consider taking it out of your pin money. Will two hundred do?"

"Two hundred will pay them all!"

"That's all you owe?"

Her cheeks heated at his astonishment, as if it were shameful to owe such a paltry amount. An amount that was a year's wages for some, and that could have cast her family into disaster.

"Consider them gone," he said. "When I mentioned two hundred, that's for your quarterly pin money."

"Two hundred pounds!"

"Guineas."

"It's far too much."

"You'll find it's not." She realized that his hand still rested on her shoulder. It no longer gripped. Now, it almost burned. "I'll pay your modiste's bills and such, but there'll be any number of smaller items you'll want to buy. In addition, as Countess of Saxonhurst, you'll be expected to support charities and other worthy causes. And there'll be social gaming. I will expect you to cover such expenses from your own money."

"I don't gamble."

His smile flickered. "I think you gambled today."

"You know what I mean."

"Yes. But your life has changed. It would be foolish to deny it. You will live in a different way. My grandmother was right in saying it will challenge you, but I doubt it will be beyond you."

She felt as if she'd been given an award. "Thank you."

"Unless you take to deep gambling—and be sure I would curb you—money is of no concern. I'll have my solicitor in to settle all these details, and settle money on your brothers and sisters, too." He smiled. "Laura is going to break hearts, soon. She must have the dignity of an adequate portion."

Meg's resolve to make him careful warred with the temptation of his generosity. "It would be wrong . . ."

"The idea of broken male hearts distresses you? I thought ladies loved that sort of thing."

"I mean your providing for her."

"Wasn't that our arrangement?"

"I meant only that you give her a suitable home. . . ."

"But then we'd have her on our hands forever." He took any offense out of it with a smile. "Anyway, I quite look forward to seeing my friends make cakes of themselves over her."

Remembering Sir Arthur, Meg felt a stab of alarm. "She's only fifteen!"

"That won't stop them. And next year, if you approve, she can make her curtsy and begin to wreak true havoc."

"I don't know. . . ." But making her curtsy sounded decorous and safe, besides implying . . .

"Presentation at Court?" she whispered, staring at him. "Surely not."

"Surely yes. You must be presented as my wife, and soon. That's essential. And your brothers and sisters in due course."

"Oh . . ." Meg felt stuffed on sugar and cream, a not entirely pleasant sensation. It was all too much. And yet, she wasn't strong enough to deny her siblings these advantages.

Somehow, the earl had come closer, and now he took her hands. Startling contact, skin to skin. "Don't worry so much, my dear. I'm sure it's been a hard time, but now you can toss your burdens onto me. They will be feathers, particularly as I'll toss them onto Owain. Give him a complete list of your debts, and he'll settle them. Do you have other matters fretting you?"

If only she could rely on him always being this earl, and never being the wild one.

"I don't think so, my lord. Oh, we do need to collect our possessions from the house. In fact, we owe rent! I forgot because Sir Arthur said we need not pay."

"Sir Arthur?"

She almost spilled out the whole truth, but thank heavens she managed to control herself. She couldn't imagine what the earl would do if he knew the truth, but it would doubtless be something extreme. "Sir Arthur Jakes. He was a friend of my father's and rented my parents the house."

"And he, too, extended your credit. Good of him. Certainly he should be paid."

Meg wanted him paid to make sure there was no lingering connection, absolutely no danger to Laura.

"Now," he said, leaping up and pulling her to her feet, "come and inspect your rooms."

Meg went with him up the stairs—he gave her little choice—but halfway up the gleaming, elegant curve, she froze. Rooms surely included bedrooms.

When he looked at her in surprise, she said, "We need to go back to our house *soon*. To collect our clothes and such."

"We'll go shortly." He tugged her onward, and down a lushly carpeted corridor hung carelessly with art.

He flung open a door and guided her into a handsome room—a boudoir. Not, thank heavens, the bedroom. It was a somewhat heavy chamber, paneled in dark wood and furnished in greens and browns. Of course, it was warmed by a roaring fire.

"It's decades out of style." He strode to tug the bell-pull. "Will you need a cart, or will a carriage do?" He gestured around. "What do you think?"

After a moment, Meg realized he was asking about the room, not the transportation. Feeling like a whirligig in a gale, she answered with a trite, "It's lovely."

"No, it's not." He flicked the faded olive brocade hangings. "This color is positively bilious. But it'll do until you refurbish it."

"That's not necessary—"

A footman entered.

"Clarence. Arrange for carriages to take us all to Lady Saxonhurst's home to collect belongings."

"Certainly, milord. Us? And how many carriages, milord?"

"Myself, Mr. Chancellor, my new family, and as many servants as necessary. Work it out." He waved the man off, and Meg noticed that the man dragged a twisted right foot as he went.

"Shouldn't the poor man be allowed to rest?"

"It's permanent. Carriage rolled over him years ago." He swept her into another room, and this time it was the bedchamber, ruled by a grand tester swathed in more olive-green brocade draperies with gold plumed finials on top of every post.

"Oh my."

"It's a heavy sort of style, but I assure you it's all dusted and aired out. Do you know how many carriages or carts'll be needed for your belongings?"

Meg tried to follow his gadfly mind. "I've never thought about how much we have. I feel as if we have little, but we've lived there nearly ten years—"

"Owain will know." He opened the door to the corridor and shouted, "Clarence! Check with Mr. Chancellor!" Then he went to open a door in the side wall. "Dressing and bathing room." Heaving back the solid top on a huge wooden box, he revealed a flower-decorated tub big enough to lie in.

"Oh!" Meg leaned over it, marveling at the interior. She'd never bathed in anything so wonderful. The best they'd had was a tin tub before the kitchen fire.

He turned her face to his and kissed her. "Enjoy." He made a bath sound like the most wicked indulgence in the world. Then he added softly, fingers still resting on her cheek, "I'll have to give Susie a bonus."

Meg could easily be distracted into positive dreaminess by the flickering warmth in his golden eyes, by the warm pressure of his fingers against her skin. Or perhaps it was just a sense of him, like the heat in a warm room on a midwinter day. . . .

"Susie is getting an inn, isn't she?" she managed. Perhaps that had only been a joke.

"She deserves more. This is turning out to be a wonderful idea." Suddenly he swept her up into his arms and twirled about the room.

Over her shriek, he said, "Imagine, I could even now be here with Cordelia Cathcart, witness to her gloating, aware of her horrible family all attaching themselves to me like barnacles. And feeling I would have to grovel forever to the chit for obliging me."

Clutching him for fear of falling, she said, "Put me down. Please, my lord!"

He kissed her. "Instead, I am in the delightful situation of benefactor, and very pleased with myself." He stilled to kiss her again, a little more lingeringly this time. "Very pleased . . ."

Meg surrendered to the play of soft lips against hers, to a closeness more intimate than anything she had ever known. . . .

But then she recognized the moves in his hunting game. Especially when he backed out of the dressing room with her still in his arms, and the plumed bed loomed over his shoulder like a threatening cloud.

"Our things, my lord," she said urgently.

"Things?" He grinned, making her words suddenly wicked.

"Clothes!"

"We have them on."

"All our clothes."

"You want them off?"

"No! From Mallett Street. Books. Toys. Pots and pans . . ."

"Intriguing," he murmured, still backing toward the bed.

She couldn't imagine how he knew where he was, but he suddenly whirled and tossed her into the middle of the brocade-covered mattress. Meg sprawled there, feeling just like a cornered rabbit eyeing the fox.

Though she was sure no rabbit ever felt this way about its hunter.

"Mmmmm." Using a hand on a post as anchor, he leaned toward her, sounding just like the twins faced with a sticky cake. But after a hovering moment—hawk, she thought—he swung back. "I'll tell the others we're off to pillage your old home."

He left, and Meg lay there stunned, trying to gather the strength in her limbs to move, and the power of her wits to think. What an extraordinary man!

The past few hours had undoubtedly been the most tumultuous of her life. She didn't really know what to think, though she did hope that occasionally her husband would have a peaceful moment. It was perhaps as well that there seemed no work for her to do here. She'd be exhausted just trying to keep up with him.

There was something about him though.

Something almost magical . . .

Then she came to her senses and wondered what he was up to. Feeling rather as she had when left in sole charge of the Ramillys' free-spirited, three-year-old son, she scrambled out of the dip and off the bed and tracked voices up to the next floor.

She found the earl on the floor of a schoolroom with the twins, rolling a miniature carriage backward and forward. He looked up with an open smile, and lifted the toy. "Isn't it grand? It's an exact copy of the town coach my parents had."

Though a bit battered, it was almost a work of art, painted blue with gilt touches and a crest on the door. Inside, it seemed perfectly fitted out with brocade squabs. It was, she realized, a replica of the carriage she'd ridden in today, and yet it must date back to his childhood or farther. Was that part of the aristocratic tradition, to keep things always the same? She'd noted that most of the furnishings in this house went back through the centuries.

"It used to have horses," he said, giving it to Richard and rising to his feet. "And figures to sit inside and out."

"Like this, sir?" Rachel dug in a wooden box and produced one carved figure, minus most of one arm.

"John Coachman!" The earl hunkered down again and placed the figure gently on the seat. He had to prop it against one of the side supports to make it stay. He looked into the box, clearly hoping for others, but then shrugged. "We'll have new made. Now," he said to the twins, rising with that strong, fluid grace that made Meg think of predators, "it's time for you to take me to explore your old home and show me your toys."

The twins each seized an arm and virtually dragged him out and down the stairs, chattering. Feeling almost weepy with dazedness and happiness, Meg followed with Laura and Jeremy.

"He seems very pleasant," Laura said, but cautiously.

"He is," Meg agreed, though pleasant wasn't quite the word. She only wished she didn't fear a turn of mood.

What, after all, if he decided she or one of her family was an enemy like his grandmother?

"Will I be able to continue my studies with Dr. Pierce?" Jeremy asked.

Meg almost said that they'd have to ask the earl, but then decided that if she was married to a wealthy earl— for better or worse—she was allowed to make such decisions. "Yes, of course. And we can buy you those Greek texts you wanted. New."

Chapter 7

They all piled into two carriages, though this time the earl made no objection to the twins traveling with him and Meg. Since the twins were capable of incessant talking, it relieved Meg of any need to make conversation.

As they approached their old home, she smiled at their commentary.

"That's Ned," Richard said, "the rag-and-bone man."

"He looks rough, sir," Rachel contributed, "but he's all right. And there's Mrs. Pickett with her dog."

"He bites, sir. You need to be careful of him. That's the haberdashery. Dull stuff."

" 'Tis not! They have ever such pretty ribbons. And buckles and buttons. All kinds of things. That's the bookshop. And the milliners."

"Hats!"

"Lord Saxonhurst's wearing a hat, so there!"

"But he gets his from a hatter. Don't you, sir?"

"I'm afraid I do. Though why there's a difference, I don't know."

"Because we wouldn't want flowers on our hats, would we, sir?"

As the twins squabbled over whether men's hats were sillier than women's, the earl looked at Meg's new hat. "Next time, it will definitely have to have flowers."

Instinctively, she reached up to touch her lovely velvet beret. "Perhaps I prefer a plainer style."

"But I sometimes like the effect of a frivolous, flowery bonnet."

Part of Meg longed for such an item, part of her resisted. Part wanted to please this man, and part of her wanted to fight.

"Oh look," Richard called, "there's our house, sir!

The one with the blue door just beyond the Nag's Head Inn."

Looking at the place with a stranger's eye, Meg was ashamed of its simplicity, but fiercely glad that it was respectable. At least they wouldn't look the complete charity cases that they were. She supposed she had to give Sir Arthur credit for that. As a landlord, he had been responsible.

She hadn't thought until now about leaving her home, and felt a pang. She'd left the house this morning, thinking for some reason to return with all their problems solved. Now they must take away their possessions so that some other family could move in.

The two handsome carriages were creating a small sensation, with strollers stopping to look, and neighbors popping out to see what was happening. Since the twins were pressed to the window, most of the watchers soon realized who was coming, and as they waved or smiled, doubtless wondered even more about things.

Meg, who'd never been comfortable with having her business known to all, found the circus horribly embarrassing. She thanked heaven that no one was likely to guess the truth.

It was as if the earl could read minds. When the carriage drew to a halt, he said quietly, "No need, I assume, to tell the whole story."

"I hope not."

The twins were totally engaged in waving to friends and waiting impatiently for the steps to be let down.

"What did you tell your family?"

She blushed for her lie. "That we'd met at the Ramillys'—the family where I was governess."

"And we fell madly in love?"

"Of course not. That would be absurd."

His brows rose. "You think love absurd?"

"No. But between you and me . . ." She felt silenced by the look in his eyes. "I mean, love at first sight. It's impossible."

"You live in a very rational universe."

"So," said Meg hurriedly, "you discovered I was in need. As you needed a wife, you suggested this arrangement."

"How delightfully cool blooded and practical. We'll stick to that. And I suggest handling further enquiries with a touch of aristocratic hauteur." He climbed out of the coach and turned to hand her down.

"Alas, sir, I have none."

"Then practice, my dear countess. Practice!"

Meg couldn't help but smile as she dug in her bag for the key. But then the door opened, and Sir Arthur appeared.

Meg's breath caught. She'd entirely forgotten that today was the day upon which their week ran out. Frozen, she might have created an embarrassment, but the twins ran at him, eager to tell their news.

His chilly eyes swept over Meg and Laura. "Is this true?"

Meg forced a bright smile. "Isn't it wonderful, Sir Arthur? And how pleased you must be not to have to worry about us anymore."

Because of the rage in his eyes, she might not have been able to approach the door, to confront him, if the earl hadn't steered her that way. For a moment, she feared that Sir Arthur would try to block their way, but then he retreated into the hall, pale, but finding a smile. "If you have found support for your family, of course all your friends must be pleased." But his eyes flickered toward Laura, and Meg at least recognized the thwarted hunger there.

He controlled himself almost at once. "You have come to show your groom the family home?"

"The countess has come," the earl said, "to collect her family's personal possessions." To Meg's surprise, the quizzing glass had appeared again. "I must thank you for your kindness to her, sir. And of course, you must submit an account for any sums owing to my secretary."

With that lesson in aristocratic hauteur, he guided Meg past Sir Arthur. "Show me around, my dear. I am very interested in the places where you played as a child."

Meg went, wickedly gleeful to see Sir Arthur treated like an upper servant. Hauteur definitely had its uses.

She gave the guided tour of their modest home, hearing the younger ones doing the same in other directions for the infinitely obliging Mr. Chancellor. It would be pleasant to have someone like . . .

She turned to the earl. "May I employ a secretary?"

"Employ anyone you wish. A female secretary might be more suitable, however. A kind of companion." They were in a corridor, and Meg had just opened a cupboard to sort good bedding from worn out. "My dear," he said, taking a yellowed pillowcase from her and tossing it back in, "we don't need more linens. Leave 'em, unless they have sentimental importance."

Meg thought of the weary hours of darning and gladly closed the door.

"Make her pretty, pure, and ethereal."

She blinked at him. "Who?"

"Your secretary."

"Why?"

"Owain's taste runs in that lamentable direction."

"Lamentable?"

"My dear, pretty is all very well, but pure is a dead bore."

Meg bristled. "I am pure."

"I don't think so."

"My lord!"

He smiled, unmoved by her outrage. "I'm not suggesting a wicked past, Minerva. But if you weren't so aware of base desires, you wouldn't be so nervous of me, would you?"

He let his gaze wander over her. It wasn't offensive exactly. His expression was too warm, too appreciative to really give offense. But it definitely made her nervous. It promised . . . things. Things she knew about without really knowing. Things that made her cheeks heat and her breathing falter.

"You see?" he said softly.

She turned sharply away. "You must have the same effect on every woman."

"I try, Minerva. I try."

So she turned back, chin up. "And if I say that I expect you to be faithful to me?"

And that knocked him on his heels a bit, she saw with

satisfaction. "Then I'd say that you will have to make yourself very available to me."

"Or perhaps you could restrain your lust."

His brows rose. "And what do you know of lust?"

"You reek of it!" Meg swung away, hands to burning cheeks. "How do you make me say such things? We shouldn't be speaking so!"

His hand circled the back of her neck, not violently, but causing her to freeze. "Certainly not here," he murmured, one finger stroking. "Later, however, such talk could be delightful."

The hand moved to her shoulder, and lips brushed her nape. "You have a charmingly vulnerable nape. A very seductive, slender nape . . ."

Then he stepped away. "I think I hear my servants clattering in." He captured her hand and tugged her down the corridor. "Come on. We'd best go through the rooms with them. You don't want them taking items that aren't yours. Or leaving anything behind."

Meg went, feeling she was leaving common sense and control behind forever.

Soon servants were carrying down whatever she wished. Aware of Sir Arthur checking each item, she was conservative. With some of the older bits and pieces she didn't know if they had come with the house or been purchased by her parents, and she didn't want to risk any unpleasantness. Anyway, as the earl said, there was no point in taking kitchen pots and worn-out furnishings.

It wasn't until she was pointing out the few items in her parents' room that she thought of the *sheelagh-ma-gig*. She could hardly see it in its bag that matched the swathed draperies, but she was aware of it as if it glowed.

How could she possibly order it taken down and removed? It must raise all kinds of questions just from being up there. And how could she explain wanting to take an old stone statue of a rudely naked woman? How could she explain to her new husband the fact that she'd have to keep it by her, but never let people touch it?

She imagined having to tell him that she'd used pagan magic to trap him in this bizarre marriage, and was appalled—as much at the fact that she *had* done that, as at the awkwardness of having to confess it.

She'd forced him into this horribly unequal match. He was being gracious, but she had *nothing* to offer him. He must certainly never suspect the truth!

Almost shaking with panic, she tried to evade him. If she were alone, she could climb up and retrieve it, then think of a way to smuggle it out of the house. Put it in a bandbox, perhaps, or stuff it in a pillow and insist on carrying it.

No, insist on Laura carrying it. She couldn't risk the effects of being that close.

But the earl wouldn't leave her side, and Sir Arthur was inspecting everything as if he thought they would steal.

She realized in the end that she *was* going to steal the *sheelagh.* Not that it would really be stealing. But she was going to have to sneak back and take the *sheelagh* secretly. She could hardly believe it.

She was staring at her parents' bed in numb frustration, when he said, "Sad memories?"

As if summoned, they came.

She hadn't thought this house particularly important to her, but now she was leaving, a kind of grief washed over her.

Of course. It was grief, grief for her parents. She'd been so caught up in managing that she'd hardly had time to be sad, but this was the final parting. The end of all the family life she had known.

Her father had died in this bed. Her mother had been found beside him. Her father's death had not been a mystery, for he'd been in ill health for many months, suffering unexplained pain and bleeding, and infections he could not fight. In the doctor's opinion, it was a miracle he'd lived as long as he did.

But the doctor had been puzzled by her mother's death. She had been healthy apart from the exhaustion of nursing. Seeming a bit ashamed of the diagnosis, Dr. Hardy had decided she'd died of grief and despair.

Meg could believe that. Her parents had been so deeply devoted.

How they would have hated to see her make a marriage of convenience, but they'd left her little choice. They'd been so wrapped up in each other that they'd not thought to provide properly for the future.

"Minerva?"

A moment later, she felt his touch and he turned her.

"Oh my dear," he said, and drew her into his arms.

She didn't say anything, for she couldn't speak of her pain to a stranger, even if he was a husband. She wouldn't cry before a stranger, either. But she welcomed the strong embrace.

"Minerva, it would be better to cry than fight it."

"I'm all right," she said, stepping free of him, chin firm.

He looked at her somewhat wryly, but didn't argue. "Very well. We need to go. I've sent the others on ahead, but Sir Arthur is waiting for you to surrender the keys."

She took a deep breath. "I'm sorry—"

He put his fingers over her lips. "Do stop saying that. If we can't comfort each other now and then, what is marriage for?" He looked around the room. "Do you want to take this bed? I noticed how sorry you seemed to leave it." He made an impatient gesture. "Plague take it, my dear, I'll buy the whole house for you if—"

"No." Meg found herself laughing, and deeply touched. "No, but thank you, Saxonhurst."

It was only as she went downstairs that Meg wondered if she'd just rejected a solution. If he'd bought the bed . . .

But no. In dismantling it, the *sheelagh* would still come to light.

Perhaps she should have let him buy the whole house, ridiculous though that would be!

If only, if only, she had thought of this before leaving for the church, she could have made any number of arrangements. What a ninny she was.

Sir Arthur was waiting, looking martyred. Meg was tempted to say something cutting to him, but restrained herself. For one thing, she was strangely certain that if she even hinted at Sir Arthur's plan, the earl would be driven to one of his rages.

She merely handed over most of the keys. "Thank

you again, Sir Arthur. It was only because of you that we've been able to survive the past few months." And that was perfectly true, making it easy to smile at him.

Perhaps he hadn't always been set on wickedness, and had only given in to temptation at the end.

"Your father would have wanted me to take care of you, Lady Saxonhurst. I only regret that I was unable to do more."

Catching his double meaning, Meg lost any desire to think kindly of him and rejoiced in the spare backdoor key weighing down her reticule. She said a firm good-bye and headed out to the street.

There, however, she found a number of acquaintances and neighbors hovering to say good-bye—and to satisfy their curiosity. For a moment she feared to be dunned by creditors. If that happened in the earl's presence, she'd want to hide under a rock. She realized, however, that she was surrounded only by smiling faces.

It soon became clear that Mr. Chancellor had spread the word that all the Gillingham family debts would be cleared. It was also clear that someone, perhaps Laura, had spread a romanticized tale of lovers parted by circumstances, but brought together in the end. A couple of the more sentimental women were dabbing their eyes with their aprons.

And of course, it didn't hurt that this was a once-in-a-lifetime chance to rub shoulders with an earl. How admirably at ease he seemed with the attention, the gawking, and the fawning. He was pleasant with everyone, and didn't employ the quizzing glass. She supposed he was used to it. How on earth was she to become used to it?

Eventually they escaped, and she settled into the seat in the coach with a relieved sigh. "We've certainly provided the neighborhood with enough excitement for the year."

"We live to amuse. What else are the nobility for?"

"Nobility?" Then she realized she was that now. "How strange."

"One becomes accustomed. Better?"

He looked only kind. "Yes, of course. It was just that I haven't had much time to mourn. And my mother's death, at least, was very sudden." But then, of course, he wanted details about her mother's death, which led to questions about her parents' lives. She wondered what he would make of the story.

However, all he said in the end was, "And how did two such wild romantics produce sensible Minerva Gillingham?"

"Someone had to be sensible." And there she was, saying something she shouldn't. She had always felt the need to be steady in the midst of her parents' almost fey carelessness about the realities of life, but she hated to sound critical.

For the first time, she wondered whether her mother had used the *sheelagh* to ease their way through life. Such fecklessness should not have been so comfortable, but though disaster had often hovered, they'd never seemed truly concerned, and the worst had never happened.

If the stone always demanded a price, however, what had it been?

Her father's horrible sickness? she asked for the first time. Their deaths?

"Do stop looking so somber," he complained. "You'll make me think myself a poor sort of husband. Clearly, I must seduce you into silliness."

Meg pushed away worries and concentrated on him. "Now there, my lord, you will fail. I've been tediously sensible since the day I was born. Exactly on time, and in the middle of the day."

He waved away her words. "We must buy you any number of things and I will insist that some of them be silly. Frivolous bonnets that serve no purpose but to drive men mad. Silk stockings so fine that they tear at first wearing. Handkerchiefs of lace that no one would ever dare to blow a nose on."

Meg could only hope that his butterfly mind would soon flit to other nonsense. "And where are your silly extravagances, my lord?"

"Women exist to give men reason to spend. But then"—and he flipped open his dark green jacket to reveal a waistcoat fabulously embroidered with glittering snakes—"we try, now and then."

Without thinking, Meg reached out to touch a snake, for the embroidery was marvelous. Then she snatched her hand back as if burned.

"But sometimes," he said softly, "frivolities are worth every penny."

Meg turned away. She'd managed rather well thus far at ignoring him—his body, that is—but in one moment the shell had shattered and she was feverishly aware that beneath elegant clothes and a light, charming manner was a hard, alarming, male body.

A hard, male body she had agreed to accept tonight. And apart from other concerns, tonight, or early tomorrow, she had to sneak back into her house to steal the *sheelagh*!

Oh dear.

"My lord . . ." she said, turning back and even trying a smile.

"Saxonhurst. I will be much easier to handle if you call me Saxonhurst."

She sucked in a deep breath. "Saxonhurst. I may have given you the impression. Earlier. When we were returning from the church . . ."

"Yes?"

Drat the man, he knew exactly what she was trying to say, but didn't intend to help at all. A tiny part of her was relieved, for it must surely indicate a trace of interest in her bodily charms. If he was repulsed, he'd take any excuse to avoid her, wouldn't he?

Then she remembered that any trace of interest was a problem, not a benefit. She had to be free of him tonight.

She licked her lips. "I might have given you the impression, my lord Saxonhurst—that I am eager for . . . that I . . ." She looked at him, begging him to take over.

Instead, he just looked puzzled—except for the wicked mischief in his eyes.

"Your snakes, sir, are a most appropriate heraldic device!"

"My snakes?" He looked down as if surprised, then ran his hand over the richly embroidered fabric. In fact, he followed one snake round and round, lower and lower. Meg watched his hand, entranced, until it stopped where the straight edge of his waistcoat met his tight buff breeches. His very tight buff breeches—

Suddenly, he seized her at the waist and lifted her astride his lap. "Having raised me to indecent heights, wife, you had best hide me for a while."

She tried to move, to struggle off, but he held her. She wanted to scream, but that would be wildly inappropriate. She was about to protest that they'd be seen, when he leaned to pull down the blinds on either side, plunging them into gloom, and making her clutch his shoulders for balance.

"My lord!"

"Of course," he said, "this position is hardly likely to help me to subside, especially if you keep wriggling and bouncing, but it is far too pleasant to give up."

Meg went still, all too aware of his "risen form."

"No more struggles?" After a moment, he let her go and lounged back lazily, as if he didn't have a woman straddling him at all.

My Lord Saxonhurst, Meg saw, liked to play childish games. She, however, was an experienced governess to young boys.

Despite heated cheeks, she spoke plainly. "I fear struggles would not help your fight, Saxonhurst."

"My fight?"

"To sink."

"Sink!" He grinned. "What a lowering thought."

She couldn't stop a twitch of her lips. "What a terrible pun."

"A critic now, are you?"

Meg was surprised to find that sitting on top of him gave her a feeling of confidence, of power, even. She settled her legs more comfortably, noting with interest how her movement made his hips twitch. "To return to our previous conversation . . ."

"Which contributed to my rising, remember. Be wary."

"I no longer think it would be wise for us to attempt intimacy so soon."

"Why not?" One hand moved to rest on the skirt that covered her knee. "We're doing quite nicely so far."

She looked at him, rather nonplussed. "Why not?" she echoed.

"You are talking of wisdom and reason, Minerva. Therefore, you must have reasons." The hand moved, stroking up her thigh to trace across the plain front of her sensible wool dress as if she had an embroidered snake there. "However, I must tell you, my dear wife, that well-risen men are as interested in wisdom and reason as well-risen dough."

His finger made a lazy figure of eight around her breasts.

She stiffened and leaned away. "It is just too soon!"

"But since we are married and it must come to the bed eventually, what difference will time make?"

"It will let me—let us—grow more accustomed to our change in state."

He moved his hips slightly and grinned. "Grow is a somewhat unwise word, my dear. And you think being accustomed is necessary to success? My present change of state is scientific proof otherwise."

He bracketed her waist with his hands, the pressure shocking despite layers of sturdy cloth, corset, and shift. She couldn't help moving, trying to escape, but seeing the flare of response in his eyes, she stilled. "Let me go, please."

"Am I hurting you?"

"You know you are not."

"Why then?" His smile teased, tempting her to delights.

Surely it was possible for a determined woman to handle even this man. "As I said, Saxonhurst, it is too soon for this kind of thing."

"But you don't object on principle?" He snared her hands, carrying them to his warm mouth, eyes fixed on hers. "You are a worthy Countess of Saxonhurst."

Meg sucked in extra air. "Because I will not play your games?"

"Because you play them so very, very well. See, my kissing your hands doesn't upset you, does it?"

She tried to tug them free. "Yes."

"No." He kissed her knuckles again and again. "It

teases at your senses, but it doesn't upset you. It doesn't make you feel frightened or attacked."

Meg had to accept that *attacked* wasn't the word. "Very well. I grant you that. but I do not *want* my senses teased. And this position you've forced me into does offend me."

"No."

"Stop saying no!"

He grinned. "Stop saying silly things. Our position makes you nervously aware of a great many possibilities. That agitates you—and very nicely, too. You flush deliciously. But it doesn't offend you. You're too sensible a wife to be offended by something like this. Am I not right?"

Meg squirmed again. Then stopped. "When you put it like that, my lord, how can I disagree?"

He chuckled. "You're adorable when you pout."

"I never pout!"

"As you say, my dear." With a final kiss of her hands, he slid her off his legs and returned her to her seat. "There, see. But I'm afraid I must insist on my right to tease your senses, even if you do pout over it." He ran a finger across her lips—pouting? Surely not—over her hot cheek, and around and around her earlobe.

Then his touch slid down her exposed neck toward her breasts. . . .

Meg closed her eyes and shivered, wondering how to find the strength to fend off this new move in his seductive hunt.

But then the coach swayed to a halt.

His touch stopped, causing a stab of wicked deprivation. "Alas," he said, "we are home." He leaned calmly past her to raise the blinds.

The door opened and Meg saw the inevitable servants waiting. The earl leaped down and turned to assist her. "We must continue our interesting exploration later, my dear."

"But I said—"

"Later." He tucked her hand in his arm and led her into the grand house that was now her home.

They were surrounded by servants, so many servants, all with attentive ears, so Meg fell silent. Part of her wanted to break free, however, to pull away and run. Run from the sensations this man seemed able to summon with a single, magic touch.

But she was being silly. Marriage was about the marriage bed, and if her husband was skillful and enthusiastic, what cause had she to complain? All the same, when he left her in her suite of rooms, she felt as if she had just escaped a hungry tiger.

She thought wistfully of her fantasy earl, the one she'd expected to marry. He'd not just been ugly and eccentric, but shy and rather gauche at *amours*. *He* would have taken weeks to gather the courage to hesitantly kiss her fingertips!

Then she realized that she was going to find it hard in her new life to be alone.

In her bedchamber and dressing room, Susie and another maid were putting away her meager supply of clothes. She couldn't detect any sneers, but she was sure they must be used to dealing with a different class of garments. And what would they think of her underwear? Never before had strangers had access to all her secrets. She didn't like it, but it was another price she had to pay for her wish.

This was her home now, her status, her future. It was no use thinking of it as just a temporary situation.

She straightened her wilting spine. Very well. These rooms were now hers. He'd said they hadn't been used since her mother's death and they hadn't been up-to-date then. It would be amusing to refurbish them, though she had little idea of current fashion.

She would have to buy new clothes to suit her station. She had no desire to be a laughingstock. Again, however, she had little idea of current tastes.

Meg accepted that most of her resistance to her new life sprang from pure fear, fear of the unknown, of admitting ignorance, of making a fool of herself.

Even—perhaps especially—in the marriage bed. What did she know of such matters? However, despite his comments about her lack of purity, he couldn't expect her to know anything about it.

She had little patience with cowards, and would not

be one. If she had to be a countess, she'd be an excellent one, in bed and out!

As a small step, she took possession of the boudoir. Though they were simple things of no value, she arranged her few small ornaments on a mahogany table that turned out to have game pieces in a drawer. Her books joined a rather fusty collection in the shelves on top of a tambour desk. She placed her mother's sewing box beside a brocade-covered chair, aware of another wave of gratitude that it hadn't been sold. She wondered if the earl would advance some of her pin money so she could buy back some of the items they had been forced to sell.

She knew, without doubt, that if she asked, he'd find them all and buy them for her. It made her smile and shake her head at the same time. She would not encourage his wanton extravagance, but he seemed to be a genuinely kind man.

All the time, however, thoughts of the *sheelagh* fretted at her. She couldn't really settle into her life here until she had it back. But then, when she had it back, where could she keep it? Nowhere here was safe from servants' eyes. The desk had keys, but no space for the stone. She couldn't possibly leave it on public display, but she must have it close and under her control.

Perhaps she could be open about it, claiming it was a family curiosity of only sentimental value. She shivered at the thought. The earl was just the sort to want to have such a thing on display, to show it to all his guests! Meg had no idea how many people had the power, but she certainly didn't want to find out.

She realized she was just standing, staring out at an uninspired garden mostly overhung by large, leafless trees. There was no point in fretting about the future. First things first. She must retrieve the stone and quickly, while the Mallett Street house was still empty.

She eyed an ivy-hung gate at the back of the garden. If only she could go now. She'd never be able to leave here undetected, however, and on Mallett Street, neighbors would follow her every move.

No, the time to go was late in the night. Or perhaps early morning. Yes, early morning, when the first servants were up and supplies were coming in from the country, so the streets would be fairly safe. But before most people were about their business.

That was when she realized that she absolutely must put off her husband. He had his own bedroom, but her parents had slept together. If they consummated the marriage, he might want to spend the night with her, and she'd never get away.

Oh dear, oh dear.

She had to put him off.

Putting off the Earl of Saxonhurst seemed rather like putting off a gale. He overrode everything she said, did whatever he wanted. And, she had to admit, he swept her along with him like a full-sailed ship.

She realized she was pacing and made herself stop. There was no point to this. She'd tackle the problem when it arose—she stifled a giggle at that—by repeating that she wasn't ready.

The earl wouldn't rape her. She felt strangely certain of that. If she just stayed resolute, if she didn't let his teasing and touching sweep her away, he would give up for the moment. All she needed was one night. After that, he could have his wicked way with her.

She nodded, settled in her mind. Tonight she would courteously turn away her husband. Tomorrow, she would rise early, walk to Mallett Street, and retrieve the *sheelagh*. Then she'd come back here, hide it, and settle in to enjoying being the Countess of Saxonhurst.

She could hardly wait!

With a guilty laugh, she went upstairs to see how the others were doing in the schoolroom quarters. She thought Jeremy at seventeen might object to sharing a room with Richard, but he didn't complain. "I hope to be off to Cambridge soon," he said.

Clearly he wasn't suffering from any regrets.

Richard and Rachel had been sleeping in the same room at home, but it was past time to separate them. Meg was glad to find that neither minded. They both considered it a sign of growing up to get to share a room with their older brother or sister. Laura pulled a bit of a face about it, for she was used to sharing with Meg, but with her usual sunny nature, she didn't object.

Since they were all happily finding places for their possessions, Meg slipped into the peaceful nursery for a moment to say a brief prayer of thanks. The *sheelagh* seemed pagan, but supposedly such stones could still be found in church walls, so she chose to see it as Godly. Therefore, her blessings came from God.

She gave thanks that her brothers and sisters were happy, and that they were going to be taken care of. She gave thanks that Laura would never be in danger from Sir Arthur or other such men. She gave thanks also for her husband being what he was. He was naughty, but also kind and generous. Most of the time.

Yes, truly, she was blessed, and if it weren't for the *sheelagh,* she could be a very happy woman.

The *sheelagh,* however, sat in her contentment like a slug in a rose. It wasn't just that she'd lost control of it and must get it back, but the fact that there was always a sting to its gifts. Pagan or blessed, it never brought untarnished benefits.

So, what could go wrong . . . ?

"Oh, stop it," she said out loud. Perhaps the problems in the past came of poorly worded wishes. She had been very careful. Perhaps she'd outwitted it and received exactly what she'd wanted. More, in fact, than she'd ever dreamed of.

She looked around the long-unused nursery, waiting through so many years for a baby's cry. She wandered over to trace the carving on the elaborate wooden cradle hung with cream brocade. Would her child lie here one day?

Hers and his.

That was part of marriage, too, and a part she longed for.

Another reason to welcome him to her bed.

As soon as she had the *sheelagh* back.

Astley's was a huge success, especially as the special New Year's show involved magic tricks with lights, water, flames, and even small explosions.

The twins clearly thought they'd gone to heaven, and over supper at Camille's, they argued about who would be the most able to stand on a galloping horse's back in order to rescue someone being carried off by a giant eagle.

"When we go to Haverhall," the earl said, "you'll have plenty of horses to try it on. But only under proper supervision."

"Real horses?" they exclaimed as one, for despite their debate, neither had ever ridden.

"Ponies, perhaps at first. But my stables are quite famous and my horses deserve respect. No heavy hands. No reckless riders. And no attempted tricks without my permission or that of my head groom."

They made absolutely no complaint about his firm orders. "Yes, sir," they breathed, looking as if the glories were beginning to be too much for them.

Meg felt tears prick at her eyes, and fear stab at her heart. The tears were from happiness at how well everything was going. The fear was in case the *sheelagh's* price was equal to the good provided.

She didn't really know that was how it worked.

True, she had trapped the earl, and she would never feel quite right about that. Perhaps that alone was the price. It was almost like stealing—stealing a person. The only way to amend for that, however, was to make sure her family was no trouble to him, and to be the best wife she could.

Including in the bed.

She wished now she could let him get on with it tonight, but first, absolutely, she must get back the *sheelagh*. Heaven only knew what might happen if it fell into the wrong hands!

She was silent as the carriage rolled home. For the short journey, they'd all crammed into one, with Mr. Chancellor going about his own business, so there was no danger of her husband's games. She just let the chat wash over her. Truth to tell, she was rather tired. It had been a long, tense day and she'd not slept well the night before.

But she couldn't afford to sleep at all, or she'd surely not wake early enough.

"Minerva?"

She started at the earl's voice, and found that the coach had halted, and the others were gone.

"We're home," he said. "You look exhausted."

Stung by her recent thoughts, she straightened and said, "Not at all!"

His brows rose, but he smiled, and said, "How delightful." As he handed her down, she knew it had been a tactical error.

"That doesn't mean—"

"In a little while, my dear," he said, leading her past waiting servants and straight upstairs. Not to her rooms. To his?

"The younger ones . . ." she said.

"Are being taken care of and put to bed. I think the twins are asleep on their feet." He led her into a room. A kind of boudoir. A private area for a gentleman, with comfortable chairs and books.

And a huge, ornate cage containing a gray bird.

The bird might have been snoozing, but it perked up. *"Hello, my lovely!"* it said, shockingly in the earl's voice. Then it added, *"Aaaargh! Woman. Eve. Delilah!"*

Meg stared at the bird, but the earl went over and fed it some tidbit, murmuring soothing, loving things. The bird almost seemed to be murmuring back!

The earl turned back to her. "I thought we'd better get the introductions over. I'm afraid Knox was trained by his previous owner to give out warnings on women and marriage."

"I'm glad he's caged."

"He's not attacked a woman yet, so there's hope."

Meg feared her words hadn't pleased him. She had to cope with a jealous, woman-hating bird? "He lives in this room?" she asked hopefully.

"He's free most of the day, particularly when I'm home,"—and indeed, he was opening the cage—"but he mostly stays in my rooms. He's from the tropics and sensitive to cold. I keep the whole house warm, but please be careful."

"Of course." Meg couldn't imagine wandering carelessly through her husband's rooms.

The bird hopped to the door, then onto his shoulder, eyeing Meg. Then the earl walked toward her.

"Knox, this is Minerva. Say hello."

"Eve. Delilah." With that, the bird deliberately turned its back.

Meg had to laugh. "I've been cut by a bird!"

"Indeed. There should be some fruit in that box on the table. Let's see if we can bribe him."

"I'm not sure it's necessary—"

"It's necessary. He's used to my company."

Feeling somewhat put out by his priorities, Meg went and found the box. It contained hothouse grapes! She took one and walked round behind her husband to face the bird, but it promptly turned.

The earl took the bird in his hands. "Pretty lady," he said, directing its attention to Meg. "Pretty lady. Show him the fruit."

Meg held it out and it was immediately snatched.

"I didn't say give it to him. Show him another."

Beginning to be fascinated, Meg held a grape out of reach.

"Pretty lady," the earl said again, stroking the bird patiently. "Pretty lady."

"Pretty lady," the bird eventually said, though it didn't sound sincere.

Without being told, Meg offered the grape. The bird took it, but as soon as the earl let it go, it hopped onto his shoulder and turned its back again.

"He'll come around," he said with a laugh, "especially if you keep feeding him his favorite treats."

"Wouldn't it be easier if I just avoided his company?"

"Not if you want mine. He'd pine to only see me on occasion." He strolled over, bird on shoulder, and opened an adjoining door.

Meg tensed, but he walked through his bedroom to open the door to another room, which proved to be hers. "Ah, Susie gets to do the honors," he said to the curt-sying maid. "How appropriate." He touched Meg's cheek and said, "I'll be back soon, my dear."

Meg stared at the door that closed behind him. "His cousin Daphne is right. He is outrageous."

Susie giggled. "But a charming devil with it, ain't he, milady?"

Meg started. She'd forgotten she'd wasn't alone. She was shaken by his promised return, but also by the fact that her chief rivals for his attention seemed to be a dog and a bird.

And she was disturbed, she must admit, by his deft handling of them. She feared that he planned to handle, train, and even hunt her with the same expertise. She had expected many challenges from this marriage, but none like this.

Susie came to take Meg's cloak, and Meg let her, but she had no idea how to behave with a personal maid. Especially Susie, who knew too much about her business.

"Come along, milady," Susie said kindly, guiding her toward the dressing room. "I've hot water for washing, and your nightgown warm and ready."

Meg realized again that all these rooms were delightfully warm. Mainly, apparently, for the parrot's sake.

The maid's nimble fingers removed Meg's bonnet and spencer, and began to undo the buttons down the front of her gown.

Meg decided that if she was a countess, she'd be an eccentric one. She stepped away. "I can manage by myself, Susie."

"I'm sure," the maid said, "but why bother?" She went on with her work, peeling off the dress and untying the stay laces as if Meg was a child.

Wrapped in so many other concerns, Meg lacked the will to resist. Anyway, presumably the maid knew the routine for preparing a woman for the earl's bed. She hadn't missed the fact that the woman-hating parrot was not kept in the earl's *bedroom.*

She doubted, however, that any of the earl's loose women had worn such a demure and weary-looking nightgown as hers, spread out waiting on a rack by the fire. In her solitary bed at the Ramillys' there'd never seemed any need to buy new, but now the heavy white cotton had become a rather threadbare yellow, and the neat repair of a tear seemed horribly obvious.

When Susie would have taken off her shift, Meg rebelled. She kept it on as she washed herself, then dismissed the maid with the dirty water. Susie, however, insisted on staying long enough to unpin her hair and brush it out.

"There, milady," she said. "Now, you just relax and enjoy yourself. Half the women in London'll envy you this night!"

With that, the maid bustled out, leaving Meg speechless. Was marriage always like this? She supposed everyone knew what the bridal couple were going to do, but to just refer to it so casually . . . !

And, she thought, covering hot cheeks, she was going to have to send him away.

She studied her appearance in the mirror. Perhaps loose hair was more becoming than her usual bedtime plait. Perhaps she should stay in her shift. It was newer than her nightgown, and trimmed on all edges with embroidery in white and pale green—

Goodness! She wanted to *deter* him, didn't she, not encourage him! Ears pricked for any sound of his approach, she tore off the shift and scrambled into her shabby nightgown, making sure it was buttoned up to the high neck and down to the snug wrists. Then she plaited her hair.

Now what?

She longed to hide under the sheets, but would that look inviting?

Her robe. Where was it?

Fearing his arrival at any moment, she scrabbled through drawers, mostly empty, then found the robe laid on a shelf in the armoire. Made of thick wool for winter warmth, and in a practical shade of brown, it would surely wither any lascivious thoughts on sight. Meg tightened the belt with the comfortable feeling of putting on armor. At that moment, the door clicked open and she turned to face her challenge.

He, too, wore a robe—a long robe of gold and brown brocade that made her think of a tiger. It buttoned, neck to knee and he was, if anything, more modestly dressed than in his tight breeches, but Meg had never seen anything more alarming.

Chapter 8

He looked her over, expression unreadable, then strolled to sit on her bed, leaning against one of the heavy posts. "You wished to talk?"

Despite a racing heart, Meg's main emotion was irritation. "You do this deliberately!"

"What?" he asked with the innocence of a hardened liar.

"Put people off balance."

"Why not? I suspect you aren't going to provide any other entertainment tonight." He stretched his legs and the lower part of his robe fell back, revealing muscular naked calves.

For the first time, Meg wondered if he was completely naked beneath the silk.

Good gracious. He was!

Because her knees had suddenly turned weak, she sat on the dresser bench behind her, fighting to look perfectly at ease with a handsome, mostly naked man in her bedroom. "A wife, my lord, is not for entertainment."

"No? I am perfectly willing to entertain you."

"My lord—"

"Saxonhurst."

"Saxonhurst. And," she demanded, "why the devil couldn't you have had a shorter name? Like Rule, or Dane, or Strand?" Then she clapped her hand over her mouth, appalled to hear such language escaping her lips.

Rather than showing shock, he laughed. "My deepest apologies, my dear. That's probably why everyone calls me Sax." With one of his special, twinkling smiles, he added, "Try it."

Like a puppet, she said, "Sax." But then she was up

and pacing. "It is not kind to tease and torment me! You expect too much. You *demand* too much."

"Minerva, I'm not—"

"This morning we were total strangers," she swept on. "You *can't* expect me to . . ."

"To what?" He looked completely innocent and puzzled, the wretch. He knew exactly what she meant.

"To permit you liberties," she stated, tugging the belt of her robe even more securely around herself.

"Liberties," he echoed thoughtfully. "Strange word, isn't it? Freedoms. Freedom with one another's person. Marriage does require that you give me the freedom of your body, Minerva. And it works both ways. You now have the freedom of mine."

As he spoke, he straightened, spreading his hands as if offering a feast.

Himself. Tawny and gold, powerful and mysterious, and so devastatingly sure of his own charms.

Oh, if only she could just surrender to his gentle wiles. Though still nervous, and still irritated by his glowing ease and confidence, Meg knew Susie had been right. Most women would envy her the freedom of this man, and she was going to have to send him away.

Clenching her fists, she demanded, "Then why don't I have the freedom to tell you to remove your body from this room?"

"That isn't quite the same thing."

"Isn't it?" She was looking at his beautiful lips and thinking about his beautiful kisses. . . .

With a snap she realized she'd been sucked into playing his games again, and as always, he was winning. Just talking about intimacy was sweeping her in that direction.

She looked him straight in the eye. "Very well, Saxonhurst. What exactly do you want? Why are you here?"

She'd never known a smile could turn so sparklingly wicked. "My dear, I don't think you're ready for me to describe my many and various plans for your enticing body."

Meg stared at him and then, to her own dismay, she burst into tears.

She was swept into his arms, and she fought him. Then

she was on the bed, writhing in his hold until she realized they were both sitting, backs against the headboard. Until she heard what he was saying.

"I'm damned sorry, my dear. Do stop crying." He rocked her, and for once, the glossy Earl of Saxonhurst sounded distinctly unnerved.

Terror was instantly replaced by embarrassment. "I'm sorry. I don't usually . . ." She sniffed, and tried to wipe away tears with her fingers. "Oh dear."

"Neither of us usually does." He brushed one tear off her cheek with his thumb. "We're making a sad botch of marriage, aren't we? I fear I've lost my touch with innocents."

"No!" Meg longed to explain. If it hadn't been for the *sheelagh,* she would have happily let him tease her into his arms, into liberties and discoveries. She sniffed again, sure she now looked a mess. "No one can botch marriage inside twenty-four hours, my lord."

He rolled off the bed and brought a towel to wipe her face. "I think the Prince of Wales managed it. But at least I haven't come to you drunk and collapsed in the fireplace."

She glanced at the red coals. "Thank heavens. You'd be a cinder."

"Probably the whole idea behind summer weddings." He dabbed one last time at her face. "Better?"

She nodded, but it wasn't entirely true. She was on her bed, in her nightclothes, with a man, similarly attired, very close. He was kneeling on one leg, and she saw naked flesh. A muscular thigh. She suddenly wanted to touch it. To see if she was right about how it would feel—hot, hard, slightly roughened by the dark gold hair. . . .

She hastily looked up at his face. "I *am* tired, Saxonhurst," she said, hearing the breathiness of her voice.

"Understandable." But he took her hand and tugged her off the bed. Oh no, what now? Meg wasn't sure how long her resistance could last. If he kissed her . . .

He simply pulled down the covers, then gestured. "My lady, your bed awaits."

Hesitantly, Meg slipped out of her concealing robe and under the sheets, pulling them well up. "Thank you."

"I am eternally at your service, my dear." But then he began to unbutton his robe.

"What are you doing!" It was almost a shriek.

His fingers paused. "Coming to bed."

"No! I mean, my lord—Saxonhurst—Sax—I need to sleep."

"Then we'll sleep together."

"But you have your own bed." Was it possible? Did aristocratic married couples with their own suites of rooms sleep together?

He undid another button. "I will enjoy sleeping with you, Minerva. And when you're more rested, we'll be comfortably situated for further investigation of marital liberties."

Meg felt like a ship in a gale and fired a desperate command. "Go away!"

He let his hands drop and studied her. "Why?"

She dragged her eyes away from the dusting of honey-brown hair on his chest. "I'm sorry, but I . . . er . . . prefer to sleep alone. I . . . I snore, my lord. And I'm very restless. Poor Laura has been black and blue sometimes."

"That's all right. I'm restless, too. We can fight the nights away." Another button opened.

Meg pulled the sheets higher. "My lord, why are you *doing* this? Is it not reasonable that we wait a day or two?"

"I'm willing to wait. I simply intend to wait in your bed."

"You simply intend to fluster me into doing exactly what you want!"

He laughed. "If I can, yes. I did warn you of my seductive plans. In truth, my dear, I don't know why you're so resistant. I promise I won't do anything you don't want."

"It's perfectly natural for a lady to be disturbed at the notion of having a strange man in her bed!"

He sat on the edge of the mattress, studying her as if she were a puzzle. "What exactly is going on in your clever head, my dear? I know women. I can't deny it. You're too sensible to think to put me off for long, and you're not at all repulsed or frightened by me. Nervous, yes. That's only normal. But rather more intrigued than afraid. You don't find my attentions unpleasant. So, why are you so desperate to get rid of me?"

Meg sought some answer that he would believe, but then he gave a sharp, surprised laugh. "Good Lord, it's your monthly courses, isn't it? Embarrassed to tell me?"

Before she could remember how wicked it was to lie, Meg nodded, her face burning hot.

He touched that heat, stroked it. "No need to blush, my dear. These matters have to be known between man and wife. Beginning, middle, or end?"

Meg wanted to slide completely under the bedclothes for mortification. Not only was she lying, she did not want to talk about these things with a man at all. Especially so *calmly*!

"Beginning," she blurted. In for a penny, in for a pound. At least that would free her of him for a week or so.

Something in his eyes made her wonder if he believed her, but he said, "Perhaps that explains your rather wild swings of mood, as well."

Meg bit back a retort. If she seemed wild, it was because she'd been forced into a hasty marriage to avoid tragedy, then found herself in the power of a man determined to torment her to death.

Smiling as if he knew just what she was thinking, he leaned forward and kissed her cheek. "Sleep well, my bride, and if these things put you under the weather, don't hesitate to stay in bed and let the servants serve." Then he pinched out her two candles and left her alone in the dark.

Meg relaxed her death grip on the sheets and blew out a long breath. She was appalled that she'd lied so easily, but she cherished a warm glow of victory, too. It had taken underhanded means, but she had won. She had fought off the tempest and was into plain sailing for the night.

And, she thought with a smile, at the right time, the earl's relentless hunt could turn out to be a truly remarkable experience.

She was dropping off to sleep when she jerked upright again. What was she doing? She couldn't afford to sleep, even though she ached for it. She'd never wake naturally before dawn.

She forced herself out of her bed and splashed cold water on her face from the carafe by the bed. Clocks around the house chimed midnight. She groaned at the thought of the many hours before she could be about her task.

Meg managed to stay awake, but only just, and only by getting dressed and walking around for most of the night. By the time the first gray hint of dawn split the sky, she was almost faint with weariness, but she had to venture out into the frosty, misty streets.

Plague take the *sheelagh* anyway, she thought rebelliously as she pulled on her warm, hooded cloak and thick, woolen gloves. It was nothing but a menace and a burden.

But then, as she slipped into the corridor, shoes in hand, she reminded herself of what might have been had the wishing stone not made the earl marry her. They would all be destitute now. Most likely they'd have been taken to the workhouse, separated male from female, and provided with only the coarsest food and shelter.

Or even worse, Sir Arthur would have approached Laura directly, and Laura, of course, would have sacrificed herself. At this moment she could be weeping in a sordid bed, violated and brutalized. Meg was quite certain that Sir Arthur intended no delicate loving of his chosen victim.

And, one day soon, the Earl of Saxonhurst was going to seduce his wife, and his wife was going to enjoy it very much indeed.

So as she crept along, Meg accepted that in this case the *sheelagh* had been a blessing. And it was definitely her responsibility. Her mother had impressed that upon her. The care and guarding of it was a sacred charge, passed down through the generations.

During the day, she had tried to memorize the large house, and now, praying that she not encounter the snarling dog, she found the door that led to the servants' stairs. Everything lay peacefully around her, as if the walls, floors, and furniture themselves slept. But soon it would wake. The first servants would rise, clattering up and down stairs, building fires, boiling water, running out to buy fresh bread at the baker's and fresh milk from the dairy.

Meg crept quietly down the plain narrow stairs to the very bottom. This was completely unknown territory. She'd seen a basement door at the front of the house, however, set below ground level and with steps from the street. There must also be a back door, probably out of the kitchen. Surely one of these had to be possible.

Heading to the front, she gingerly opened a door, wondering what she would find. She let out a held breath and stepped into a small room containing only a plain table with chairs around it, and a dresser lined with plates. Perhaps the servants' dining room. It was cold here, for the fireplace held only ashes.

Beyond the table, pale light glowed through the glass-paned door she'd sought. Through the glass, she could see the stone steps beyond, the ones that climbed up to the street.

The door was locked, but the key hung on a string from the knob. She inserted it, and the lock turned smoothly. What should she do, however, when she was outside? She couldn't leave it open. It might be dangerous, and it would show that someone had left the house in the night.

After some thought, she took the key, string and all, and locked the door from the outside, putting the key in her pocket, where it jangled a chime of guilt against the one to Mallett Street. What an expert thief she was becoming.

She had no choice, however. A missing key would be a mystery, whereas an unlocked door would cause serious questions.

She pulled on her shoes and hurried up the stairs, her breath puffing white in the freezing air. She was glad to tuck her gloved hands into her padded muff.

She heard the faint chink of the two keys in her pocket. If she returned quickly, she might be able to return the Saxonhurst key before it was missed. The first servants would be about by then, but perhaps she could just drop it nearby. Then, when it was found, it would look as if it had fallen off the knob. With this in mind she moved the key from her pocket to her muff. As she hurried along, she picked and rubbed at the string to wear it through.

It distracted her anyway from the eerie quiet of the frosty morning. She'd never before ventured out at this gray hour. Far more than deep night, it seemed a time for ghostly spirits. Revelers, hawkers, and lurkers had all surrendered to sleep. When a cat slid across the street in front of her, she froze with a nervous gasp.

She went on, telling herself that the lack of people on the street was a good thing. No one was about to hurt her. Even so, her skin crawled. She tried to believe that the night prowlers—the thieves and housebreakers, the villains who snatched girls for brothels—would be home by now, but every misty corner or dingy shadow held a threat.

Slowly, however, the sky brightened and London came to life around her hurrying feet. A cart rumbled by, dragged by a plodding horse, hauling cabbages to market. She had to wait to cross one street, as a laden mail coach charged by, swaying and racketing along the cobbles, chased by excited dogs. Servants banged and clattered out of sight, or appeared to stagger yawning to wells and bakers' shops. The first vendors appeared with the rising sun, crying milk, or eggs, or oranges.

When she arrived at her old home, however, Mallett Street was still quiet, except for a bit of activity in the inn's stables. The people here had few servants, and everyone rose a little later to start the day together. Meg slipped down the familiar back lane and into the small garden of her old house.

Only yesterday morning the house had been her home, so she shouldn't feel like a criminal. Even so, when she turned the key in the back door, the click sounded like a gunshot to her, and she looked around, expecting someone to cry the alarm. Nothing stirred. Blowing out a relieved breath, she turned the knob and slipped into the cold, dark house.

How deserted it seemed. How empty.

She looked around the kitchen. Battered pans and chipped crockery still sat in place, and she supposed the stone crock in the cupboard still held a little oatmeal. She'd felt so unsure when leaving for the church, that she'd not given away any of their meager supply of food and wood. She could light the familiar stove and make porridge now if she wanted. . . .

With a shake, she pushed aside mental wanderings and went about her business. Still, nonsensically, trying not to make noise, she hurried up to her parents' bedroom, carried a wooden chair over to the bed, climbed up, and stretched for the heavy, brocade bag.

She couldn't find it!

Muttering about the dim light, Meg teetered on the soft, unstable mattress, groping around.

It wasn't there!

Frantically, illogically, she checked all four sides of the bedframe. Nothing. She scrambled down, and looked around the outside of the bed curtains, but her heart raced with sick panic. It wasn't there!

How? Why? Who?

The answer shot back.

The "who" had to be Sir Arthur.

Shaking with shock and bone weariness, Meg slumped on the edge of the too-familiar bed. She gazed all around as if by some miracle the stone might be on the floor, the table, or the washstand. Pushing to her feet, she checked inside drawers and cupboards, and under the bed.

She knew, however, that it wasn't there.

But how could Sir Arthur even *know* about the *sheelagh-ma-gig,* never mind that it was important?

Her mother would never have told him. Her mother, however, had kept no secrets from her beloved husband. Walter Gillingham had considered Sir Arthur Jakes his friend. In those long weary months of illness, had he said more than he should?

Meg leaned against the walnut armoire, trying to make her foggy mind follow the puzzling path.

How much did Sir Arthur know? Clearly enough to believe the stone had some value. Surely, though, he'd not know about the magic, or believe it if he did.

That didn't matter at the moment. The pressing question was, how was she going to get it back?

She hated to leave the room, because a foolish part of her mind said that the *sheelagh* had to be here somewhere. She couldn't resist one last hunt, as if the statue might suddenly have returned to its rightful place, or to some other nearby.

Of course, it hadn't, and time was racing by.

She had to leave.

Anyway, she remembered now that she could sense the *sheelagh* if she was close to it. There was something like a tingling in the air. She'd not been aware of it until she'd left home, and slowly realized the presence was gone. It had been a huge relief.

She certainly should have known from the first that the *sheelagh* wasn't in the room.

In the corridor, she rubbed her head wondering if she should search the whole house. But the sun was up, and the earl's house would surely be stirring by now. She had to get back before her husband rose and asked for his wife.

Then what?

Sir Arthur had taken the *sheelagh,* and she had to get it back. She was too weary now, however, to even think about that problem. She needed to get home and into her bed.

Bone tired and aching with disappointment, she dragged down the familiar stairs, fighting tears. Why did everything seem to be going so dreadfully wrong? Was it because she'd given in to temptation and used the *sheelagh*?

It must be. The sting in the—

A *click*?

She froze.

Someone had just unlocked the front door.

Shocked alert, she knew it could only be Sir Arthur.

She stiffened, impelled to confront him and demand the return of her property. But then she realized that was folly. Heaven only knew what he would do. He might drag her off to the constables in revenge.

She had to get out!

Out!

Whirling around the bottom of the stairs, she raced toward the kitchen, even though her shoes clattered loud

on the floor. She hurtled through the back door, down
the path, and out into the lane, expecting at every moment the cry of *"Stop thief!"*

Nothing pursued, neither cry nor person, but she raced
on anyway, around the corner into Graham Street.
There, she made herself stop. People were about their
business, and they'd notice a wild woman racing by.
Anyway, now that the first burst of wild panic had faded,
she was winded and almost faint.

She leaned against a railing, still seeking through the
surrounding noises for the hue and cry. They hanged
people for housebreaking! It wouldn't come to that, and
she knew it, but she had to get farther away. Sucking in
deep, panicked breaths, she pulled the hood of her cloak
over her face and walked rapidly down the street.

A countess wouldn't hang, she assured herself.

A countess probably wouldn't even be hauled into
court for such a petty crime. But she didn't feel like a
countess. She felt like Meg Gillingham, who had so recently skulked around to avoid creditors, and who had
come within an inch of being a beggar on the streets.

They'd hang Meg Gillingham for theft.

Her steps quickened, carrying her back, back to Marlborough Square and the earl's house. It didn't feel like
her house or her home, but it felt like sanctuary. She'd
be safe there. The Earl of Saxonhurst would never let
the law drag his wife away to jail. . . .

But then she groaned, appalled at the thought of him
having to protect a lowborn, criminal wife from the
authorities.

And it was her wicked wish that had embroiled him
in this.

As she hurried along, Meg earnestly prayed that he
never find out what she'd been up to. He had been, was
being, so good to all of them. He deserved a decent wife,
not one so deeply, deeply unworthy.

She'd even lied to him. A barefaced lie!

At that point, if she'd had anywhere else in the world
to go, she might have changed her route. As it was,
tears trickled down her chilled cheeks as she forced her
unsteady legs to carry her back to Mayfair and Marlborough Square.

How had she come to this? She had always been an honest person, able to face the world without shame. Now here she was, a housebreaker who had lied to her kind husband, and was probably going to have to lie again in order to get that dratted *sheelagh* back.

Had it been Sir Arthur who'd entered the house? Who else? He couldn't have rented it already. What had he thought? With luck, that the intruder had been a common housebreaker surprised at mischief. Let him not even dream that he'd almost caught the unlikely Countess of Saxonhurst looking for her wishing stone.

Deluged by worries, she was back in Marlborough Square almost without realizing it, but then she came to a horrified halt. Life stirred in Mayfair much earlier than she'd thought.

The square was already busy with hawkers and servants. A man led two milk cows down one side of the square, while a woman led four nanny goats down the other. Servants popped in and out of the houses with jugs to be filled with warm, fresh milk.

Meg longed for some of that milk.

Other sellers strolled up and down with baskets and panniers, or pushing handcarts. Clearly in this wealthy part of town, the mountain came to Mohamet!

Meg made herself walk toward the house, hoping that in her plain hooded cloak she looked like a servant herself, and turned to go down the steps to the basement door. Her hand was tight around the heavy key on its frayed string.

Through the door, up the stairs, and into her room. That's all. She was so close—

Oh no! She backed up the steps and hurried away.

The small room was clearly the dining room for the lower servants. Five people had been sitting around that plain table, digging into eggs and sausages.

Stupid, stupid, she berated herself, hurrying on, for to stop now would be conspicuous. Of course, the servants would be up and about. Where had her wits been?

What on earth was she to do?

The back.

Weak-kneed with panic, Meg hurried down a mews lane into the area behind the big houses, seeking that ivy-covered gate into the earl's garden. It was tricky to find it from the back, but she chose what she thought was the right gate and tried it. Thank heavens, it opened with only a faint creak.

Even so, lurking behind some bushes, Meg wasn't entirely sure she was in the right garden until she saw the limping footman come out the back door and go down a path.

Doubtless on his way to the privy.

Swamped by relief, she slumped against the wide trunk of one of the beech trees. All she had to do now was to slip into the house unobserved. Surely that couldn't be impossible.

The earl's back garden was bigger than the one at Mallett Street, but crowded with large trees. Though leafless, the trees and some evergreen shrubbery offered concealment. Meg waited until the footman—Clarence, wasn't it?—limped back to the house, buttoning his breeches, before creeping, tree to tree, bush to bush, closer to the back door.

A lad came out to chuck a bowlful of water on the ground.

Meg ducked behind the last wide tree trunk, balefully considering the open space between herself and the house. She even muttered some words a lady shouldn't know. This was never going to work.

Moreover, at this time of day the kitchen area would be busy. As if to prove it, a maid came out, went to a small shed, unlocked it, and took out some supplies. Probably root vegetables.

Meg was so weary she was ready to slide down onto the ground, pull her cloak around her, and go to sleep right there. She didn't even care that she'd be missed, that her family would search for her. She just wanted to go to sleep.

It was too cold, though. She'd freeze to death.

They'd find her corpse in the garden.

What would they think?

Probably only that she'd foolishly gone out for a walk in the garden.

Like a beam of light, she saw the way.

No one except the earl had any right to control her

movements. If the eccentric Countess of Saxonhurst wanted to walk about in the winter garden at an unearthly hour of the morning, that was no concern of the servants' at all.

It took almost more courage than she had, and the dregs of her energy, but Meg drew a deep breath, squared her shoulders, and strolled out of concealment, heading straight for the door. When it opened again, she made herself stay calm, preparing a casual comment for a servant.

She came face-to-face with her husband, the strange dog snarling at his side.

"Good morning, Minerva," he said as if this was the most normal thing in the world, but there was definitely a question in his eyes.

Meg knew her cheeks had flared a guilty red, but she tried. Clutching her trembling hands inside her muff, she said, "Good morning, Saxonhurst. Winter morning air is so invigorating, isn't it?"

He stretched and yawned and she was suddenly aware that he only wore dark pantaloons and white shirt, carelessly open at the neck and loose at the wrists. He must be freezing. Their breath was puffing, and yet he seemed as careless of cold as a healthy animal.

She gulped. If she'd thought herself aware of his body before, she'd been wrong. This was awareness. She could glimpse his contoured chest, and imagine the rest of the torso so lightly veiled by fine white cotton. No imagination was needed about the shape of hips and legs in form-fitting black wool. She could even see the round shape of his male parts.

As he stretched, her attention was dragged to his elegant hands, and the strong lower arms exposed by his unfastened cuffs.

His neck. His jaw. His rumpled, beautiful hair.

His golden eyes watching her with wry amusement.

Watching her watching him.

Even then, she couldn't stop. She felt drunk and completely out of control.

Astonishing though it was, this magnificent man was hers. By his look, by his tolerance of her look, he was accepting it as he had last night when he'd offered her the freedom of his body. She ran her gaze over him again in a way she had never imagined looking at a man.

She'd certainly never imagined a man being willing to be looked at like that by her.

Hers. Hers to command.

Oh, how she regretted her false monthly flow! But it only forced a minor delay.

"Invigorating?" he said at last, in that way he had which gave even innocent words a spicy edge. "Perhaps it is at that. However, being unacquainted with winter morning air, I'm damned if I know what it is except freezing. Are you always so sprightly so early, my dear?" With a distinctly wicked look, he added, "I find the idea delightful."

Meg heard herself say, "I don't know."

He'd think her a complete idiot, but she didn't know. She was answering his underlying question, which had something to do with the marriage bed, and she was too tired to make sense. Whatever force had carried her home, then carried her to the door, had now drained away. Her head swam and everything seemed a distance away, and not quite real.

Even he seemed unreal. Too beautiful to be real. Too beautiful for Meg Gillingham, idiot, liar, and thief.

"I am determined to reform." She hadn't meant to say that out loud. She struggled to make sense of it by adding, "Morning walks, you know, my lord. Not lying around in bed . . ."

Oh, how she wanted to be lying in a bed!

"How admirable. If you are determined on early morning walks, you will like Haverhall, even in the winter. Brak enjoys walks there, too. Do you need to commune some more with nature now, or are you ready to come in and have breakfast?"

In. In was good. It led to warmth and a bed.

Meg walked forward, then absorbed the word "breakfast." She hadn't thought that people would expect her to go through a normal day. She couldn't!

Perhaps she swayed, for his arm came around her. "Are you unwell?"

There was only one thing to say. Sickened at her own lack of integrity, she picked up her lie again. "It's the time of month, you know. I think I should go back to bed."

He swung her into his arms and carried her, carried her past the startled servants in the kitchen, and up the stairs to her room. Against his hot chest, hand on his shoulder, with only fine lawn and her glove between their skin, Meg fought tears of weary hopelessness.

Nothing good could come of lies.

And she wanted something good with this man. Wanted it very badly.

He placed her carefully on the bed, extricating her from her cloak and hat as he did so. Instead of summoning her maid, he pulled off her gloves and shoes himself, then brushed straggling hair off her face. "There. Shall I send Susie to help you undress?"

He looked so concerned, and his dog had its head on the mattress and might even be concerned too. "Yes please. I'm sorry—"

Again, his hand sealed her lips. "It's my fault for demanding instant marriage. Or rather, the duchess's fault. If we'd been able to follow tradition and let the bride choose the day, we could have avoided this."

Meg felt Satan should appear at that moment and drag her straight to hell.

He kissed his fingers and touched them gently to her lips. "It's no bad thing, really. You were right, my dear. Last night was too early, and now I can woo you in proper form. I do want you eager, Minerva, not exhausted or frightened."

"I'll try."

"I hope it won't be too much of an effort." He snapped his fingers and he and the dog left, but before obeying, the animal licked once at her hand.

Tears stung Meg's eyes, both at her husband's dry tone, and that gesture of sympathy from one coward to another. What a wretch she was.

If only she'd said she was at the *end* of her monthly flow.

Oh, if only she'd not lied to him at all.

And it had all been for nothing. The *sheelagh* was gone.

Chapter 9

By the time Susie bustled in, Meg was sniffing back tears. She'd lost the *sheelagh* and lied to her husband, and was probably going to have to lie to him again, and again, and again. . . .

Now even Susie was frowning at her.

Of course. A personal servant knew everything, even when a woman bled. Susie must think Meg had lied about it just to escape her wifely duties.

Well, she had in a way. Just not that way.

Why on earth hadn't she claimed a migraine headache?

As Susie helped her off the bed and out of her dress, Meg responded to the frosty disapproval. "I don't have my monthly."

"Thought not, miss. Sorry—*milady*."

Oh yes, Susie was definitely disappointed in her.

"I didn't mean to lie. It just slipped out."

The dress was off, and Susie was untying the stays. "Well, it's your business, milady."

Yesterday, Meg would not have believed that she could feel so chastised by the disapproval of a servant. "I'm so tired," she said.

Susie turned her, frowning. "I don't know what you've been up to, but I hope it's not wickedness. It was you as went out the front basement door, wasn't it?"

Of course, the servants would know. She should have realized that servants know everything. Meg nodded, feeling like the most base sinner. "I had something I had to do."

"Something to do with the earl? I do feel sort of responsible, milady."

Meg saw the real worry on the maid's face. "Oh no.

Nothing that would affect him! Truly. Just a personal matter I had to settle. After all, the marriage was done in a rush. I didn't have time to tidy everything."

After a moment Susie nodded. "All right, then." She dressed Meg in her nightgown and brushed out her hair. "But it'll all come out, you know. You'll be really having your courses soon."

Meg was close to drifting off to sleep, but at that she came alert. "Oh no!"

"Oh yes." Quick fingers wound Meg's hair into a plait. "Unless you get in the family way. You'd best hope to do that right off, if you ask me." She steered a dazed Meg under the covers and tucked them around her, but her next words were no comfort. "Sax isn't a stickler for much, milady, but he don't like liars. Now, where's that key?"

Keys. Keys to heaven. Keys to disaster.

Despite looming disaster, Meg couldn't resist the pull of sleep. "In my pocket," she muttered, eyes already closed. "I was going to try to drop it . . ."

"I'll take care of it. Go on to sleep now, but let's have no more of this foolishness. If you need something done, one of us servants'll do it for you."

Meg hardly heard because she was obeying the first command. Anyway, she doubted she'd be able to obey the second. One way or another, she still had to get the *sheelagh* back, and it wasn't something she could leave to servants.

When Owain Chancellor went down to breakfast, he was astonished to find Sax lounging at the table, reading the *Times*. Knox was on his chair back, eating something.

"Good morning, my lovely," the bird said.

"Good morning to you, too, Knox."

Brak sprawled over Sax's feet and just waved his tail in greeting. The dog always reminded Owain of one of those awful, snarling bear rugs. For himself, he really didn't think he'd be able to keep it around. But Sax was Sax.

And Sax was not an early riser.

Owain glanced at the mantel clock to be sure he

hadn't overslept. No, it was not yet nine and Sax had clearly already eaten.

"Interesting wedding night?" he couldn't resist asking.

"Fascinating." Sax put aside his paper. "What do you know about women in their monthly time?"

Owain felt his cheeks turn red. "Less than you, I'm sure." He turned to help himself to kippers, damning himself for sounding like a maiden aunt coming across a hound with a bitch in heat.

"Perhaps not. After all, the ladies of my intimate acquaintance avoid me during that time. Don't you have sisters?"

Owain sat at the table as Monkey, with perfect timing, hurried in with a pot of the *café-au-lait* Owain preferred.

Sax turned to him. "You know much about women during their courses, Monk?"

Now Monkey looked like the maiden aunt. "You should ask one of the females about that, milord, I'm sure." Nose in the air, he stalked off.

Sax chuckled. "The male reaction to these matters is very interesting. I'll have to raise it over dinner at the club one dull day."

"Coffee please!" Knox demanded.

The only interest the bird ever showed in Owain was because of the milky coffee it had a fondness for. As he poured a little into a dish and put it on a spare chair, he had to admit to an idiotic pleasure that there was one thing he did better than Sax.

He was as mad as everyone else around here.

Once the bird was sipping, Owain eased fish off fine bones. "Do I gather the countess is . . . er . . . inconveniently indisposed?"

"That's one way of looking at it. She's taken to her bed. But I found her skulking about the garden this morning, dodging from tree to tree."

Owain couldn't help feeling a little smug. "If you pluck a bride out of nowhere, you must expect a few surprises."

Knox raised his head to give a routine warning. *"A bride is a bridle."*

Sax shoved his cup over. "Pour me some more coffee, even if it is that damnable stuff."

Owain obeyed. "What were *you* doing in the garden in the early morning?"

"Does it matter?"

Owain returned to his kipper. "You raised it. I assumed you wanted to speak of it."

"Damn your impertinent eyes," Sax said without heat. "I wasn't in the garden. Or not at first. I woke early. One of those times when we're not sure if we're dreaming or not. I wasn't sure the whole thing hadn't been a dream, so I went into her bedroom. She wasn't there, but she clearly existed. Her things were all around." He sipped from his cup and pulled a face. "Monk!" he called. "Cover your blushes and fetch more coffee. The real stuff this time!"

"So you wondered where she was," Owain prompted.

Sax pushed his cup far away. "Don't know how you can stand that pap." Knox immediately hopped up to drink that, too, but Sax put his hand over it. "No." Only when the bird had gone back to its dish did he pour a little more coffee into it. "I don't know what I thought other than it was damned fishy. Was she stealing the silver? Had she turned coward and decided to run away? Was she a sleepwalker? Anyway, I pulled on some clothes and investigated."

Monkey returned, bearing a steaming pot and poured black coffee into a fresh cup, stirring in just the right amount of sugar.

Sax said, "Monk—"

"If it's about the front downstairs door, milord, that I mentioned, and the missing key. Not to worry. The string just wore through. The key was on the floor."

"Good try. But the countess was in the garden. Did she shimmy out a window?"

Monkey reddened again. "I wouldn't know about that, milord."

"Servants know everything." Sax sipped his fresh coffee. "Therefore, let it be known that the countess likes the early morning air. She is, of course, free to come and go as she pleases."

Monkey relaxed enough to wink. "Right, milord. Not that any of us would talk outside the house, as you know."

"I certainly hope I know."

The footman left, and Owain put down his knife and fork. He was beginning to be seriously concerned. If Sax's wife was mad or bad, it was a disaster. "What *do* you think she was up to?"

"I have no idea. I wonder if one day she'll explain."

"You know, Sax, you are responsible in law for her criminal acts."

"Only if I can reasonably be assumed to have ordered or condoned them." He gave Owain a rueful smile. "All right, all right. This was a foolish route to take, which I may well regret. Unfortunately, it was the only one left me by the dragon. Now I'll have to deal with the many secrets of my mysterious bride."

"A bride is a bridle," announced Knox again, adding a hopeful, *"Coffee?"*

"No, you've had enough." Sax extended a hand, and when Knox hopped onto it, he stroked the bird's chest. "Don't you think, my feathered friend, that sometimes a horse enjoys being ridden?"

He grinned at Owain. "I'm finding marriage fascinating."

Meg awoke to see daylight through the crack in the middle of the dark curtains. Clocks started to chime, telling her it was one-thirty. She'd had perhaps five hours of sleep, so it wasn't surprising that she still felt awful.

She mainly felt awful, however, because her life was pure disaster.

The *sheelagh* was out of her control, probably in the hands of Sir Arthur, and she had to get it back. She was its guardian, responsible for keeping it safe, and for keeping the world safe from it.

Then there was her husband, whom she had lied to, and who had caught her out in the garden. What was he thinking? He hadn't been surprised, which meant he must have seen her from the window.

She scrambled out of bed and went to look down at the bleak and frosty garden. The view from here must be similar to that from his window two rooms away. An evergreen tree blocked sight of the mews, but he could easily have seen her dodging behind the trunks of the others. She must have looked the picture of insanity, or like someone with a very guilty conscience.

If only she'd thought to walk around boldly from the beginning! She was no good at all at these nefarious doings.

And what about the key? Had anyone told him it had been missing? Had Susie managed to return it?

And then there was the tangled problem of her monthly courses. Now she could think straight, she wondered if he'd guessed that she was lying, and had put it down to nervousness. Perhaps she could just tell the truth on that one and be forgiven.

She didn't relish the notion of confessing to an untruth, however. . . . No, to two! She'd repeated the lie this morning. Hands over her face, she had to admit that Susie was right. The only true way to conceal her lie was to get with child immediately so that her courses stopped.

The thought, she had to confess, did not displease her, either in the act or the consequences, but she had no idea how likely it was to happen so quickly.

If it didn't work, he'd soon know that she'd lied.

And apparently, he didn't like liars. They were in accord on that. She didn't either.

Oh dear. Perhaps it would be safer to keep him at a distance for months and hope he lost track of the dates. She laughed aloud at that notion. Judging from her husband's behavior thus far—and hers!—keeping him at a distance was as likely as keeping Jeremy away from books.

She'd just have to get it over with and confess the truth.

She felt better for a moment, as if she'd shed a weight, but then the burden dropped back upon her. Even in her confession she'd be lying, because she'd have to tell him she'd lied out of maidenly modesty.

She couldn't tell him about the *sheelagh*.

She wished she could. She tried for a moment to imagine a way to tell him the truth.

I own a magic statue, my lord.

She could see his look of disbelief, and how could she

prove it, especially when she didn't have the *sheelagh*? Even if she did, she shuddered at the thought of using it again.

You might think you married me because of your grandmother, but really I trapped you into it through magic.

She shook her head. It was impossible.

And if she did convince him of the truth, it might be disastrous. He loathed his grandmother for trying to rule him. He'd warned Meg yesterday never to try to change or control him. How would she react if he believed that he'd been a puppet of her magic will?

So, she'd have to get the *sheelagh* back without her husband suspecting a thing. She leaned her aching head against the chilly glass of the window, wondering what sin she'd committed to end up in this state—

A knock on the door had her whirling around as if her guilty conscience were about to stalk in, finger pointed. "Come."

It was only Susie, followed by an anxious Laura.

"Feeling perkier, milady?" the maid asked. "Would you like a bath? A luncheon up here? A decanter of brandy?"

For all her cheerfulness, the last offering showed that Susie was still not sure about her. "A bath, please," Meg said meekly, attracted by such indulgence in the middle of the day.

Ah, the luxury of high living.

And how little she deserved it.

Susie bustled off and Laura perched on the edge of the bed. "Are you all right?" After a moment, blushing, she added, "Was it so very terrible?"

Meg almost groaned. Oh, what a tangle. "I'm perfectly all right," she said, trying to exude contentment. "I just felt very tired."

"Oh. I suppose that's natural." Before Meg could think what to say, she added, "The earl was up early, though. We weren't sure what to do about breakfast, so we all dressed and went downstairs. He was already there, with Mr. Chancellor. And a bird. It called me Delilah!"

Meg had to laugh, and she tried to explain a little

about the parrot. She'd heard a question in her sister's words, however. A question as to why the husband should be so energetic in the morning when the new wife was worn out. Since Meg didn't have a notion how to respond, she avoided that. "I hope they fed you."

"Oh yes." Laura dipped her head and looked up, seeming younger and unsure of herself. "I heard something . . ."

Meg couldn't turn away her sister when troubled. She sat beside her. "What?"

"When we were approaching the morning room, I heard him say something. The earl, I mean. Something about it being foolish to have married you. That he regretted it. And about finding out all your secrets. What did he mean, Meg?"

Though she suddenly felt achingly hollow, Meg made herself laugh. "I'm sure it was just one of those things people say. After all, our marriage was foolish by the world's view. Or perhaps he meant he regretted the rush of it."

"And secrets?"

"When two people are strangers, they are bound to have secrets. When we marry someone, we begin to learn more about them."

"I think I'd rather find out beforehand."

Meg silently echoed that, but all the same, she knew she didn't regret marrying the Earl of Saxonhurst. If only she could make it work.

Susie returned then to say that the bath was ready, and Meg was grateful to escape her sister's concern and curiosity.

As she sank into the warm, delicately perfumed water, however, she was fighting tears again. Of course, the earl was disappointed in her, and suspicious, and regretful. Not only had she sent him away on their wedding night, but he'd then caught her wandering the garden in the bitter early hours of a winter's day.

What did he suspect?

She dreaded to think.

Rubbing soft, creamy lather over her body, she wondered if he'd want to consummate their marriage at all. If she were him, she'd be having serious doubts. She had to swallow tears at the thought that her impulsive, idiotic, wondrous marriage might be over so soon.

After all, the Regent had separated from his arranged bride within days of meeting and marrying. It could happen.

Susie brought her some meat, bread, and fruit, and placed it on a small table by the bath, then topped up the water with new hot.

Meg smiled at this pampering. "I feel as indulged as a barbarian princess."

The maid stiffened. "I wouldn't know nothing about that, milady!"

Meg suppressed a giggle at the things that shocked people.

She languished there as long as she could, but eventually, she had to go out to face the world. More precisely, to face her unlikely and suspicious husband.

"Is the earl downstairs?" she asked Susie, who was tidying up.

"Yes, milady. But he has guests."

"Guests?" Had he already summoned his lawyers to find a way out of his marital mistake?

"Just old friends. If you want, someone can take him a message."

Feeling like a person reprieved on the gibbet, Meg shook her head. She couldn't imagine sending a message to ask if she could join her husband. "I'll go down shortly. I'll just check on the others."

As she hurried up to the schoolroom, she knew she was running away from things that must be faced.

She found the twins doing arithmetic under Laura's supervision, but all three leaped up.

"At last!" Rachel cried. "You've been in your bath *forever*!"

Richard explained the eagerness. "Cousin Sax—he said to call him that—said that when you're up, he'll take us to see London. And we did do lessons this morning!"

"You've lived in London all your lives," Meg pointed out.

"Not *that* London," Richard said. "The Mint. The Tower. Perhaps even Bedlam."

Meg stared at him. The mental hospital? "Saxonhurst suggested *that?*"

He colored. "No. But—"

"But no! The very idea. But if the earl is waiting, we had best all go down. Where's Jeremy?"

"At Dr. Pierce's, of course," said Laura.

Of course, but Meg wished he were here. As they descended the stairs, she blushed for yet more cowardice. She was deliberately facing him in company because she already knew the earl well enough to know he would not ask difficult questions in front of the children.

She'd forgotten that he already had company, and when they entered the drawing room, she found two other men with him, laughing at something. In her guilt and discomfort, she immediately thought they were laughing at her. Or rather, at the ridiculous marriage.

When Knox screeched, *"Eve! Delilah!"* it sounded like a true accusation.

She froze, even thinking about retreating, but the earl rose to greet her with an apparently genuine smile, even if the parrot on his chair had turned its back. "Ah, Minerva! Come and meet these fellows."

She had to go over and be introduced to Viscount Iverton and Lord Christian Vale, both tall, athletic-looking men of the earl's age, one brown, one black haired.

Both were polite, bowing and offering congratulations and best wishes for the marriage. Both, however, looked surprised and curious. Meg supposed she'd have to get used to people wondering how the Earl of Saxonhurst had ended up with such a dowdy dab.

"And this is my new family," the earl was saying, introducing Meg's siblings so easily that it heaped coals of fire on her head. He was being perfect, and she was a lying and conniving wretch.

She was pleased to see that the twins were on their best behavior, even though she knew they were fascinated by the parrot, and itching to ask about their promised exploration of London.

Saxonhurst winked at them and said to his friends, "I have to throw you out. I've promises to keep."

The guests left amiably enough and the earl took his

discourteous bird on his hand and turned to the twins. "Now, the truth is that your slugabed sister has wasted the best part of the day. It will be growing dark soon, so we'll have to put off our explorations until tomorrow. You're not to sulk about it."

Richard put on his affronted face. "We *never* sulk, sir!"

"I'm pleased to hear it." He stroked his bird and made it at least face them all. "And I promise that we'll go on our jaunt tomorrow, even if we have to drag your sister out of bed by the hair."

The twins giggled. "She's always up first anyway, sir."

Saxonhurst cast her a brief, but slightly amused look. "So she is. Now, before the daylight fades, why don't I show you all around this house."

Accompanied by the dog, which sidled out from under a sideboard as if it would rather no one knew it had been there, and the parrot tucked inside his jacket, presumably for warmth, the peculiar Earl of Saxonhurst gave them a well-informed guided tour. Meg marveled at the beautiful items that were, to him, mere furnishings. Tables inlaid with polished, jewellike stones. Enameled cabinets covered in pictures made from tiny pieces of inlaid oriental woods and ivory. Table items of silver and gold. Chandeliers with hundreds of faceted crystals.

Everything was so beautiful, so unlike her. She found Brak a comfort. Anyone who was fond of such an ugly dog should be able to tolerate Meg Gillingham, who at least did not look as if she were snarling all the time.

"I suppose," she said, "that you inherited all this."

"Most of it, yes." He'd stopped off to leave his bird in his warm rooms, and now led them back downstairs. "The collection of paintings was sparse, so I've been adding to it. And other items that take my fancy here and there."

As he ushered them into a library full of books, he gave her a rueful look. "I doubtless should have pointed this room out to Jeremy straightaway. If you see him before I do, assure him he has the freedom of it."

"You're very kind." An understatement of the first order!

He shrugged it off. "It would be unthinkably churlish

to deny such a scholar the use of the books, most of which are never opened."

Everyone was wandering around studying the titles behind the glass doors, or the valuable ornaments on every surface. With half an eye on the twins, Meg admired the paintings hung wherever the shelves left space on the wall.

She didn't know a great deal about art, but she could tell these were all by masters and indicated depressingly high standards. Which had he chosen?

"Sir!" That was Rachel's voice. "Why does this lady have a bird's face?"

Meg turned and saw that the twins were fascinated by a particular painting. When she went over, she saw that indeed, the richly dressed woman in the portrait had a hawk's face. Not far away was a picture of a man with a face made of fruit.

"Allegorical?" suggested the earl, strolling over. "I have no idea, but I found the pictures intriguing. The artist is called Fuseli, and you may meet him one day. Despite his work, he is fairly normal. As normal as any of us, at least."

Well, thought Meg, studying the disturbing pictures a while longer, she shouldn't be startled. She knew the earl was eccentric.

She thought of the pictures in her rooms—mostly conventional landscapes and still-lifes. They'd doubtless been consigned there as boring. There was a very quiet little Dutch interior that was snaring her interest, as if it were a magical window into another world. That painting was to her taste, and yet her husband liked pictures of people with strange things where their faces should be.

She shrugged off her worries. She'd expected to pay for the *sheelagh's* solution, and the price wasn't too high. His behavior thus far had been tolerable. A little wild now and then, but no more than that. Whatever caused his behavior with his grandmother, it clearly wasn't his normal way of going on.

When they'd toured the house, Saxonhurst declared that they all needed a quiet evening at home. He ordered an early dinner and then invited the Gillinghams to show him how they were used to passing a winter's evening.

With glee, the twins found their pieces for the game Fox and Chickens.

"Ah, I remember playing this," he said, and proved it with his skill, even though he often had to be reminded of the rules. Meg thought that sometimes he forgot on purpose. Life was complicated by the fact that the parrot was back and wanted to play with the pieces as much as they did.

He'd spoken the truth about the time he spent in the bird's company, but she did think there was true affection there. Perhaps devotion on the part of the bird. Such devotion carried obligations, and she should be glad that he respected it.

In fact, she was glad, especially when the bird decided to make overtures of friendship to Jeremy and Richard by plucking holly leaves off the mantel and bringing them over as offerings.

Soon the two of them had little piles of holly leaves, and the mantel was looking decidedly bare, and everyone was laughing at the bird's antics.

Enjoying her family's high spirits, Meg let herself appreciate the moment. Even if life was troubled, such moments were to be treasured, as was the man who brought them like holly sprigs into her life.

She was very tired, however, feeling as if she might close her eyes and slide into sleep at any moment. Perhaps he noticed, for he commanded a supper and suggested an early night for all.

Meg wondered if he would try to seduce her again, and shivered with weariness at the thought. But he merely escorted her to her bedroom, kissed her cheek, and left her. Meg was happy to let Susie prepare her for bed, to finally settle to a solid night's sleep.

She still had problems, but she had so many blessings as well. Not least of them her unpredictable, glossy, entrancing husband.

Chapter 10

After breakfast the next morning, Saxonhurst gathered them all for the projected tour of London and commanded a carriage. "I think we can squeeze five into one vehicle. It's cold out there, though. Coats, hats, gloves, and scarves." When the twins rushed off, pursued by Laura to keep them in order, he said to Meg, "You'll have gathered that your brother has gone to his tutor again. I tried to tempt him to leisure, to no avail. A serious student, isn't he?"

"I'm afraid so."

"No need to apologize. I'm sure the world needs some people who think translations of Horace of great importance."

They were alone, and there was a look in his eye. Rested and refreshed for battle, Meg retreated a few steps. "I should go and get my cloak. . . ."

"Not at all." He tugged the bell and a footman stepped in. Or limped in.

"Milord?"

"The countess intends to go out."

"Very well, milord." The man left.

"I can get my own things."

"Be charitable. They need employment."

"But that one shouldn't be asked to climb stairs."

"Clarence? How is he to work if he doesn't climb stairs? He would hate being pensioned off as an invalid."

Meg supposed that was true.

"His leg doesn't pain him much. It just makes him awkward. So," he added, "how are you today?"

Her fictitious monthly! She knew she was coloring with guilt. "Very well, thank you."

"It won't inconvenience you to drive around London for a while?"

How delicately he phrased these questions. "Not at all."

"Good. I hope you'll also feel up to visiting a modiste for measurements and design choices. The sooner the better."

He was ashamed of her appearance. Well, of course, he was. "I have no objection, my lord."

He *tsked,* and she hastily said, "Saxonhurst."

"Sax."

She stared at him. "Not yet."

Surprisingly, he grinned. "Good for you. The last thing I want is terrified obedience. Send me to the devil whenever you want."

If she heard "without lying excuses" it was doubtless just her guilty conscience speaking.

She expected questions then—about keys and what she'd really been doing out in the garden yesterday— but he chatted about the weather, and about a diplomatic mission to Russia mentioned in the day's papers. He asked if she favored a particular news-sheet, saying she should order it.

"Oh, and magazines, I suppose. *La Belle Assemblée. Ackermann's.*"

Meg had to again stop an instinctive protest. These magazines wouldn't be wanton indulgence. In order to be a suitable countess, she doubtless needed all the advice she could find on fashionable living. And Laura would love them.

When her brother and sisters ran downstairs, bright-eyed, ready for adventure, she experienced another burst of happiness. She was likely to turn dizzy with them all, and they all came from Saxonhurst.

As Laura dimpled innocently at some teasing flattery from her brother-in-law, Meg offered a full-hearted prayer of thanks—a prayer directed sacrilegiously to the *sheelagh* and the earl as much as to God.

No matter what it took, she was going to become a countess worthy of him, and make him happy.

In every way.

*   *   *

They rode first to the Tower, where Mr. Chancellor had arranged a private tour by a Beefeater. The man knew plenty of gory tales suited to ten-year-olds. For her part, Meg was interested, but rather saddened by the many tragedies that had been played out here. Languishing prisoners had scratched messages into stone and glass, and some had been taken out to lose their heads on the mound. High rank had accorded them privacy from the howling mob, but she doubted it had been much comfort in the end.

She swallowed at the thought of how close she'd come to the gibbet, and at the thought of the risks she might still have to take. How *was* she going to get the *sheelagh* back?

When they emerged through the stone gateway, the carriage was waiting to drive them to a tea shop for refreshments. Meg was becoming fascinated by the way the earl was surrounded by perfect service. She rarely saw him even express a wish. His servants seemed to pride themselves on providing for his needs without being asked.

When everyone had eaten and drunk their fill, the earl announced that it was growing late for another major expedition. He suggested instead that Monkey, who had ridden on the back of the carriage, should escort the twins home on foot. He promised that the footman would show them some interesting spots along the way.

Then he turned to Meg and Laura, "Fair ladies, let us go and spend a great deal of money."

Meg was still trying to protest when they entered the establishment of a fashionable dressmaker. As soon as she saw the gowns on display, however, she abandoned all attempts to be sensible. She'd never pined for pretty dresses, not being one to pine for what she couldn't have, but if he was going to insist it was her wifely duty to be clothed in such fairy-tale garments, who was she to refuse him?

She let the earl and Madame d'Esterville play with her like a doll, choosing designs and draping her with fabrics so beautiful she could almost weep to think of them being cut. By the time they left, she seemed to have ordered dozens of outfits but had no clear idea what they would turn out to be.

Laura was in a daze of delight, since she, too, was to have new gowns suitable for social occasions.

When Meg gave the earl a worried look, he said, "They'll be as decorous as you could wish. But she's old enough to come to the theater with us now and then, and perhaps even to attend a party in the country."

"Really?" Laura gasped.

"Really." His twinkling, indulgent smile and Laura's happy laughter made Meg even more intent on being worthy of him.

"Now," he said, offering an arm to each of them, "we'll let the carriage trail along and visit a place I know you'll like. Mrs. Sneyd's."

"And what, pray, is Mrs. Sneyd's?" asked Meg.

"A haberdashery. But a haberdashery, my dear ladies, such as you have never enjoyed before."

And he was right. The place was a vast emporium, displaying every item imaginable. Dazed by hundreds of styles of stockings, thousands of gloves, by lace, and ribbon, and braid, by shifts of silk and shifts of linen, by nightgowns and robes, and even by cheaper types of jewelry, Meg was literally spoiled for choice.

Again, he took over. She wasn't sure she had drawers enough for the stocking and shifts he bought for her, all of the finest quality.

"My lord," she protested, watching him gathering silk stockings like someone picking berries, "I will need cotton hose, too."

He smiled at her. "Of course. I was thinking of me."

Laura turned, startled. "Do you wear silk stockings, my lord?"

His lips twitched. "With court dress, yes. But not like these." He held up a pair made of finest flesh-colored silk with tiny butterflies embroidered up the back. He winked at Meg, causing a fiery blush. Her legs would look naked in those. Naked, with butterflies!

Clearly, however, he had not developed a disgust of her, and she couldn't help but be fiercely glad.

Conscience eased by his extravagance, she began to choose for herself, or in fact, mostly for her brothers and sisters. She happily equipped them with new under-clothes, stockings, and night wear.

As Mrs. Sneyd's delighted employees ran out to the carriage with pile after pile of purchases, the earl sighed with the satisfaction of a job well done. "I think we'll command the shoemaker to the house. But I'd like to stop by a certain millinery I know."

As they strolled into the busy street, Laura asked, "Do you have sisters, my lord?"

"Only my new ones. Why?"

"You know so much about ladies' clothing."

Meg had to bite her lip, and Saxonhurst seemed a little strained as he said, "I have a great many female friends who ask my advice."

"Oh," Laura said. "How strange."

Meg found herself sharing a suppressed grin with her husband, and blushed. But it was a pleasant blush. She liked him, and she thought that perhaps he might like her.

She wasn't even shocked or offended at his rakish admission. He'd been right in saying she wasn't pure. It must be all the reading she'd done, that and her natural curiosity. Thank heavens her husband didn't seem to mind.

It was ironic that they shortly encountered one of his female friends— a fashionable woman on the arm of a dashing, red-coated soldier. With clustering golden curls under a high, elaborate bonnet, and cheeks and lips that clearly owed something to paint, she made Meg feel like a hedge-sparrow.

"Sax, *darling*! What a lovely surprise. I was just wishing I had your advice on silks." She presented a cheek, and he obliged by kissing it, then nodded to the officer. "Redcar."

The woman ignored Meg and Laura as if they were servants, and stepped a little closer to the earl. "I'm trying to decide on just the right material for some very *intimate* apparel. . . ."

"Then you'll have to rely on Redcar's advice, Trixie." He turned to Meg. "My dear, let me introduce you to Lady Harby and Colonel George Redcar." To them, he said. "This is my wife, Lady Saxonhurst, and her sister, Miss Gillingham."

Two jaws literally dropped.

The silence was embarrassing, but Saxonhurst didn't seem to mind. It could only have been seconds, anyway, until manners clicked in and both lady and officer smiled, greeted, congratulated. Then they hurried on, carrying a promise of invitations to the ball the earl would be holding shortly to introduce his wife to the *ton.*

"Ball?" Meg queried, rather shaken.

"I confess, I hadn't thought of it till then, but we might as well puff it off in style rather than in dribs and drabs. A Twelfth Night ball. We'll make sure you have that apricot gauze thing to wear."

Meg tried to distinguish apricot gauze from the rest of the rainbow of fabrics. . . .

"Our wedding announcement was in the papers today anyway," he was saying as he stopped in front of a familiar shop. "But Trixie Harby never reads anything."

Meg seized her courage. "Will you invite your family to the ball?"

He turned at the door. "Family?"

She knew this wasn't wise, but had to do it. "Your grandmother and—"

"No. Come along." He shepherded them through the door of Mrs. Ribbleside's, and Meg's brief spurt of courage faded. It was early days. She'd heal his family's wounds later.

The pretty milliner gushed and glowed again, but with a calmer eye Meg didn't entirely like the way the woman smiled at Saxonhurst as she curtsied. Theoretical tolerance clearly didn't extend to actual examples. Meg wished she knew another fashionable milliner to suggest. An elderly one. Or one with warts, or crossed eyes, or an enormous sausagey nose.

She didn't however, and Mrs. Ribbleside was clearly skilled at her trade. As Meg was determined to make up for her moral shortcomings by being a perfect wife in every other way, she could not object. Soon she was a mere head under a parade of toppings, bombarded with questions about brims, height, ribbons, fruit, flowers, feathers. . . .

The earl, lounging on a chaise, gave most of the responses. "Not that one. Too heavy round the face. . . . Try another pink. Ah yes. Very becoming . . ."

Eventually, hat boxes were stacked to be delivered later, and the earl gave Laura carte blanche to choose some headwear for herself under Mrs. Ribbleside's advice. He drew Meg over to the window.

"Tired?"

"A little," she confessed, feeling a poor creature when he hummed with energy in a way that reminded her of the *sheelagh*. "But I must thank you—"

"Devil a bit. I'm having enormous fun." He turned to watch Laura angle her head to admire a wide villager hat of white lace trimmed with cream roses. "Take that one, for sure, pet. Come spring, you'll slay all London."

Laura chuckled, but ordered it, eyes brilliant with excitement.

"She's going to be wonderfully dangerous," Saxonhurst said.

"Dangerous?"

"To men. And," he added with a twinkle, "to our peace of mind. She won't even need a fortune to be hunted. You're lucky to have me, you know. I'm not sure you could have kept the predators at bay."

Meg stared at him, forcibly reminded of Sir Arthur, of what might have been.

He deserved so much, this generous man she had trapped. She wished she could be completely honest, but she didn't dare. She could, however, try to put one thing right.

"The other night," she whispered, glancing to be sure Laura and the milliner could not hear, "I lied about . . . about my courses." She wouldn't give him an explanation, for that would need a new untruth.

He smiled, apparently unshocked and unoffended. "I thought so."

Oh dear. "I am normally very honest, Saxonhurst. I assure you."

"I believe you."

Meg had to turn to stare through the small-paned window at the bustling street before she could go on. "Tonight," she whispered, even more quietly.

"Yes?" He leaned his head close to hers, as if he were having trouble hearing her.

She cleared her throat. "Tonight. It will be all right." She flicked one glance at him, then stared away again. "Tonight."

She felt him take her hand, and as he raised it to his lips, she met his eyes.

"My dear Lady Saxonhurst," he said, "tonight it will assuredly be all right. I pledge my life on it."

"What do you think—?"

Meg snatched her hand free and turned to Laura, just as Laura broke off her own words. Both she and the milliner were looking at them with bright-eyed interest.

Had they been overheard? Meg felt her face flame at that.

No. But probably the tone of their conversation had been noisily obvious.

Sax, unconcerned, strolled over to her sister and adjusted a saucy toque that seemed entirely composed of ribbons. "Laura, my dear, there should be a law against it. I think I shall put a bill before the House that all pretty young ladies be compelled to wear veils and wimples like nuns."

Laura gurgled with laughter. "Then veils and wimples would be all the rage, for who'd want to rank themselves with the un-pretty?"

"And poor Mrs. Ribbleside would lose most of her custom. However, since I suspect we've stripped her stock for today, let us be on our way home to prepare for the evening."

Meg, still standing by the window, felt a jolt at those words, but a moment later she knew they were mostly innocent. He'd planned a trip to a pantomime tonight.

As they left to return to the carriage, however, she knew by a look in his eye that they hadn't been entirely innocent. He had other plans, and though deeply nervous, quiveringly so, Meg couldn't wait to end up in this particular fox's jaws.

He wooed her. Slowly, over the remainder of the day, Meg was aware of her husband leading her toward the promised night.

In the carriage, despite Laura sitting opposite, he took her hand. It was no more than that, and they both wore gloves, but throughout the short journey to the house, she was aware of his fingers wrapped around hers.

Then, for the last few minutes of the journey, his thumb slid beneath the edge of her glove to rub against the skin of her inner wrist. She had never felt anything so dangerous in her life.

At the house he, not a servant, removed her cloak and bonnet, his ungloved hands whispering briefly against her neck. As they went toward the room where tea awaited them, his hand rested lightly against her back—so lightly and yet so unignorably.

They conversed. Jeremy was home and had things to say. Laura and the twins were keen to tell their brother all about their adventures. The earl made the occasional comment. Mr. Chancellor played his part, and so did she, she thought, though her mind was completely tangled in intimate matters.

He sat beside her, not touching, but almost seeming to. She felt like a piece of metal placed beside a powerful magnet, as if she could quite easily slide right up against him, locked there.

He served her, plying her with tea and cakes. Sometimes his fingers brushed hers. Occasionally, his eyes lingered on her lips like a phantom kiss.

Sipping at tea, she realized that this was seduction! This was what happened when a man like Sax singled out a woman and began to invite her to his bed. They were married, and yet she felt perched on the edge of wickedness, secretly being invited into sin.

She had to put down her cup before her unsteady hand created a spill.

Despite the fact that the others were still chattering and nibbling, he rose, holding out a hand. "If you've finished, my dear, let us go upstairs for a while."

No excuse. No explanation, despite the sudden hush, and the interested looks. Mr. Chancellor suddenly picked up the conversation again.

Now?

She'd thought tonight.

She wasn't *ready* yet!

But she wouldn't dodge him again.

Her legs astonishing weak, she let him guide her up the stairs to her bedroom.

No! To his. She'd thought it would happen in hers, though it shouldn't make any difference.

Again his hand on her back gently guided her to her fate.

Once in the room, she looked around nervously, desperate for something to talk about. "Oh my!" she gasped, before she could stop herself.

Who would paint a camel figurine green, and then ornament it with orange spots? Who would purchase such an object? What kind of man gave it a prominent place on his mantelpiece? What man had as a clock a gilded face stuck in the belly of a fat white figure wearing a pink and gold wrap?

And what of the oval platter beside them? She had to go closer to be sure she wasn't mistaken. Indeed, the picture in the middle showed the starving poor breathing their last by the roadside.

"You admire that plate?" he asked.

Meg looked around, trying to conceal dismay. What a contrast to the rest of his elegant house! And yet this, and his bizarre paintings in the library, must be his true taste. And his dog, of course. And his bird.

Clearly Saxonhurst, despite appearances, was not entirely sane. Yet she was tied to him for life.

And he *was* being so very kind to them all.

She looked from him to the plate. "Is it supposed to create a guilty conscience, perhaps? To deter gluttony."

"I have no idea. Do you not care for it?"

From a range of possible answers, Meg said, "It is not to my taste, no."

She'd caught sight of another peculiarity—a stand of some sort composed of tortured bamboo painted bright pink but topped with green leaves. Apart from its other problems, it clashed horribly with the gold-papered walls.

She shuddered, wondering if she might eventually be allowed to throw these objects out and choose more suitable ones for the poor man. If she was to engage in all her marital intimacy here, it would be essential.

With sudden alarm, she wondered just what sort of clothes she'd let him choose for her. Her memory told her they would be in good taste, but now she wondered.

She glanced at him and saw that he was watching her, perhaps amused. "You haven't admired the painting over the bed yet."

Meg had been deliberately ignoring the bed, but now she faced it, and stared. On the back, above the headboard, set among swags of golden brocade, was a huge and extraordinary picture of naked women. Astonishingly muscular naked women.

"Amazons, of course," he said, coming closer. "You'll note the absence of the right breast."

"It's hard to avoid." Meg couldn't take her eyes off the outlandish painting. It wasn't the nakedness that disturbed her most, or the breastlessness, but the fact that the women hurtled shrieking in all directions, bearing blood-drenched swords and assorted severed body parts, and that all the corpses were men.

She feared he really must be mad to sleep under a thing like that.

With a forced smile, she turned to him. "You admire military subjects, my lord?"

"I admire strong women." He was close, and came closer. "Like you."

He took her hands, and her heart tried to race to a stop. "I don't feel at all strong just now," she whispered.

"Of course not. Nature doesn't work that way." He was drawing her into his arms. A protest trembled on her lips, a protest stimulated in part by his unbalanced decor, but she suppressed it. This was her duty, the payment she must make.

And beyond duty, she *wanted* it. She wouldn't lie about that.

Mad or not, the Earl of Saxonhurst stirred her wanton senses.

Pressed lightly against his body, held gently there by his arms, she steadied herself and turned her face up for a kiss.

His skin was not so smooth this close. She supposed no skin was. His honey lashes were long, however, and his eyes were yellow as trees are green, created by a million shades. He smelled of a faint perfume, and also of something much more earthy that she knew was him.

Doubtless, she had her own smell. She hoped it was as pleasing.

"We are still going to wait for the night, Minerva," he said, snaring her attention for his lips. "But I cannot wait that long to kiss you again."

This was unlike his other kisses. Meg had not known there were so many types of kisses. His lips pressed upon hers, warmly, softly, playing there a little, but meaning— she was sure of it—more.

He angled his head and teased her with his tongue. "Open to me, Minerva. Explore me. . . ."

With a little noise that startled her, Meg obeyed, driven by the fact that he had turned passive. What she wanted, she would have to take.

She touched his teeth with her tongue, almost groaning at the shocking intimacy, then felt his tongue against hers, a gentle greeting, a welcome.

He sucked at her. At her tongue. She made another noise. It might have been a protest. He ignored it, drawing her in, pulling her close so she could tumble deep into his kiss.

Then he was carrying her. To the bed!

He seemed to settle her there, to settle beside her, without any interruption. His leg came over hers, his torso pressed her down as he captured her mouth and her soul. One hand caressed her breast, his gentle touch like fire despite layers of cloth and corset.

She'd thought they were going to wait, but had no real objection to doing it now if he was being carried away by his animal nature. She'd quite like to get the first time over with so she could stop worrying about it.

In case he needed encouragement, she raised a hand to the back of his neck and became enraptured by the sweet, potent feel of hair and skin against her fingers.

His leg settled between her thighs, pressing through layers of petticoats and skirts. She couldn't help but shift against him, and he raised his head to make a murmuring, approving sound, almost like a big cat purring.

He smiled, and she smiled back.

Meg remembered once—so long ago—yesterday—

thinking she knew about this sort of thing from the *shee-lagh,* and that she was immune.

She'd been wrong.

And he'd known she'd been wrong.

There was a connection, yes, but one as frail as teased silken floss, disintegrating here in her hands.

Grasping her courage, she raised her head and kissed him on the lips. He laughed with a delight that could break hearts.

"You're going to change for the theater, aren't you?"

"The theater?" She blinked at him dazedly.

"Remember. We're not going to consummate our marriage now."

Meg just stopped herself from saying, We're not?

Wailing it.

She was going to be the perfect, conformable wife. Whatever he wanted, she would do. Even control herself. "You want me to get ready for the theater? Now? I only have one silk gown. . . ."

"Begin to get ready. As in taking off the gown you have on." He was already shifting, rolling her away from him. Undoing the buttons down the back of her dress, slowly, one by one.

She sprawled there, knowing she could stop him and he would obey. He demanded willingness of her, a willing surrender of prey to predator. He'd already won that battle, though. She was completely, bonelessly his.

Lips. Lips against her bare back above her corset. Playing there. Tracing circles and spirals, making her arch with simple pleasure and complex delights.

Then he pushed the gown forward, baring her shoulders, and kissed her there, too, all along the broad straps of her corset. A hand slid over and down, slowly following the strap down inside the sanctity of boned linen and buckram, to touch the top of her breast.

She reached up instinctively to protect herself from that significant invasion, but for a crucial moment her hands tangled in the cloth of her gown, and then she didn't want to stop him at all. He began to play with her, hand inside her corset, big body lying all along her back, thigh between her legs, breath hot against the side of her neck where he kissed and nibbled.

Meg arched again, hands limp now, and surrendered to the strange, stirring sensations so like and yet so unlike the magic she had feared.

When he slowly slid his hand free, she moved her hands, this time to stop him from stopping. But he turned her into his arms, kissed her parted lips, her neck, and the upper edge of her tingling breasts. "Tonight . . ."

And Meg said, "Not now?"

He grinned. "Not now. But your body will remember."

"It would be impossible to forget."

He stroked down her body as if she were a cat, his eyes sparkling like fireworks on a frosty night. "Wonderful, isn't it?"

"So why not now?" She was hungry, she realized. Sharp-toothed appetite nibbled at her innards. "Why not?"

"Ah, Minerva, I love your frankness. I love your hunger. Always be this honest with me. Always. But you know what the French say. *'Bon appétit.'* Things are best enjoyed with a hearty edge to the appetite."

"And how is your appetite, Saxonhurst?"

He seized her hand and pressed it to him. "See?"

Meg suspected that a proper lady, even a proper married lady, would snatch her hand back from that shape. She didn't. She didn't even want to. She reveled in the hardness, in what it promised for the aching void he'd created inside her.

"Then you don't think *I* have enough edge to my appetite?"

His smile turned wry. "In truth, my dear, yes. You have surprised me. In only the most delightful ways, I assure you. But we don't have time just now for a feast, and I am determined that your first taste of these delights will be a splendid feast. In years to come, we will be able to enjoy many a light repast between tea and dinner. Hasty puddings, even. But not today."

He'd continued to stroke her, she realized. In some way that different touch and his words had reduced her biting desire to a seething hunger that could be satisfied, just, by the promise of food to come. She let her hand fall away and enjoyed just lying there as the winter day faded, and her husband, lounging beside her, soothed her sizzling senses.

They could almost be two people side by side in a drawing room.

She had to suppress a smile. Well, not really, not with her gown still loose and her corset straps exposed. But she felt astonishingly comfortable, uninhibited by expectations of how she should behave.

"In a proper world," she said, "perhaps the man and woman would come to marriage equally ignorant and explore the mysteries together."

His lips twitched. "You are not comfortable with being the neophyte?"

"It is my nature, I'm afraid. I like to be independent and in control."

"I share your tastes."

"But for a man, it is easy."

"Is it? Few men are independent, or control their destiny. I am one of that lucky few."

"And treasure that."

"When one has a treasure, it must be guarded."

Meg suppressed a sigh. She'd feared as much. It made it even more impossible to tell him he was here on this bed with her because of a magic spell.

"And yet," she risked, "you were forced to marry me."

He tilted her chin and looked at her, and she knew even that casual comment had caught him on the raw. "I married you to avoid worse fates. That's choice of a kind."

"Then everyone has choice in everything, if only whether to die or submit."

"Minerva Saxonhurst, you are not at all the mouse you at first appear, are you?"

"I never tried to seem a mouse. But I do confess that being horizontal seems to have a loosening effect on the mind."

He laughed, a sharp hoot of amusement. "Perhaps it does, at that." Watching her—and she knew he'd turned hunter again—he pulled looseness into the bodice of her gown and began to unhook the front of her corset.

Then he looked down, and his hands stilled. He pulled

down her gown a little further, and Meg bit her lip. She was so used to her underwear that she'd forgotten it. Now he was tracing the lines of vivid scarlet embroidery she'd worked along the stiffened seams of the corset.

"How beautiful." He ruffled the white frill at the top that was part of her shift, and that she'd vandyked with tiny stitches. "Pure above, wanton below."

She saw something different on his face, something more than desire, or amusement, or pleasure. "You are a creature of magical surprises, my sweet Minerva. I tremble at the thought of peeling you layer by layer down to your innermost secrets."

The word "magic" jabbed like a needle in her conscience, and "secrets" jerked her with alarm, but Meg was mainly concerned by what he would think if he investigated too far.

Most women didn't wear drawers. Most people thought them wicked, a sign that a woman wished to ape a man's role. And to make it worse, she'd embroidered hers, never thinking they'd be seen.

He was still tracing the design of her corset, his touch shivering through her torso. "This is your work?"

"I could not afford to pay someone for such frivolity."

"Why?" He looked up and she saw only open curiosity.

It was a simple question with a simple answer, and yet Meg balked at revealing her private thoughts, at exposing the most vulnerable part of her soul. She sat up, turning away, pulling up her dress, knowing she was being foolish, foolish, foolish.

"You don't have to tell me if you don't want," he said from behind her.

"I just like pretty things." She struggled with unsteady fingers to rehook the one wanton fastening at the front. "A governess cannot wear fanciful clothes, but no one knows about her corset—"

She was seized, dragged back, forced down under his power. For a moment she fought, but then she remembered her resolve. And anyway, he was too big and strong for her, as she'd always known.

He dragged her gown down even farther then before, tracing the fine, vivid stitchery. Meg lay powerless, hating the invasion, but biting her lip on a complaint. She would do his will.

Then a thumb rubbed her lip, loosening it. "Don't. If you want me to stop, say so."

She looked into his frowning eyes. "Stop."

After a still moment, he gently pulled her gown back up. Not all the way, but as far as it had been. Then he undid that one top hook of her corset again, and kissed between her breasts.

She looked at him and laughed, close, in truth, to tears. "You are so very strange. How do you understand?"

His lashes lay thick on his cheeks for he looked down at her covered breasts. "We all have places that are private. Sometimes places that make no sense to others." The lashes rose, revealing darkened, brilliant eyes. "But I hope to explore your private places soon, Minerva. Every wicked inch."

He began to loose more hooks on her corset, slowly, one by one. She knew without looking that he was keeping her gown over her corset even as he exposed her breasts.

She felt him slide his hand in to raise her right breast free of constraint, felt the air play cool upon it. Felt no shame or embarrassment at all. He kissed the tip gently, then looked up at her. "What a delightful mystery you are."

Then he lowered his mouth again.

She waited, expecting something fierce, but felt only the brush of his tongue around her nipple, and the chill when the air found the dampness. He brushed her again, over the very tip, and she shivered. Not from cold.

He put his teeth to her, abrading her slightly so she raised a hand to protect herself. He captured it. Stayed it. Without word, he asked her to trust him and she let her hand fall back to the bed.

He sucked her, one long, slow suckling that stopped her breath and made her tense in places she hadn't known she could tense. And then he was gone.

Or not gone. On to the other breast.

Gently, it too was freed of constraint, dampened,

teased, and suckled. Meg clutched the rough silk of the bedcover so that she wouldn't clutch onto him.

Then slowly, he settled her breasts back inside the corset, fastened up the hooks, and pulled up her dress.

He looked at her, smiling with what could only be contented pleasure. She lost any wish to hide her helpless reactions.

"They will remember," he said. "You will remember. All through the evening. Through the meal, at the theater, during the carriage ride back home. They will remember. You will remember. It wouldn't be fair if I were the only one suffering as we wait."

Then, in one of his changes of mood, he was off the bed and tugging her to her feet. He turned her and fastened her buttons without any play at all.

"Normally we'd go late to the theater, but I'm sure the twins would think that poor fun, to miss the early shows." He put a friendly arm around her and walked her awakened, hungry, aching body through his dressing room into her bedroom.

She had entirely forgotten that she wasn't in her own room. She'd lost all awareness of spotted camels, tortured bamboo, and shrieking Amazons.

She was, as he had intended, now solely aware of one thing.

Him, and the coming night.

Susie was already laying out clothes for the evening. The maid looked them over with clear understanding, dimples forming in the round cheeks. "Are you wanting to change for the evening now, milady?"

"Er . . . yes," Meg said.

Her wicked husband put his head against hers, hand curling to hold her there, lips close to her ear. "Tonight," he whispered. "Remember. Here. Away from the Amazons. But don't prepare for bed. I want to undress you, my wife, layer by wonderful layer. . . ."

Meg watched him leave, shivering as if she'd just made the most wicked, clandestine assignation. Indeed, except for the minor detail of them being married, she had!

Chapter 11

Somehow, Meg survived dinner with dignity, perhaps because she and her husband were seated at opposite ends of the table. She couldn't say she ate much.

In the carriage, they sat side by side, and while conversing with Jeremy and Laura—the twins following behind with Mr. Chancellor—he somehow made her think of kisses and touches all the time. It was always possible the wickedness came entirely from within herself, but she doubted it. The Earl of Saxonhurst was a wizard in these matters, able to spin magic spells and entrap poor mortals into forbidden ways.

To make, as he had promised, the prey long for the hunter's killing touch.

She entered the theater in a daze, her attention wholly focussed on matters some hours ahead. She could only pray that she wouldn't do something excruciating embarrassing during the waiting time. She was so completely distracted, that it took her some moments to realize that the earl was talking to Sir Arthur Jakes!

Meg was sure she must have given something away, for she felt as if she'd been suddenly pitched into a torrent of icy water. Perhaps she even made a noise, for she caught a slight, perceptive look from her husband. Sir Arthur, however, was oblivious, for he was being claimed by the twins, who wanted to tell him all their adventures.

She was reminded that he'd been a family friend for years. She'd been as fond of him as the twins when younger, for he'd always been generous with pennies, or small treats, or trips to the nearby tearooms for sticky cakes.

It would take very little to convince her that she had

dreamed it all—his proposition about Laura, and his theft of the *sheelagh*. But then she caught one tiny glance he slipped toward her sister and she knew she hadn't dreamed it all.

His look wasn't one of love lost, or distant adoration. It was angry, frustrated, corrupt greed.

Smiling, he detached himself from the twins, and turned to Meg. "Quite the happy family. I am delighted to see you all so well set up, Countess."

The title jarred her, and before she thought, she said, "Oh, you must not. We are still old friends, I hope."

A moment later, she wished the words stopped, wished them scrubbed away. They had come from the past, from pennies and sticky buns, and from her own discomfort with her new rank, but they were so very foolish.

She'd surprised him, too. He was unable to hide it. But a moment later, he was easy again. "I consider myself honored," he said with a bow, "and not because of your rank. Your parents were dear friends, and they would want me to keep an eye on their children. I hope you will not mind if I call now and then. And perhaps take the younger ones for a treat, as I used to do for you."

Sinking in quicksand, Meg said, "The twins will miss you if you don't." She hoped he understood that he had no permission to be alone with Laura. Ever.

But was even Rachel safe from such a monster?

"My dear," the earl said, touching her elbow gently, "we must gather our flock and take our seats. Sir Arthur." With just a nod, he dismissed the man and Meg could only be grateful.

As the earl guided her along the carpeted corridor toward their box, she wondered if she could tell Saxonhurst about Sir Arthur and ask his advice. Not about the *sheelagh*. Just about his designs on Laura.

She suspected, however, that the earl would do something drastic. Perhaps even a duel. She could not bear that.

No. All she needed to do was to warn Laura. Laura had clearly begun to be uneasy with Sir Arthur, and would not seek him out. If Meg made sure she wouldn't be caught by some trick, all should be well.

In fact, Sir Arthur had no power over them anymore.

Except if he had the *sheelagh*.

Drat the stone. Drat Sir Arthur. The magic was gone. Not the *sheelagh's* magic, but the spicy enchantment her husband had woven through the day.

Monkey—she must remember to call him Monk, as Saxonhurst did—was in the luxurious box, clearly having made sure all was ready for them. A small table held wine, tea, cakes, and a bowl of oranges. He took coats and cloaks, then stationed himself there, ready to serve.

Meg had never been in a theater box before, and she marveled at the comfortably upholstered seats and the iron stove at one side which kept the area cozy.

"One thing I've always wondered," she said to Saxonhurst as he settled her into her seat in the second row, leaving the front for the excited younger ones, "why are there curtains at the front, and why are they sometimes drawn? Is that because the box is not in use that night?"

His lips twitched. "Not at all, my dear. It means it is very much in use."

His look filled in the details, and Meg blushed. "In the *theater*?"

"Indeed."

"But why?" she asked, very sotto voice. "I mean, there must be many other places. . . ."

"Not for illicit lovers."

"But everyone would know. And know whose box it was. And who was inside."

He grinned. "Frankly, unabashedly curious. How very wonderful you are."

She stared at him, aware that the magic had not died.

"I hope you are always so intensely curious, my wife. About everything." He took her hand and kissed one finger. "Perhaps the gentleman who owned the box might not mind his exploits being known, and the lady could join him once the curtains were drawn."

"Or"—he kissed another finger—"the owner could be a lady. Some famous ones ply their trade here."

"Not a *lady*," she pointed out with what voice she had remaining. The wizard was definitely at work again.

"Probably not. But"—he kissed her ring finger—"since most owners do not use their boxes every night, it could be rented by anyone. That box up there for example . . ."

Helplessly, she looked at the next row up and opposite, at drawn curtains.

". . . belongs to the very staid Viscount Newnan, who I know is celebrating Christmas with his family in Wales." He gently turned her face toward him. "And now, I know, you are wishing you could see through that heavy cloth. . . ."

"Not at all!"

A finger against her cheek prevented her sharp turn away. "Don't lie, Minerva. Never lie. I want you curious. I want you interested in everything. I want you trembling with it, with the need to know, the need to touch and taste."

And she was trembling, but not entirely with the effect he could have on her. She was trembling from that comment about lies. Susie had said he didn't like lies. He'd forgiven her the one about her courses, but would he forgive others? The continuous, entangling lies . . .

The finger moved, stroking her cheek. "At times, you seem troubled, Minerva. I know this is not easy. Am I troubling you?"

"No." It slipped straight out, but it was essentially true.

"I desire you," he said, still touching her in that delicate, distracting way. "Tonight." With a quirk of the lips, he added, "To be honest, now. But I can wait. Wait even for another night if need be."

Even now, he was offering her escape.

She thought about her words this time, for deep inside quivered a place that feared him, feared his power over her, feared the breaking of barriers that she knew must come with intimacy. But she said, "I don't want to wait."

His smile showed pure delight. "I'm glad." But then he added, "So, is there anything else troubling you?"

It was so tempting to tell him everything, but she knew temptation must generally be resisted. "Nothing in particular," she said, but looked away. Oh lord, she might as well paste a sign to her chest saying LIAR!

He moved his hand, letting her turn to look out at the noisy, crowded theater and be comfortable. If someone so troubled could be comfortable.

"What about Sir Arthur?" he asked.

She turned back. "What?"

"You don't seem easy with him."

She hated the hint of watchfulness and doubt in his eyes and gave him what truth she could. "He's an old family friend. I was quite fond of him when I was young, but later"—she looked away again, but this time just from remembered embarrassment—"he . . . he made me uneasy. Before I left to take up my post."

"Did he do anything?"

She looked back. "Do?"

His lips twitched again, though his eyes were not particularly amused. "The sorts of things I have done. Kiss you. Touch you."

"No!" At the sharp word, Laura twitched to look behind, and Meg smiled for her. "No," she repeated in a quiet voice. "Nothing like that. Just a change in his manner. It made me uncomfortable. And I am a little concerned about Laura."

Though it was slight, she sensed his sudden tension. "Has he done anything there?"

After a moment, she lied. "No." It wasn't really a lie. He hadn't done anything. Yet.

"Certainly, Laura seems at ease with him. Most likely the man's harmless, but to be safe, we won't allow him to be alone with any of them. With so many idle servants eating their heads off, that's simple to arrange."

It was so complete a solution that Meg felt tears sting her eyes. "Thank you."

He reached to brush beneath her eyes. "I wonder if you told me the whole of this."

With despair, she knew he had to know she had not.

The finger trailed down to her lips and tapped once there. It was almost a chastisement, though a very gentle one. "Marriage is for sharing problems, my dear, and for finding solutions. Though it's early days, I will be hurt, I think, if you continue to fight battles alone."

Then Meg did want to burst into tears and spill out every detail, but the muted orchestra surged into full volume, playing a rollicking music for the clowns of the first show. As she turned and watched the curtain rise to reveal the glittering scene in front of a gaudy oriental palace, she was glad to have escaped that folly. She fiercely resolved, however, never to hurt her kindly husband again if she could help it.

For his part, Sax watched his strange wife, rather than the performance. He noted the excited pleasure of the younger ones, and enjoyed their enthusiasm. It was easy to become jaded. His new family was breathing life into stale pleasures. Mostly, however, he was fascinated by his wife. She, too, was breathing new life into stale pleasures. How long had it been since he had anticipated sex quite this much?

She seemed to be enjoying herself, too, but she was definitely troubled.

He wondered how bad it was.

He didn't judge Sir Arthur Jakes to be the type to forgo months of rent, even for an old family friend. What payment had he demanded? Minerva herself? Was it possible that she'd had to give the man her virginity, and that her nervousness about consummation was simply a fear of being found out?

He thought over their encounter in his bedroom, trying to see if she'd acted like a woman who'd never been touched before. It was hard to tell. She'd been surprised, but in the end, eager.

Sir Arthur might be an insensitive lover who had simply used her, so that more subtle attentions were new.

He might have raped her.

Careful not to startle her too much, he put a hand on his wife's shoulder, to the place left bare by her modest evening gown. She started a little and glanced at him, nervous, but not truly fearful. He doubted Sir Arthur, or any man, had abused her, thank God, but it was still possible that she'd had to pay for shelter with her body.

He wanted to be the first, and he wanted the freedom to carry her high. After this afternoon, his marriage bed lay before him like a delicious promise, like the smell of baking bread or roasting meat, bringing saliva to the mouth, and the spiciest kind of keen appetite.

His wife. His unexplored domain.

Ah well, even if she wasn't a virgin, she was unawakened in all the ways that mattered.

She turned back to the stage, but he knew she had to be aware of his hand against her skin. He let one finger tease her nape, and as keenly as she watched the antics on stage, he watched her every reaction—her parted lips, her warming cheeks, her hand flexing suddenly on the arm of her chair.

Ignoring Monk behind them, he moved a little closer and put his lips to her neck, just behind her ear, hearing her catch her breath. "If we were long married," he whispered, "and alone, I'd draw the curtains."

She raised her chin—the tiniest, revealing arch of surprised desire. When her lips parted more, he put a finger between them and grinned when she set her teeth into it. Passion. His wife was a creature of passion. No matter what little secrets she was hiding, he was a very lucky man.

He moved closer to first lick, then bite, then suck her lobe. She almost rose out of her seat, her hands tight on the arms. "We have a bed waiting, however," he whispered. "And tonight, I think we need a bed."

Letting his tongue play around the curve of her ear, he inhaled, taking in her scent, warm and womanly and personal, except for the most prim hint of lavender. Would he adorn her with richer perfumes, or was she best as she was, so proper on the surface, but all fire and spice beneath?

"Your bed or mine?" he whispered.

She turned to him, drowning, he could see, in her senses, just as he wanted her.

Wanted her.

By Hades, it was true. If they were alone, he would not wait. He was master of this game, however, so if they were alone he would not be playing with this fire until it was time.

"You said mine," she said dazedly.

"So I did. Does that please you?"

"I don't think I mind anymore."

"Yours." He kissed her soft, parted lips. "The Amazons might give you ideas. Your bedroom, where I will undress you by candlelight and firelight, and uncover every secret of your senses."

"I think you already know them."

"Every woman is a new mystery."

She stiffened slightly, as he knew she must. Something had to cool things down.

The music changed and on the ignored stage, a magician began to make flags appear out of nowhere.

Her lips pressed together, and she straightened in her chair. "No woman likes to think of herself one of many, my lord."

"I've known plenty who'd prove you wrong. A man's no use to them unless he's desired by many others."

"I suppose they queue at your door."

He'd swear she had sniffed, and he grinned. "No, but I receive some interesting invitations by correspondence."

She turned pointedly toward the stage. "I wish to watch the performance, my lord."

Thoroughly put in his place, Sax silently laughed and stretched a hand behind him. Monk put a peeled orange into it. Sax ate one segment himself to be sure it was sweet and good, though he trusted Monk's abilities in these matters. Then he put the next segment to Meg's tight lips.

She glanced at him, frowning, then after a silent struggle relaxed enough to let him feed her. But it was grudging. She was punishing him. He loved it. When she swallowed, he presented another. "If you want to own me, Minerva, you will have to earn it."

She chewed the orange and swallowed, still looking at the stage. "I am your wife."

"You think that gives you property rights?"

She turned then. " 'Forsaking all others'?"

"My confession was just about my unruly past. The future is yet to come."

"Can a leopard change its spots?" She took the orange from his hand, peeled off a segment and presented it to his lips. "I think, my lord, I must learn how to behave from you."

As he took the fruit and chewed it, he had to suppress

a growl of approval. Oh yes, marriage to Minerva was going to be a lot of fun. "Are you saying you intend to take lovers?"

She put another piece of fruit against his lips. "That depends on what *you* earn, doesn't it, my lord?"

He seized her wrist. "Fidelity," he challenged quietly, surprising himself. "Both of us, for each other alone. Forever."

He was undoubtedly mad. It must be a primitive instinct about the woman whose children would legally be his, but his own words startled him, as did the intensity of feeling behind them. She was his—her secrets, her fighting spirit, and her fascinating underwear.

His.

The thought aroused him to a point perilously close to disaster.

Perhaps she sensed it. Her eyes grew huge, but not afraid. Like a wild creature she was excited by an instinctive knowledge of his desire. "That is what I said in the marriage vows, Saxonhurst. I take such vows seriously."

He nodded, released her, and took the piece of orange she was still offering just as the burst of applause warned him that the early show was over.

The younger ones turned around, bright-eyed and excited, and demanded oranges and cakes. Monk served them all, giving the adults wine.

Sax sipped his, consciously cooling himself down. The promise he'd just made could prove to be very awkward if he'd judged his wife amiss. But no. Watching her as she laughed with her brothers and sisters, he didn't think she'd surprise him in bed, except in the most pleasant ways. Any other little secrets she might have were irrelevant.

His unexpected countess was a woman of deep and honest passions, or he was a celibate monk. In his years of lively investigation of women, he'd learned that many apparently ordinary women were deeply passionate, while many flamboyant ones were all tinsel, with no true interest in the earthy side of life.

He'd also learned that random sexual encounters, no matter how expert, could become tedious, something he'd never have believed when a wildly liberated twenty-one. A lengthy sexual voyage with his mysterious wife would not, he was sure, be tedious at all.

She suddenly swooped forward to prevent Richard from tossing a piece of orange peel into the pit. Her dowdy silk skirt shifted to reveal her shapely ankle and a hint of embroidered petticoat. The plainest white on white, but a complex design, beautifully worked. Passion concealed by lack of color, and obvious only to those of keenest sight and instinct.

That earlier glimpse of her corset had shown lush green vines bearing scarlet blossoms.

Lush, embracing, secret passions.

He relaxed back. He was a very, very lucky man, and had no doubt that in a few hours he was going to be in an extreme state of connubial ecstasy.

Meg saw that the twins were restless, and suggested that they all stroll the corridor a little. She needed a respite, too, for the box, though large, seemed closed in and hot, especially when she glanced at the earl and saw the way he was looking at her.

Anyway, she hoped for a moment alone with Laura to deliver her warning. Despite Saxonhurst saying they wouldn't let Sir Arthur be alone with any of them, she wanted Laura alerted. Now. Though logic said her fear and urgency was ridiculous, she wouldn't feel safe to let her sister out of her sight until she was warned.

The fashionable crowd were arriving, however, to see the main performance, and the crush in the corridor was too great for private talk. Family excitement was running too high, too. There'd be time when they were leaving, or when they returned home.

Before . . .

She glanced at her husband, and he smiled.

Before.

Then she was being introduced to people, people whose names she would never remember, especially as their faces were all the same—astonished.

Sir Arthur appeared again. "Just visiting an old friend in his box," he said, with a wave behind him. "I can see you are all vastly pleased with the performance."

The twins proceeded to tell him just how pleased, with

more decorous agreeing noises from Jeremy and Laura. Meg noted her husband watching hawkishly for a moment before his attention was claimed by a fashionable middle-aged couple.

That predatory alertness helped her to relax. He would guard them, and she trusted him to do it well. None of them was vulnerable to Sir Arthur anymore. Eased, she even joined in the conversation with their ex-landlord.

He behaved impeccably, and yet she still felt his interest in Laura, and a simmering anger toward herself. She hoped she was imagining it, but was relieved when the bell rang to announce the next act.

Like leaves blown by a sudden breeze, the crowd shifted toward their boxes. Meg turned, but for a brief moment she and Sir Arthur were side by side and alone, as the earl took farewell of the older couple.

"Housebreaking is not very ladylike, Meg."

"I have no idea what you're referring to."

The older couple moved off. Sax turned.

She stepped away, toward her husband, but behind her back, Sir Arthur's hand seized her gown. Still smiling, he said, "Make an opportunity to speak to me in private, Meg, or you will deeply regret it. I have something you want."

Then he loosed her and bowed, and she staggered forward to take her husband's offered arm.

"I hope he wasn't distressing you," Sax said.

"Not at all." She made herself smile, and sank helplessly into another lie. "But he says there were a few things left behind at the house that he thinks are ours. He wants me to go and look."

"Not without me." He was calm, but implacable. "There's something about that fellow I can't quite like."

Perhaps that was why he played no more games with her during the first act of the pantomime. Meg was partly grateful, for he could so easily upset her equilibrium, and partly fearful that she'd somehow given him a disgust of her.

How many times could she lie to him and not shatter what they had?

Meg couldn't stop thinking about Sir Arthur's threat.

How could he make her regret not speaking with him? How?

The worst he could do, surely, was to tell Saxonhurst about the *sheelagh*. It would be embarrassing to have to admit to possession of an obscene statue, but that was all.

Unless Sir Arthur knew about the magic.

But even if he did, he couldn't know she'd used the magic to trap the earl into marriage.

He might guess.

If he knew about the magic.

No one knew. *No one.*

He *couldn't* make a viable threat against her, and yet she quaked inside. She'd have to find out what he was up to before she could have a moment's peace. And, of course, she had to get the *sheelagh* back.

At the intermission, she looked around, hoping for another encounter with Sir Arthur, for the chance to find out what he'd meant. She didn't see him. She didn't have a chance to speak to Laura. Saxonhurst seemed almost to be ignoring her!

Oh, *why* had Sir Arthur turned up here to spoil everything?

Blindly watching the last act, Meg could have wept for the loss of the earlier warm, bubbling anticipation.

Why had Sax stopped paying her any attentions?

Did he know?

Had he overheard?

Then, as the performance wound to its end, he took her hand.

With a mere whisper of his thumb against hers, he seemed to bring the magic back. Losing interest in the wild action on the stage, and pushing aside all thought of Sir Arthur Jakes, Meg turned eagerly to her husband.

Looking startled, then pleased, he raised their linked hands to his lips, and kissed hers. Then he pushed their hands back toward her own lips.

She noticed again how elegant his fingers were, reminded of their first moments together, when his hand had prevented her fleeing the church. She kissed each elegant finger as he presented it to her lips, then when he extended one, she obeyed, and kissed the tip.

His other hand suddenly came to rest on her back above the seat and one finger stroked there, stroked down her spine, sending a shiver right through her. He gently turned her attention back to the stage, and she watched dazedly as disguises were stripped away and true loves found, while villains came to abysmal ends, and heroes were rewarded.

And as a clever, subtle, magical hand wrote promises on her back. That was all he did—write secret promises there but in that simple way, he captured her. When the final applause died, he stopped and took her cloak from Monk to drape around her shoulders, talking easily to the others.

She clutched it to herself, feeling shivery and raw, but in the sweetest possible way. How long now? Less than an hour, surely. But then, back at the house, a supper would probably be laid out.

She couldn't possibly eat.

She expected him to arrange for them to travel back alone to the house, but he had the twins ride with them, and encouraged them to chatter all the way. He even gave up his seat to Rachel, so they sat opposite, not beside each other.

But that way, she discovered, he could send secret messages with his eyes and mouth, messages that kept her nerves humming.

"Are you all right, Meg?" Rachel asked at one point. "You look funny."

"I'm fine." She pinned on a smile.

"I think we're all ready for bed," her mischievous husband said. "So much excitement."

"No, we're not!" Richard declared. "We're not at all sleepy."

Even as the boy yawned, the toe of Sax's shoe found Meg's ankle. "True. We're not at all sleepy."

Once in the house, he firmly sent everyone to bed. His tone was so pleasantly authoritative that even the twins didn't protest, especially when promised their supper in the schoolroom. Jeremy had suddenly remembered his books, and was already on his way. Laura flashed Meg a wicked glance, but turned to the stairs.

"Laura!" Meg called, suddenly remembering that she

must be warned. Sir Arthur might try some trick, and what would Laura do if he used the *sheelagh* to blackmail her, perhaps in the morning before they could talk?

Her sister turned three steps up. "Yes?"

"I need to speak to you." She stepped forward, but the earl caught her hand.

"It can wait," he said, in that same pleasant, implacable voice.

Meg, however, pulled her hand free and turned a smile on him. "Only for a moment, Saxonhurst!" Then she hurried up the stairs, tugging her astonished sister with her.

"What are you doing?" Laura whispered. "The earl—"

"Don't argue." But at the top of the stairs, Meg looked back to send him another reassuring smile.

He was staring up at her through his quizzing glass!

Chapter 12

Meg put that aside—it would be easily sorted out—and bustled Laura into her own boudoir.

"Why are you doing this?" Laura asked, wide-eyed. "What's the matter?"

"Sir Arthur."

"Sir Arthur?"

Meg made herself concentrate on this one thing, then she could make all right with her husband. "When I was your age, Sir Arthur started to behave strangely with me. Touch me in ways I didn't like. Say things that weren't quite proper."

Laura colored, and looked down. "Yes."

Meg pulled her into a hug. "Oh, I'm sorry I didn't say anything sooner. I just want to be sure that you will never, ever let yourself be alone with him. No matter what he promises, or threatens. . . ."

"Threatens?"

To truly warn her sister, she'd have to tell her the truth. "Laura, he has the *sheelagh*."

Laura put a hand over her mouth. "How?"

"I couldn't see how to take it out of the house with the servants there. And Saxonhurst stuck to me like a teasel. So I thought I'd sneak back later. In fact, early yesterday—"

"Oh. Was *that* why you were so tired? Not . . ."

"Not. Yet. Not yet. Never mind." Meg stopped gibbering. "Sir Arthur said something in the theater that makes me think he's going to try to use the *sheelagh* to get something from me. I don't know what. I just want to be sure he can't trick you into meeting with him, or going anywhere with him. Promise."

Laura looked at her, a surprising maturity in her

steady gaze. "What could he threaten that would be so bad?"

"I don't know. He might guess . . ." She'd have to tell all. "He might guess what I did. About this marriage."

Laura's lips parted. "You *didn't*!"

"I was desperate! I had to. But the earl must *never* know how this marriage came to be, Laura. Never. He would hate it. . . ."

Sax quietly reclosed the door.

He'd not intended to eavesdrop. He'd gone to his room, then decided not to let his wife's strange nervousness interfere again. He'd passed through her bedroom and opened her boudoir door, intent on getting rid of her sister and picking up his seduction. He knew by now she was not seriously unwilling.

It hadn't occurred to him to knock. He hadn't tried to be quiet. His house, however, was damnably well made and well run. Nothing rattled or squeaked.

He stood, staring almost sightlessly at her bed, the bed that had been his destination this night.

Had been.

It wasn't just the words. It was the tone.

Desperate.

He moved on, back to his own rooms, going over what he'd just heard.

What I did. About this marriage.

The earl must never know how this marriage came to be.

He would hate it.

Physical desire still thrummed in him, quite uncomfortably in fact, but mental desire—the important part—was sheathed in ice.

Surely not.

It couldn't be.

He sought refuge in brandy, his shaking hand causing the decanter to bell-chime against crystal as he poured. The burn of fine spirits cleared his head a little.

His wife's words had to be innocent. Of course, she'd been desperate to marry. He knew that. Desperate because of poverty.

But what had she done that he would hate?

He thought again about Sir Arthur. Perhaps that was it. Perhaps she'd sacrificed herself with the man for food and shelter. He'd hate that on her behalf.

But not on his own.

It didn't feel right. Ringing clear through her remembered words was the implication that he, Saxonhurst, would particularly hate whatever she had done to bring about the marriage. That he'd been tricked.

There had to be a logical explanation. Not the one that seethed like a pack of snarling beasts deep in the swamp areas of his mind.

Debts?

How could she possibly have acquired debts that could distress him? But if she had, how could she think to repay them without his knowledge?

There must be something else he would hate, something she'd feel she had to keep hidden. Other than—

The beasts hurtled free.

The dragon.

He just stopped himself from smashing his glass, placing it with painful care on a table before pacing the room.

No. No!

But what if the duchess was even more duplicitous than he'd ever imagined. Could she have set this up, using Susie and Minerva as tools? Was Daphne a mere red herring? Had the duchess been laughing at him during that confrontation in the hall?

No. *No!*

But he would hate that. He would hate it with all the loathing implied by his wife's tone.

He put his hands to his head, feeling as if monsters were loose in it, raging and snarling. How had Minerva reacted to that scene in the hall?

Remember.

Remember.

She'd wanted him to be kinder. Was that suspicious? He was sane enough to know it wasn't.

The dragon had dismissed his new wife as unworthy, but that could be acting. God knows, the old witch could act.

They appeared to be total strangers—

"Saxonhurst?"

He whirled to look at her, hovering uncertainly in the doorway.

He'd have to see about getting the doors fixed in this house. Fixed so they squeaked.

"Do you have a headache?" she asked, frowning in concern.

He dropped his hands. "No." He could speak normally if he tried. "I was trying to remember something."

She came a little farther into the room, looking wary and slightly guilty, but surely not guilty enough for the plot he envisioned. "I'm sorry. About earlier. I had to speak to Laura."

"About what?"

"About Sir Arthur. I wanted to warn her."

He forced himself to relax, to chain the beasts. His suspicions had to be nonsense. He knew he wasn't quite sane on the subject of the duchess. Or that others would think he wasn't quite sane.

He went over to her. Took her hand. Led her toward the fire. *Make it make sense to me, Minerva.* "You could have spoken of that in the hall."

She looked away and, sickeningly, he knew she was about to lie. "Servants could have been listening."

"As I intend to warn them about Sir Arthur, that hardly matters." *Tell me the truth. Please.*

"I hadn't thought of that." She looked back, the very picture of honesty and concern.

Clearly, he was mad. He'd constructed her guilt out of nothing. Could she have acted that panic in the church? Would Susie betray him?

Trick! howled the demons, fighting their chains. *She said "trick"!*

He drew her into his arms. "Forget Sir Arthur. Unless, that is, he has done enough to desire punishment. In which case, we will hound him to hell together."

"No. Nothing so bad." But she kept her face down against his chest.

He gently turned it up, so he could see her eyes. "Then forget him. You need never even speak to him again."

Worry shadowed her, but surely not guilt enough. "But the twins are quite fond of him."

"Is it a fondness you want to encourage?"

"No. But what am I to do if he calls?"

"You will never be in."

"And if we encounter him?"

"Cut him. In fact, I'll have a word with him and make it clear that—"

"No!"

And he couldn't dismiss the flash of wild panic in her eyes. Devil take it, was the man blackmailing her over some sin? Over her lack of virginity? That had to be it.

He pushed her slightly away, but kept his hands on her shoulders. "What *do* you want me to do about Sir Arthur?"

There was a hint of tears in the corners of her eyes, and he longed to wipe them away. She was honest. He'd pledge his soul that in all ways that mattered, she was honest.

But frightened. Why?

"Perhaps we can just go on as we are," she said. "Probably Sir Arthur will not seek us out. And if he does, I'm sure he will not create any trouble."

Yes, the man was at the root of her concern.

She was staring at something behind him, however, and he turned to see Brak's snarling face peering up from beneath the bed. He hadn't even realized the dog was here.

"Come out of there, you idiot."

Brak moved forward perhaps an inch. No farther. How did the dog sense Sax's devils so well?

He looked back at his wife, his wife who surely wasn't the villainess he'd thought.

She raised her chin. "I thought we were going to . . ." Then her boldness clearly failed her, touchingly so.

"You are not afraid?" If she'd lost her virginity, wouldn't she be less eager? More? Did it matter?

Her eyelids fluttered in confusion. "Should I be?"

"I don't know."

She moved very slightly back. He supposed his reactions might seem odd if she were innocent. Or threatening if she were guilty.

He took her hand to stop her from moving away. They had to deal with this. "If—through no fault of your own, my dear—if you were not untouched, you might—"

She blinked at him for a moment, then snatched her hand free. "Not untouched! What sort of a woman do you think I am?"

"A desperate one." He could hear that his voice was calm, which was a minor miracle.

He believed her.

She was a virgin.

But if she was a virgin, he was back to seeking the trick she had played.

"Desperate?" she repeated, voice rising. "You think . . ."

He couldn't answer. He was fighting the beasts.

What would he hate?

Only one thing.

In a butterfly life he had only one certainty, one firm purpose. Opposing the dragon. To the death. Refusing her any effect on his life. If there was the slightest danger that his wife was the dragon's tool, he could not surrender to her.

Not even with her here before him, willing and desirable.

He'd built appetite in himself as much as in her, and now it flared, but he couldn't. Not now. Now, it would be ruled by the beasts, poisoned by the dragon, whatever the truth of it all.

With the slightest chance that he was wrong, he couldn't let their first time be tainted like that. And he knew he could be wrong.

He wasn't sane on this subject.

He brushed a loose tendril of hair from her smooth brow, willing his hand not to shake. "I'm sorry. It had occurred to me that your nervousness might be because you were not a virgin. I wouldn't have blamed you."

Sax wondered what his frowning wife was seeing. She wasn't a stupid woman and he knew he couldn't seem entirely normal. "I am a virgin, Saxonhurst. It's almost as if you would prefer that I not be."

"I don't care." That didn't come out right, and he saw hurt flare in her eyes. He had to make that right, but couldn't seem to find the words. This was only going to get worse. He had to get rid of her before something terrible happened.

"I won't blame you. Whichever . . . Damnation. The mood has gone awry, my dear. We have a lifetime. No need to hurry."

She regarded him steadily, the very picture of honor. "I did it, didn't I? When I went to speak to Laura."

"Did what?"

"Spoiled everything." But then she shook her head. "No, it's more than that. You sense my secrets, don't you? You're always talking about them."

"God, Minerva. Don't –!" But then he looked into her eyes. "If you have secrets, tell me now. Tell me, and they will have no power."

"If I thought that was true, I would have told you already."

"So," he said, heart racing with despair, "you think I will 'hate' your secrets." Deliberately, he quoted her.

And she flinched. "Some things are better not known."

"Surely you know the story of Pandora's box. Merely knowing you have secrets starts the rot."

Her chin rose. "Do you not have any?"

Oh, she was remarkable, this chance-found wife. "Yes."

"I'll tell you my secrets if you'll tell me yours." After a moment, she smiled wryly. "See? I think marriage allows us a little privacy, does it not? Both of us."

When he said nothing, she turned away. "Good night, my lord."

Lust conquered. Lust and optimistic faith. He lunged after her, pulled her back hard against him, ignoring her shocked cry. Head down in the curve of her neck, he said, "To hell with secrets. Just tell me it's nothing to do with the duchess."

"It's nothing to do with the duchess." She said it in a choked whisper, and he realized he had his arm tight around her throat. Appalled, he let her go.

She staggered away and turned, pale with shock, to face him. Her hand went up to her throat. "Why should it be? To do with the duchess?"

Dear God in heaven, he'd hurt her. He'd almost throttled her! The least he could give was honesty. "Because I couldn't hate anything as I hate anything to do with her."

She shook her head. "You can't hate an old woman, Saxonhurst. And hate hurts most the ones who hate."

He laughed at that, turning to seize his brandy glass and refill it. "Oh no, my dear. My hate hurts the dragon, despite her tough scales." He drained the glass, feeling the rich, burning liquid scour away some of the dross.

It brought back sanity. She'd told the truth. Every sense and instinct said that. He put down his glass and walked toward her, smiling his relief. "If your secret has nothing to do with her, we can be happy." He reached gently for her. "I'm sorry if I frightened you."

She went stiff. "No."

He drew her in for a kiss. "Forgive me. Come, let me—"

She twisted free. "No."

Laughing, he caught her and pulled her back. "Remember earlier. Let's—"

She hit him on the shoulder hard enough to shock. *"No!"*

Dazed, he read certainty in her fierce lips and eyes.

"No," she said again. "Not like this. Not with distrust between us. Not with you hating your family so!"

He let her go and rubbed where she'd hit. "Devil take you, woman, this all started with your secrets. Don't throw distrust at me!"

"But you're the one who hates!"

He moved away before he lost control of his raging body. "You've known since the beginning that I hate the duchess. Why throw it up now? An excuse for cold feet, my nervous little chicken? Or are you just a tease?"

She turned as sallow as her dreadful dress. "I didn't see how deep it went."

"You expect me to believe that you're refusing me your bed just because I don't get along with a relative?"

"Because you hate your grandmother. It poisons everything!"

He stared at her set chin and fierce eyes. Pure Ardent Reformer, damn her to Hades.

He picked up the brandy again. "Well, Minerva, if you're going to deny me your bed until I'm a sweet and loving grandson, this is going to be one hell of a marriage. Good night."

After a moment, she whirled out and slammed the door.

Sax almost threw the crystal decanter, but had control enough to put it carefully down. It was a beautifully made piece of Waterford.

Brak whined and disappeared back under the bed, wise dog.

Sax chose the revolting maggot-white, sneering clock figure and hurled it at the howling Amazons.

Meg fled into her bedchamber and turned the key in the lock. A moment later she felt foolish. Her husband certainly wasn't coming after her.

Then, in the distance, she heard something shatter. She ran back to the door, thinking to offer help. But the noise was followed by another crash, then another. . . .

Oh, dear lord! The children!

Shaking with shock and fear, she opened the door to peer into the corridor. Deserted. Taking the opposite direction to her husband's room and the terrifying racket, she picked up her skirts and raced up to the higher floor and her family.

She hurtled into the schoolroom. All her family sat at the schoolroom table, finishing their supper and chattering.

At her arrival, Jeremy shot to his feet. "What's the matter?" A moment later, he asked, "What's that noise?"

"Don't ask." Meg closed the door, and the sounds were muted. But they could still be heard. She gathered the twins into her arms. "And don't go downstairs! Any of you."

Jeremy halted by the door, staring at her.

She realized almost at once that she was making them frightened, and that she was hugging the twins for her own comfort, not for theirs. She let them go and forced a smile.

"I'm afraid the earl is a little bit upset."

"He's breaking things?" Laura asked, wide-eyed.

"Yes."

Rachel suddenly pressed back into Meg's side. "I'm scared."

Meg made herself calm, and stroked her sister's silky hair. "Don't be. He won't hurt you. He's just smashing things." She hoped that was true. She was beginning to have morbid imaginings about Clarence's crippled leg, and Susie's blind eye.

"Why?" Rachel asked. "What's made him angry? Us?"

"No! No, of course not." Meg sat and pressed her sister close. She needed another lie. Well, perhaps just a half-truth. "It's to do with his grandmother, dear."

"He doesn't like her, does he?"

"No."

"Why not?"

"I don't know, love. But it's nothing to do with us, you see, so nothing will harm you." Then the faint noises stopped. That should be reassuring, but Meg tensed, listening for angry footsteps pounding up the stairs.

The door opened.

She clutched Rachel closer, but it was only an enormously fat maid, with three chins and a merry smile. "Ready for bed, Miss Rachel?" she asked as if nothing was amiss.

Rachel looked up at Meg, who remembered to let her go. A part of her wanted to keep all her family in this room and barricade the door.

She kissed her sister. "Good night, love. It's all over now."

Laura took Rachel's hand. "I'll go, too. It's been a long day." Meg silently blessed her.

They all had to look out for each other. They were all they had. But who would look out for her if her husband came, as was his right, to get her?

Now the maid had left, she saw a manservant hovering, clearly for Richard.

"Peter," Jeremy said to him, "did you hear breaking noises just now?"

"Just the earl in one of his states, Master Jeremy. Not

to worry." But he did give Meg a funny look, clearly having some ideas about the reason for the state.

Jeremy, bless him, asked the question Meg wanted to ask. "Does the earl do this often?"

The man shrugged. "Depends, it does. But it's only ever in his room, see. So you don't ever need fear he'll bust up anything outside. You ready, Master Richard?"

Already soothed by the man's cheerful acceptance of it all, Richard said his good nights and left. Meg had to wonder, however, how much she should trust servants who took all this in their stride.

Jeremy eyed Meg. "I don't think this is any of my business."

"Or you hope it isn't."

He shrugged, and went over to where his books lay open, waiting.

"Don't your books provide anything useful in these cases?"

He gave her a wry grin. "Fathers eating sons. Mothers sacrificing children. Men driven mad by songs."

"And they call it education." Meg sat, and sighed. "You're right. It won't affect you. I hope."

"It's bound to. A bit."

She wished he were older, that she could shift some of the burden onto him. She didn't know anyone, however, who could help her in this. For a brief time she'd thought she'd found a colleague in the earl, but not now.

Perhaps she had been right in her first macabre suspicions. Despite his charm and generosity, her husband was probably not quite sane. It was tragic, but she didn't know what to do about it.

She pushed wearily out of her chair. "I'll leave you to your studies."

"Are you sure you should go back down?"

"You heard what the servant said. Only in his room. I'll make sure to keep out of there."

"Don't you sleep together as Mama and Papa used to?"

Meg knew she was red-faced. "No. We have separate suites."

"Strange." But then he plunged back into infanticide and cannibalism.

Meg would like to stay up here, but she knew any
sense of safety was illusory. She was married to the earl.
For life. Her family couldn't protect her from him, and
by lurking up here she might put them in danger.

"Don't forget to make sure the candle's dead," she
said to her brother.

"I always do."

With a sigh, she left the schoolroom, closing the door
quietly. She knocked, then looked in on her sisters, who
were both in their nightgowns. The maid was brushing
Laura's hair, while Laura brushed Rachel's. Meg remembered how often she and Laura had brushed and plaited
each other's hair and longed for simpler times.

"Sleep well," she said, and they both turned to wish
her good night. Only Laura looked a little concerned.

Bracing herself, Meg made herself return to the main
floor. She crept down the stairs, every sense alert for
danger. Was that another crash? A cry? What was he
doing?

When she was near the bottom, however, the faint
noises clarified into chattering. And laughter? It almost
sounded like a party in the corridor. Perhaps *she* was
going mad!

Peering around the corner, she saw a parade of servants with brushes, dust pans, and buckets, filing through
a door and down narrow stairs. One maid carried bits
of the spotted camel, another mangled works of that
ugly clock. Clarence, the limping footman, bore a
twisted, ruined, pink stand like a trophy. "Five guineas
from the kitty for this, mates! Thought I'd never see
the day."

Meg pressed back. They were all mad! What had she
done to bring her family here?

"Like to know what set him off this time," said one
voice, receding.

"We all know *what*," said the woman's voice. "Silly
titty. Just not why."

The door clicked shut, cutting off all sound.

Weak-kneed, Meg slithered down to sit on the stairs.
Was she going to have to live here, with everyone speculating on everything she did, thinking her silly for not

rushing into bed with him? And with her husband hurled into a fit of destruction whenever crossed?

The answer of course, was yes. As the old saying went, she'd made her bed and must now lie in it. The only thing to do was to try and work some of the lumps out of the mattress.

Hugging herself against the chill, she contemplated her problems.

The biggest one was the rift between the earl and his grandmother. She'd have to find a way to heal it. True enough, the duchess seemed to be a tartar, and family wounds could linger, but the duchess was just an old woman. She couldn't do her grandson any harm.

She pulled a wry face at that. The duchess had tried to marry him off to that walking nose-drip. But that was the sort of thing parents and grandparents did—tried to push the younger ones into marriage, not always wisely. It wasn't ground for unremitting hatred.

Nothing was, short of murder.

Or rape. Or threatened rape. She hated Sir Arthur. But she wouldn't fly into a rage at the mere thought of him.

She made herself consider whether the earl really was unbalanced. Irrational.

Mad was the word she was dancing around.

That might explain this obsession.

And what did that offer for their future?

Chapter 13

She sat there in the dim light provided by a wall lamp in the corridor, pondering the past couple of days. She stayed there because she was too scared—she was honest with herself—to go into her bedroom where he might find her. Yet he hadn't behaved like a mad man most of the time. Despite his teasing, she'd never been afraid of him until now.

Perhaps he was just irrational on this one point, like someone afraid of spiders, or sickened by the color blue. He'd said that he could only hate something to do with his grandmother, though why he'd think there was any connection between herself and a dowager duchess she couldn't imagine.

Clearly she was caught in one of these vicious family feuds one read about in books. The earl and his grandmother likely hadn't spoken calmly in years, and family quarrels did have a way of getting out of hand. Look at her mother and her Aunt Maira.

Perhaps if she arranged for Saxonhurst and the dowager to meet. For tea. In some unalarming, neutral spot. . . .

She was still sitting there, chin on hands, planning her strategy when a candle flame shone into her eyes.

She started, and saw Mr. Chancellor looking up the stairs. "There you are!"

Meg straightened, alarm darting back. "If he's sent you to fetch me, I'm not going."

His eyes widened slightly, but he said, "Not at all. I . . . er just wondered where you were." After a moment, he added, "Do you want to talk about it?"

I didn't seem quite right to discuss these matters, but Meg certainly needed someone to talk to. Mr. Chancellor gave every impression of being sane, and must know more of his employer than she did. "In the drawing room?"

"It'll be icy now the fires have died. Why not your boudoir?"

Meg rose. "Won't it look . . . strange? If . . . if my husband . . ."

"Sax knows I'd never offend in that way."

He sounded so calmly certain that she wondered if it was just another aspect of endemic madness. But she needed some insights here, and Mr. Chancellor was her only hope. A boudoir, after all, was just a fancy name for a parlor. The fact that it adjoined her bedroom was surely irrelevant.

Once there, she sat in one chair by the fireside, while he took the other, crossing his legs, and looking so very normal, she could have hugged him.

"So, Mr. Chancellor," she said, "explain the earl."

"Lord, Lady Saxonhurst, never in a lifetime! Sax is Sax."

"Is he mad?"

Humor faded. "Do you think he is?"

"I don't know. I don't even know what madness is. I can understand, I think, why he became upset, but not the extent of his disturbance. And it is not normal to destroy things when thwarted."

He cocked his head. "Haven't you ever wanted to? Wanted to express your feelings in a very direct way?"

Meg thought about it. "No, I don't think I have. I can't imagine breaking something in a fit of temper. I'm not highly emotional, I'm afraid."

"Perhaps as well. Two in one house might be a bit much."

She considered the man opposite, the one with calm manner and kind eyes. The man she'd thought as normal as she. "You've felt the urge to violence, Mr. Chancellor?"

"Certainly, my lady."

"Oh, please. Call me Meg."

He stared. "Meg? Not Minerva?"

At his expression, Meg put a hand over her mouth. "Oh, dear! And he's doubtless heard the others calling me Meg. But he wouldn't think . . . He wouldn't take *that* as a hurt, would he?"

Mr. Chancellor shrugged. "Hard to tell. But he wouldn't like it. Why lie to him?"

Meg let her hands fall, a kind of hopelessness pressing down on her. "I didn't mean it as a lie. It is my name. And he assumed . . . It's just that he is so very *forceful,* Mr. Chancellor. I wanted to keep a bit of myself in reserve."

He smiled. "I can see that." He uncrossed his legs, and touched his cravat in a clearly nervous way. "Was that why? I don't mean to pry. But earlier . . . everything seemed to be roses."

Meg knew she was blushing, but met his eyes. "Yes. Indeed. I don't really know quite why. I did go to speak to Laura, but I can't see why that should throw him into such a state. Does he always go wild if thwarted?"

"No. In all truth, Sax is generally an easygoing man. Tolerates more than I would from his miscellany of servants, for example."

"They are strange, aren't they?"

"He takes on needy cases."

Meg would have liked to explore that more, but she must try to find her way through more crucial matters. "So why would my going for a few moments to speak to my sister create such problems?"

"I don't know. Generally, the only thing likely to truly upset Sax is his grandmother."

"And that is silly." But then she stopped herself from such a hasty judgment. "Perhaps not. Can you explain the situation?"

He leaned back, worrying his thumb with his teeth. Then he let his hand drop. "Some of it's public knowledge anyway. The earl's mother was Lady Helen Pyke-Marshall, daughter of the Duke of Daingerfield. She ran off, when only sixteen, with the second son of the Earl of Saxonhurst. Rupert Torrance was by all accounts a charming rogue with only a few feathers to fly with. The sort of man her parents, her mother in particular, would never let within a mile of her."

"Oh dear."

"Oh dear from the duchess's point of view, but apparently they were delightfully happy. Despite the duchess's best efforts."

"What could she do?"

"Blackened Rupert Torrance's name in society, for a start. He'd been something of a rascal and she used that to make sure no club would take him, no reputable hostess would let him over the threshold."

"Are you sure it wasn't true?"

"You do like to use a cool head, don't you? This was when I was in the nursery, so I don't know. It didn't matter anyway. The happy couple settled on a small estate near Derby and never came near London or other fashionable spots."

"Perhaps they had no choice."

"Perhaps, but I've spoken with enough people who remember them to think they didn't suffer. I'm told Lady Helen tried repeatedly to reconcile with her mother, but was refused unless she left her husband and children and sought a divorce."

That didn't seem to offer much hope for Meg's plans.

"The old . . . the duchess even managed to turn the Torrances against them, but then they're a funny lot. One great uncle still won't communicate with Sax. Of course, that just made it easier for the duchess to spread tales about mental instability in the family. When the old earl shot himself—"

"What?" Meg definitely didn't like what she was hearing about her husband's family.

"True, he did. And in one of the anterooms at White's stripped down to his underclothes. A notorious scandal twenty years ago. Anyway, the duchess convinced a lot of people that he'd done it because of the wicked behavior of his second son. And when the new earl—Rupert Torrance's older brother—broke his neck out hunting, she made that out to be suicide, too."

"Well, it could have been."

He quirked a brow. "No man of sense tries to put an end to it all by attempting a tricky oxer in the Shires. Failure rate would be high, and chance of ending a cripple even higher. And anyway, this was ten years after the marriage."

"Mr. Chancellor, you can't claim that the Torrance family is noted for sensible, moderate behavior."

"An understatement, dear lady. Sax's grandmother kept over a hundred cats, and nearly as many canaries. Though she may, I suppose, have kept the birds to amuse the cats. And one of his Torrance aunts clothed all the nude statues at Haverhall."

"Mr. Chancellor, the duchess was clearly right to have misgivings about the match!"

"Perhaps. But what does a rational, moderate person do in that situation? I submit, make the best of it, not try to destroy people."

Meg slumped back in her chair. These stories were not increasing her comfort. "And she still holds a grudge after all these years, and is taking it out on their son? I suppose it's easy for her to spread scandal about him, too."

"It's worse than that. Do you know that Sax's parents and his younger sister were killed when he was ten?"

She straightened. "How awful. Killed? How?"

"A carriage accident. The family were in London for some reason. Staying in this house. Sax's father was the earl by then and they'd had to change their quiet life and take up their responsibilities. His parents drove out to pay a visit, and they were held up. His father was shot and the horse bolted. Tipped the whole thing into a river, and his mother and sister drowned."

Meg covered her mouth with her hand. "Oh my God! He was left alone."

"Not entirely. I'm not sure who Sax's legal guardian was, but the duchess seized control. Her husband was dead by then, and her son—the present duke—always was an ineffectual nodkin. Sensible Torrances were thin on the ground."

"Poor little boy." Meg thought of the twins' grief over their parents' death. "To be orphaned so young has to be terrible for any child. I don't suppose the duchess provided much comfort."

"An understatement."

"But the earl is a grown man now, and free of her. It is folly to let his feelings toward her rule him."

"Yet that is why you are married to him."

"Which I am beginning to regret."

Then Meg had to stifle shock. Could the *sheelagh*, with its bizarre disregard of time, have actually *caused* these tragic events? Therefore, had *she*? No, she couldn't think that way.

"I see you shake your head. So you should. You can't seriously regret your marriage in the light of your desperate situation."

She had no answer, for he was completely correct.

He leaned forward. "Sax won't hurt you, my lady. My word on it. You or your family. Even in his anger, he only ever smashes things. But you can hurt him."

"I?" Meg moved slightly back.

"You are his family now, you and your brothers and sisters. He feels strongly about such things. If you hold yourself aloof . . ."

"I don't *want* to."

"But clearly you are. You must have done something to set him off! Are you really saying that your problems came all because you spent a few moments speaking with your sister? Sax isn't a man to be upset by foibles."

"He did seem very upset by it. But it . . . it led to other things. He spoke of his grandmother with such *hate*. So I told him I could never . . . never be wife to someone who felt like that."

" 'Struth." He looked stricken. "That does rather put you in a pickle."

"You're as bad as he is! Whatever she's been in the past, the duchess is now a frail old woman with few years left to her. I don't require that the earl be doting, just that he treat her with the civility due a close relative."

"Then it's an impasse. He won't."

Meg sat up straight. "Then *I* won't! I don't see why I should make all the accommodations here."

"Lord. You're as bad as one another."

"Not at all, for I am willing to work toward a solution. I will act as mediator."

He stiffened as if someone had rammed a rod up his spine. "No, my lady. Please! Trust me on this. If you approach the duchess, that will only make the situation intolerably worse."

Meg shot to her feet. "Mr. Chancellor, this is ridiculous! It's like being trapped in a melodrama. Where is Christian charity and forgiveness?"

He rose, too. "Buried somewhere at Daingerfield Court." He suddenly sighed. "I'm sorry things are happening this way. I hoped for better. You have only been married for days, however, and everything must still be very strange. But I beg you, Lady Saxonhurst, don't do anything impetuous."

"Mr. Chancellor, I never do anything impetuous. I am known for my cool, rational behavior."

"Indeed? Then what took you coolly and rationally to wander in the frosty winter garden a couple of mornings ago?"

Meg halted. "I suppose it did look a little strange."

"And perhaps an indisposition that wasn't an indisposition?"

Meg blushed. "I assure you, sir, I am normally the most truthful of women. And I have confessed that lie to the earl."

"That one but not the other ones?"

Meg felt as if she'd been slapped. "Yes, I have secrets, but none are too terrible. It's just that they might upset the earl a little. Therefore, I would rather keep them from him. I hope to soon have things sorted out—"

"You expect me to be reassured by that? Lady Saxonhurst, I have known Sax since we were boys, and I'm sure you can have no stain on your past that he could not overlook."

When she didn't respond, he added, "Have you met Peter, who is serving your brothers?"

"Yes."

"He was pilloried for embezzlement. Hardly escaped with his life."

Meg stared at him. "And the earl has him here in his house? Attending my brothers!"

"He's not going to embezzle here, is he? And he'd never hurt the youngsters. Why should he?"

"But still . . ."

"See, you're as bad as most people. In Sax's opinion, no one can be expected to reform if he doesn't have the means of survival. But you see that he can overlook a great deal."

Meg's jaw dropped. "Mr. Chancellor, you can't think . . . ! I assure you, I have nothing illegal to hide!" She decided her one foray into housebreaking didn't count.

"Then moral? I'm sorry, but we are bound to speculate. Even so, I doubt you could have done anything to outrage Sax. Whereas, secrets and lies can destroy him.

"Mr. Chancellor, unlike my husband, I have led a life of unquestionable propriety. And you forget, this rift has nothing to do with my secrets, or my strange behavior. It is simply caused by the earl's refusal to be reasonable about his grandmother!"

He raised his hands. "I give up. I just offer you some straight advice. The duchess made his youth hell. She used Sax to punish Lady Helen for disobeying her, for escaping, and for daring to be happy in her rebellion. And for dying. Don't try to bridge an unbridgeable gap. Don't place impossible conditions on this marriage. And don't keep secrets, or tell lies."

"Oh, wonderful! And what stern instructions will you give him? Or is it all for me to do?"

He rolled his eyes and headed for the door. When he opened it, Meg saw her husband standing outside.

"I could not help but hear your raised voice, my dear," he said, cool as an icehouse. "Are you all right?"

He carried a single candle that flared in the draft of the opening door. In contrast to the decorous Mr. Chancellor, the earl had discarded his jacket, waistcoat, and cravat, and his loose shirt gaped riotously at the neck. With disordered hair and the strange leaping shadows of the candle, he looked like a golden angel from hell.

"She's just trying to smash the air with words," said Mr. Chancellor curtly, "though she assures me she is very unemotional."

"Ah. I thought you were supposed to give me stern instructions."

"Certainly." Mr. Chancellor walked forward and the earl politely stepped back so he could pass. The flame danced wildly again. "Tell her all about your grandmother."

Then he was gone, and Meg was left facing her husband through the open doorway.

"I don't think so." Saxonhurst spoke as if his friend was still there. The flame steadied, gilding his handsome face. "You never did understand women, Owain. It will only encourage her in her virtuous meddling." He gave Meg an ironic, courtly bow. "Good night yet again, sweet wife."

He closed the door between them.

Meg stumbled back into her chair. She didn't know why that brief exchange had been so terrible. He'd not been violent. He'd not even seemed angry. Yet she felt as if he'd driven something cold right through her heart.

She realized that Susie had left a decanter of brandy in the room. Wise Susie. Meg's mother had used brandy and water to settle an upset stomach, but clearly people used it to settle many other things. Meg mixed half a glass of brandy with half a glass of water, wishing she had a bit of honey to make it palatable. Then she screwed up her nose and made herself drink the whole glass down, despite the burn.

After a minute or two, when she had her breath back, it did seem that her problems were fading. Not going away exactly . . . Or yes. Moving away like a receding shore. Still real, but distant. Misty.

Interesting.

She drank another glass of the magic potion, then struggled out of her clothes, glad to be wearing an old gown designed for a life without maids. She had no intention of ringing for Susie. At this point, the maid probably wanted to slip her some hemlock.

She giggled at the thought, aware that it really wasn't a giggling matter.

In the end, she tumbled into bed in her shift.

How wise her mother had been. Brandy was almost as powerful as the *sheelagh-ma-gig*.

When she woke, however, Meg discovered that magical spirits have a sting in the tail, too. It actually felt as if her head was expanding and contracting with each heartbeat. Not surprisingly, this caused intense pain. She put her hands to her skull, astonished to find it still, and carefully opened her eyes. The curtains were drawn, but the thin slice of white, winter light cut into her eyes like a blade.

She closed her eyes again and moaned.

She'd have lain there forever if not for a burning thirst.

She rolled off the bed, attempting the impossible task of moving her body without moving her head, and fumbled for the carafe of water. After draining the glass twice, she felt a tiny bit better. Perhaps just well enough to stagger back to the bed.

No wonder they said drunkards went to hell. It was astonishing that they did not know it when every step was so tortured.

She drank another glass of water, moaning when she realized the carafe was empty. Stretching, she pulled the bell-cord.

She was sitting on the edge of the bed when Susie arrived bearing a jug of warm water covered with a clean cloth. "Good morning, milady."

Meg thought of drinking the warm water. Then she realized she needed to use the commode chair. "Cold water, please, Susie."

The maid stared. "You want to wash in cold water, milady?"

"I want to drink cold water."

The maid's clever eye took in the evidence. "Lord save us. You a drunkard, too?"

Meg knew she should be outraged, should send the maid off with a blistered ear, but she felt ill, and stupid, and wicked. "I've hardly ever touched brandy before. And I never will again."

The maid sighed. "Just you lie down, milady. We have a powder for these things. I'll soon have you better."

She left, taking the brandy with her as if she didn't quite trust Meg's words.

Meg wanted to lie down, but her needs were urgent. She staggered over to use the commode. As she made her way back to the bed, she realized that she was beginning to feel better. Not well. She wasn't sure she'd ever be well again. But better.

Which meant that all her problems rushed back into her poor, mangled brain.

She lay down and moaned again, but not with physical pain—with mental anguish. How could everything have gone so terribly wrong within a couple of days?

Sir Arthur had the *sheelagh* and was up to something. Her husband knew she had a secret, and distrusted her. With reason, she must admit. He, however, was seriously unbalanced, and subject to ungoverned rages.

It was all very well for his servant—the pilloried embezzler, for heaven's sake!—to say he only unleashed his rage in his room. What might happen to her or one of her family if they happened to be in his room when he cracked? And could such a restraint be trusted in such an unrestrained man?

And he hated his poor grandmother.

In many ways this was the silliest problem, but for that very reason it dominated Meg's mind. It was so trivial that the earl should be able to shrug it off. He should realize that the duchess was a frail old lady who could only bluster, never hurt. Clearly the dowager was a bitter woman with a nasty tongue, but so were many, particularly when they thought their children had disappointed or betrayed them. Younger, stronger people should put up with them for the few years they had left.

That the earl could not do that, that he seemed willing to throw away any chance of happiness in his marriage in order to hold on to his bitterness, made Meg fear that he was beyond hope. She had no idea what to do if that was the case.

Susie came back with a tray of stuff. She poured a glass of water, and tipped the contents of a paper into it. She stirred it briskly and handed it to Meg, still swirling. "Get it all down fast, milady."

Reckoning it couldn't taste any worse than the cause of her pain, Meg pulled a face, and drank it all down. Thank heavens, the bitterness only hit at the end. "Ugh! It's foul!"

Susie put another glass into her hand. "Orange juice. It'll take the taste away."

Meg hastily drank the juice, and it did clear her mouth of the worst of the bitter edge. However, her stomach rebelled. "I think I'm going to be sick."

"Sometimes takes people that way," Susie said with

disgusting cheerfulness. "Lie back for a little while and it'll probably settle. I'll go and get your breakfast tray."

"I can't eat."

"You'll change your mind in a while."

Meg wasn't up to arguing. "What time is it?"

"Ten o'clock, milady. Master Jeremy is off to his tutor, and Miss Laura is giving Master Richard and Miss Rachel a lesson. Mr. Chancellor would like to speak to you at your convenience about hiring a tutor or governess for them."

Meg opened her eyes a crack to stare at the maid. She'd been imagining the whole house in the same wrecked state as herself. Could everything really be going on as normal?

Was the earl, too, acting as if nothing had happened? She wished she knew how to ask without asking.

"Would you like your breakfast in here, milady?"

Meg still didn't intend to eat, but wasn't going to argue. "I hate eating in bed. Put it in the boudoir."

"Very well, milady. And what gown will you want to wear?"

Chivvied into the mundane essentials, Meg made that decision, then let Susie ease her out of bed, into her warm robe, and onto the chaise in the boudoir. Meg conceded that she could get used to being a pampered member of the nobility, even if she wasn't entirely sure this state of affairs could last.

Her every need was anticipated and taken care of. Everything around her was of the highest quality.

Here it was, January, and yet she hadn't needed to shiver once, not even when in just her shift. The corridors were cool, but every principal room was heated in readiness for her. No need to build a fire with chapped fingers. No need to make clothes, or launder, or iron, or mend them. Certainly no need to cook.

In fact, she thought with a sharp sense of loss, all the things that had filled her days were now taken from her. She'd never dreamed she would miss them. What was she to do with her days? Lie on a chaise?

She'd known all along, hadn't she, that this was a ridiculous situation for plain Meg Gillingham and she was proving it. She was failing to live up to her side of the bargain.

A different maid came in bearing a tray, and set out breakfast on a small table. Meg eyed the ordinary-looking, middle-aged woman and wondered what defect or peculiar past she hid so well. "You eat up, milady," she said with a motherly smile. "It'll all work out in the end, you'll see."

It was certainly nice that someone thought so. Perhaps that was what made the breakfast slightly appealing. Meg picked up a piece of toast, and nibbled at it tentatively.

When she thought about it, her head was hardly pounding at all, and her stomach didn't seem inclined to reject the toast. In fact, the poached eggs looked almost tempting. Was it chance or genius that the cook had not sent up the usual fried food today?

When Meg realized there was hot, strong tea as well, she decided she might well live. That meant, however, that she had to start dealing with her problems.

Thinking as she ate, she decided that she was going to have to trust Mr. Chancellor about the general safety of herself and her siblings. After all, despite the strangeness of the servants here, they all seemed good-hearted and unafraid. It was hard to imagine them standing by while the earl hurt anyone.

Given that, she could consider other aspects.

She had to heal the breach between the earl and his grandmother, and she'd have to do it while the old lady was in London. She'd never be able to drag him to wherever the dowager lived in the country. Perhaps she could arrange something at the Twelfth Night ball, if that was still to go ahead. Saxonhurst wouldn't invite the dowager duchess, but Meg could.

After a little thought, she decided she'd have to meet with the duchess first to prepare the ground. Her unreasonable husband was not going to like that, and she had vowed to obey him. Did such vows hold when he was so clearly wrong?

She admitted, too, that she was frightened of provoking another rage. It was all very well for everyone to assure her that he only broke things, and in his room, but it didn't comfort her. There was always a first time. And what if she was in his room at the time?

Look at the way he'd seized her last night to drag her back against him. His arm had almost throttled her and she'd been powerless against his strength. She undid her robe and pushed up the short sleeve of her shift. As she'd expected, her arms were bruised.

He'd sounded truly deranged when he'd asked if her secrets concerned his grandmother.

She'd had to hit him to get free.

She put down her empty cup, wishing the earl had taken his friend's stern advice and told her why he felt so strongly about his grandmother. Perhaps he did have reasons to be irrational and wild, though she couldn't imagine what they could be. Even if the dowager had been a harsh guardian, the earl had grown up healthy, wealthy, and well-educated. His grandmother hadn't done too bad a job.

She would plan to get the earl to tell her the truth if she was sure they were on speaking terms. She sighed. Despite her uneasiness, after just four days of marriage, the idea that her husband might not seek her out, might never again try to seduce her, could break her heart.

She sternly put that aside. They were married. They had a lifetime, and such a breach couldn't go on indefinitely. Then she remembered the Regent and his wife, intractably separated almost from the moment of marriage. That, she told herself, was because it was an ill-considered arranged marriage between two people who could never suit.

And what was different about her case?

She sat back, cradling her empty cup. Despite the many ways in which she and the earl were different, despite his wild behavior and her wariness, she didn't think they were incompatible. Not at all.

She slid into some misty daydreams in which the earl came into her room in his most charming guise, to apologize, to explain, and to seduce.

Chapter 14

A tap on the door jerked her out of fantasy.

Meg sat up, heart racing, straightening her dressing gown. "Come!"

It was Laura. Of course. He wouldn't knock.

"Is everything all right?" her sister asked, coming in.

Meg sighed and decided to have as few lies as possible in her life. "Reasonably."

"I haven't seen the earl today."

Meg smiled. "Well, I haven't eaten him like a black widow spider, I promise."

Laura giggled, reassured, and sat in a chair. "What about the *sheelagh*?"

Meg sat bolt upright. "Good heavens, I'd forgotten all about it!"

"But last night . . ."

"I know, I know. I think I'm going mad."

Laura eyed her. "Do you think the earl . . . ?"

"No! No, of course not. He's . . . eccentric."

"Well then, perhaps he'll help you get the *sheelagh* back. I'm sure he can handle Sir Arthur."

Meg was, too, but there were problems. "I'm not supposed to tell anyone except other women of the family about it."

"I'm sure Mother told Father."

"So am I. That's doubtless how Sir Arthur found out. Mother would never tell him directly."

"So you *could* tell the earl," Laura suggested. Clearly, Saxonhurst had not fallen far from his pedestal in her sister's eyes.

"Tell him what?" Meg asked with a sigh. " 'My lord, I am custodian of an ancient, magical statue which Sir

Arthur has stolen. I need your help to get it back.' He'd clap me in Bedlam!"

Meg wondered with sudden alarm whether he'd like an excuse to clap her in Bedlam. It was one way to get rid of an inconvenient wife.

"But when he saw that it was true . . ."

"Laura, even if I went with the earl to Sir Arthur to demand the *sheelagh* back, Sir Arthur would deny all knowledge. I can't prove anything, even that the *sheelagh* existed in the first place."

"I could say it did."

"I don't think that would impress the authorities, and as far as I know, no one else ever saw it. Certainly no one could say it is magic, and if they did . . . can you imagine how strange it would all sound? I'm not even sure it's not still illegal to practice magic."

"Like witchcraft?" Laura exclaimed.

Meg shuddered. She'd never thought of the *sheelagh* in quite that way before, but now she knew that making it public could be disastrous.

"If it's not illegal, they'd think it proof of madness to believe in such a thing. I have to go to Sir Arthur and see what he wants." Not Laura, Meg prayed. But that, thank God, was now impossible. Mad or sane, Saxonhurst would never permit it.

"I wish you didn't have to," Laura said. "I don't like Sir Arthur anymore. I hope we never see him again."

"I wish I didn't have to. Try if you can to discourage the twins from wanting to see him. They'll have treats enough these days to not be easily tempted."

"What do you think he wants? Money?"

"I hope so. That would be simplest, though how I'm to find it, I don't know. The earl has promised me generous pin money, but I don't have it yet. I have to get the stone back, though. I can't begin to straighten out other things until I do."

Suddenly, temptingly, came the notion to ask the *sheelagh* to heal things between the earl and his grandmother. Surely, that had to be good. Couldn't carry a sting . . .

She started, realizing Laura was frowning at her. "Things aren't all right, are they?"

Meg smiled wryly. "Not entirely, no. But there's nothing wrong that will affect you. Now, shouldn't you be back with the twins?"

"Peter is helping them with arithmetic. He's much better at it than I am."

Meg made herself stay silent. She supposed an embezzler would be good with figures. She rose. "I'd better speak to Mr. Chancellor about a proper tutor. Then I'll go and see Sir Arthur."

"Won't the earl object?"

If he knew, Meg thought. How to sneak out of the house in daylight? But then she stopped that. "Laura, we're not prisoners. You, too, may go out if you wish. Just remember to always take a servant with you."

"Will you take a servant? To Sir Arthur's?"

Meg hadn't planned on it, but it was the sensible thing to do. "Of course. Don't worry. I'm not going to do anything foolish."

Laura went away looking relieved, and Meg went into her dressing room where Susie was waiting. "What jewels, milady?" Susie asked when Meg was ready.

"Jewels? I'm afraid I don't have any." She thought wistfully of her mother's locket and pearls, simple things, but treasured, and sold to support them all.

"The earl sent the jewel box, milady. Not the grand ones, of course. Mr. Chancellor has care of those. I think they're in the bank vault." She unlocked an inlaid wooden box that sat on a small table.

The maid lifted out a series of trays, each containing different items—rings, pins, brooches, chains, necklaces, aigrets. . . .

"Good gracious." Like a child with a box of toys, Meg couldn't resist. As Susie had implied, nothing here was fabulously valuable, but it was all a great deal more than she'd ever had before. Holding a pretty necklace of pearls and some pale blue stone set in silver, she realized that her estranged husband must have sent this sometime after their chilly encounter.

How extraordinary. Would she ever understand the man?

Perhaps he *did* do it deliberately, enjoying making others feel off-balance.

She made herself stop playing. "I don't think I want any ornament today, Susie. Pack it up. We'll have to find a place for it."

"No one here would steal, milady, but there's a safe in your bedroom."

Meg followed her and watched as she swung aside one of the small inset bookshelves. "I didn't know about this, milady. Mr. Chancellor showed me just now when he brought the box."

Meg sighed. The jewels had doubtless been Mr. Chancellor's idea entirely.

Behind the shelves lay a metal door with a lock. Susie dug in her pocket and produced a key. "Here you go, milady."

Meg inserted it, and turned. The door opened to reveal a wide space about six inches deep and two feet high, set with two shelves. The box would fit on a shelf. However, Meg's main thought was that the *sheelagh* would fit in it on its side.

Susie put the box away and Meg locked the safe. "Who else has a key to this?"

"Likely Mr. Chancellor."

It was definitely a possible hiding place, and the best she'd found so far. First she had to get the statue back. "Susie, you are doing quite well out of this marriage, aren't you?"

The maid turned from where she was tidying Meg's nightgown, a rather wary look in her eye. "I suppose, milady. Though Monk says we can't get on with things till things here are settled."

"Does he? Then I assume the two of you would like to help me settle things."

"Perhaps, milady." From the tone, Susie was still very undecided about her. In a strange way, Meg rather liked being thought unpredictable and dangerous. It was certainly novel.

"After I've spoken with Mr. Chancellor about a tutor, I need to visit our old landlord. I want Monk to accompany me. Is that possible?"

"Of course, milady. You can't be going off on your own."

Meg tried to think of a way to put it gracefully, but couldn't. "I don't want the earl to accompany us."

"He went out early, milady. Gone for the day."

Meg turned away to hide coloring cheeks. So, he was avoiding her. Doubtless, the jewels had been Mr. Chancellor's idea.

She put the key in her pocket, praying she'd be able to mend things later.

"There's this key, too, milady." Susie picked up one from a side table. "It was in the pocket of your blue gown."

The back door key to Mallett Street! She'd thought she'd left it in the door, but clearly not. She took it, and dropped it to chink against the other one. Clearly, Sir Arthur knew that she'd been to the house, so she'd return it. Despite her minor illegal activities, she wouldn't keep someone else's property.

The key dragged in her pocket like a guilty conscience, however, as she went in search of Mr. Chancellor.

She found him in an office on the ground floor—a surprisingly businesslike office. The room was lined with glassed-in shelves over drawers, and Owain Chancellor was not alone. An elderly man and a gawky youth sat at tall desks entering something in ledgers.

Mr. Chancellor rose. "Have you come to talk about a tutor, my lady?" He waved her to a chair.

"Yes. Or a governess," she said, sitting. "Which do you think would be best?"

"We could have both, but we thought the twins would prefer to take their lessons together for now."

We? Had the earl and his secretary had time and inclination to think about educational matters since last night? Perhaps in this household, a night of destruction and melodramatic confrontation was all washed away with daylight.

"Perhaps a well-educated woman for now," Mr. Chancellor was saying.

"Very well." She made herself pay attention.

"Shall I arrange for you to interview some applicants?"

Meg was daunted at the thought of assessing other

young women doubtless very like herself, but it was her responsibility. "Certainly. As soon as possible." She rose, but hesitated.

"Do you require anything else, Lady Saxonhurst?"

Uncomfortably aware of the clerks, Meg lost the courage to ask for money. Anyway, she couldn't possibly ask for enough to meet any price Sir Arthur might set on the *sheelagh*. She had a few coins, and the earl had said the servants would pay for incidentals.

She couldn't help one question, however. "I gather the earl has left the house for the day."

"He had a standing arrangement to race at the Heath."

"I see." Meg was quite sure the arrangement would have been altered in other circumstances. Other circumstances, such as him having spent the night in his wife's bed, completing the wonderful seduction he'd begun.

She suppressed a sigh and left before Mr. Chancellor asked about her plans. In the hall, she found Monk waiting, small but dignified in his braided livery and powdered hair. "You required my services, milady?"

The stately butler stood nearby, and though he appeared uninterested, Meg had the feeling that he might step forward to prevent her leaving the house.

"Yes, Monk," she said in as ordinary a manner as she could. "I have a few errands."

The big dog was lying by the door like a very shaggy rug, probably waiting for his master to return home. Meg could sympathize, though she was pleased—she had to be pleased—to have a day free to settle the matter of the *sheelagh*.

Brak turned his snarling, woeful face to her, heaved up, and came over, as if he'd decided she'd do as a very poor second. She fondled the dog's ears and its tail stirred.

"How did the earl come to have Brak?" she asked Monk.

"He was like he is from birth, milady. None wanted him."

And that was complete explanation?

"I'm surprised the house isn't full of such unwanted creatures."

Monk glanced at the butler as if checking how far he could go. "There are more at Haverhall, milady. But mostly, we makes sure he doesn't come across too many."

"Do you require the carriage, milady?" interrupted the butler in the tone of one who expects the answer to be yes.

Brought back to the matter in hand, Meg said, "No, thank you. . . ." Bother, she couldn't remember his name.

Pringle, mouthed Monk.

"My errands are all close by, Pringle. But I do want my outdoor clothing."

"Very well, milady." Meg saw the flickered look he cast at Monk before departing. It surely carried the message, *Watch this one.*

Even in this house, the hall was a little chilly, so she waited in a warm reception room, shadowed by Brak, until Susie appeared with her hooded cloak, bonnet, gloves, and muff.

Then, of course, the dog wanted to come with her. She said, "Stay!" and pointed to a spot on the floor. Mournfully, he flopped down there and she could escape.

"He is well trained," she remarked as they went down the steps.

"Sax won't have untrained beasts around."

Meg wondered wryly about untrained wives. Looking back on last night, she couldn't decide who'd been most at fault. Perhaps it was beyond the line for a wife to disobey her lustful husband. Oh well, if only she could get the *sheelagh* back she was sure she could sort out all the other problems.

An icy wind whipped down the street, lifting her skirts and chilling her legs. She asked Monk if he was warm enough with only his livery.

"I don't need much to keep warm, milady. Just me gloves. Where to, then?"

They were approaching an exit to the square. Meg glanced at him. "I didn't tell the butler the truth, Monk, but I didn't want to use one of the earl's carriages. Take me to the nearest hackney stand."

"Very well, milady." His manner was as chilly as the January air. Meg wished she could explain. She wished she could tell everyone about everything, but she couldn't. Once she had the *sheelagh* back, she could start to act like a proper countess and they'd soon realize she wasn't a wicked adventuress.

Because of the nippy wind, Meg was glad to settle into the hackney carriage, even if it smelled of many past users and had hard seats. Just a few trips in the earl's carriage and she was spoiled. Monk would have ridden outside, but she commanded him to join her.

"Now," she said, as the coach jerked off, showing that the springs were not the best, either. "I am about to visit my old landlord, Sir Arthur Jakes."

"Very well, milady."

She ignored his distant manner. "You are to stay outside and out of sight while I go in."

"Yes, milady?" His skinny, monkeyish face expressed profound disapproval.

"I've known the man all my life. I'll be perfectly safe. But I don't want to arrive with an escort." She couldn't explain it, so she didn't try.

"Very well, milady."

They sat there in silence, bouncing and rattling across London.

When the carriage stopped, Monk leaped out to pay and collect the ticket. Then he turned back to hand her out.

"Which house, milady?" he asked, looking at the row of tall stuccoed residences. Only a few streets separated them from Mallet Street, but these were clearly gentlemen's residences.

"It's number three, down the other end. You stay here."

He almost stood to attention. "As you say, milady."

Meg walked a few steps, then sighed and turned back. "Very well, Monk. I'm not absolutely sure of my safety. If I don't come out again in a half hour, you may send for assistance."

"Oh, right," he said, relaxing into something close to a glower. "And Sax'll skin me alive! Now, milady, let's rethink this one."

"Not at all! You can tell the earl it was all my doing."

She walked briskly away, but heard him say, "Fat lot of use that'll be."

She paused for a moment before Sir Arthur's house. Even though he'd visited her house many times, she'd never been here, and she felt like a fly about to rush into a spider's web.

That was silly. She couldn't imagine what he was up to, but he wouldn't try to do her harm.

She rapped the lion's head knocker briskly, then again, and again, wondering why no one was answering. Could he have been suddenly called away?

Then the door was opened by a dark-haired woman in black bombazine and a severe cap. "Yes, ma'am?"

Despite the woman's dress, Meg found something faintly improper about her. Perhaps it was her full lips, or her heavy-lidded eyes. Meg reminded herself of Brak. Not every housekeeper could look like starched propriety.

"I wish to see Sir Arthur." When the woman's dark brows rose, Meg realized she'd have to give her name. No, her title. How strange. "Tell him Lady Saxonhurst is here."

"Lady?" The woman's bold eyes passed over Meg's serviceable gown and brown cloak. Then they flicked beyond, clearly checking for carriage and servants. "Pull the other one, dolly."

Meg stood straighter. "I am Lady Saxonhurst, and well known to Sir Arthur. I assure you, he will be very distressed if you turn me away." With exasperation, she added, "I used to be Meg Gillingham. My family rented the house in Mallett Street."

"Oh, that one." The woman stepped back and invited Meg in, but without any sign of increased respect. Meg wished desperately that she had a quizzing glass and the earl's ability with it. Injury was added to insult when she was put to wait in a frigid reception room lacking any kind of fire.

Meg paced to keep warm, but also to work off anger and nerves. She had to get the *sheelagh* back. She tentatively checked for the feel of the thing, but the air here seemed dead of it. Never having studied this aspect of the magic before, however, she had no idea how close she had to be to sense it.

What if Sir Arthur *didn't* have it? What then?

But he'd said he had. . . .

Hadn't he?

How much did he know? Did he know about the magic, or just that the *sheelagh* had some value? He couldn't possibly know that she'd used it to trap the earl, could he? No one knew that but herself and Laura.

It was becoming such a burden of guilt, however, that she felt as if it were branded on her forehead!

"My dear! Having to exercise to keep warm!"

Meg whirled to face him. He was still elegant in clothes and smile. He still made her flesh crawl.

"You must be turning to ice. Come upstairs." As they passed through the hall, he called out, "Hattie! Hot tea for her ladyship."

His use of the servile title was clearly ironic. If only she knew what he wanted!

On the upper floor, he opened a door. Meg hesitated. She'd expected to be taken to a drawing room, but this was a more private kind of sitting room. It could be attached to his bedchamber. She walked in anyway. It was warm, and he'd made it clear before that he had no wicked designs on her aged body.

Determined not to show any fear, she put aside her muff, and stripped off her gloves. "You wished to speak to me, Sir Arthur?"

"No, no, my dear. *You* wished to speak to *me*, or you would not be here. All alone, as well." Cruel humor glinted in his eyes. "Did you have to steal out of the house? Would your exalted husband not approve?"

"I left the house openly." Doing her best to appear unconcerned, Meg sat in a chair by the fire. "Sir Arthur, there was an item missing from our house. I am here because you implied that you have it."

He sat opposite, flipping his coat tails out of the way, then crossing his legs. "Missing? But you took all you believed was yours, did you not?"

Meg prayed not to blush. "I forgot something."

"Then it could hardly have been important. . . . Ah, the tea. Thank you, Hattie." As the housekeeper set down the tray, he said, "Lady Saxonhurst, would you pour?"

Meg did so, glad of a moment to collect her thoughts. "Milk, Sir Arthur? Sugar?" When she'd added them, she passed him his cup.

She took her own and sipped. Let him make the next move.

"So," he said at last, "what is this important item that slipped your mind?"

"A stone statue. More of a bas-relief."

"I don't remember seeing any such item around your house."

"It was in my parents' bedroom."

"But I visited there often in those last months when poor Walter was so ill."

Meg took another sip, hoping to conceal that she'd overlooked that. "It was kept out of sight." On the slim chance that he had no idea what it really was, she put on a coy smile and leaned forward. "You see, Sir Arthur, it was somewhat improper, and so it was always kept hidden. However, it has been in my mother's family for generations, and thus has sentimental value."

"Improper?" His brows rose. "In what way, my dear?" Someone else might have thought him merely curious, but Meg knew he wanted to embarrass her.

She thanked heaven for her recent sparring exercises with the naughty Earl of Saxonhurst. "It is of a naked woman," she said bluntly, "legs spread wide."

She could have laughed at the startled flush that hit his cheeks. "My dear Meg! I would think you'd feel well rid of such a thing."

"As I said, it has been in our family for a long time. I feel I should keep it, even if concealed, as my mother did. Do I understand that you have it?"

She had gained control. He put down his cup with a sharp *chink*. "What remained in the house could be assumed to be mine. And, of course," he added, "anyone entering the house illegally would be a criminal. Subject to court and transportation."

Meg took another sip of tea. "I hardly think they'd transport a countess, Sir Arthur."

"But perhaps the Earl of Saxonhurst would divorce a wife convicted of the Black Arts."

Meg managed to swallow without choking. "Black Arts? What on earth are you speaking of?"

Now he settled back in his chair, once more at ease. "Your father was a very sick man, my dear, weakened by the disease and the opium he took for the pain. Weakened into speaking of things he might not otherwise have mentioned. He was very concerned that your mother might do something wrong. Something to do with an old Irish statue that, he said, had pagan magic, but that should never be used."

Meg prayed that her face wasn't giving her away. "If my father was so sick, perhaps his mind was wandering."

"I doubt it. He even told me where the item was. Said he was glad it was over his head where he could keep an eye on it." He smiled, and she braced for trouble. "When your brother found them dead, he sent for me as well as for the doctor." He made her wait, then added, "I found the statue out, on the bed, between their bodies."

Meg spilled her tea. She put down the cup and saucer her shaking hands could no longer manage. She kept silent, but inside she was screaming. The suspicion had lurked in her like bad meat, turning her stomach. Now it was confirmed. Her mother had tried to use the *sheelagh* to save her husband, and had ended up dead.

But if the *sheelagh* could *kill,* what might come from her own use of it? Her father had been right. It should never be used.

"Of course, I put it carefully away," Sir Arthur continued. "Back in its hiding place. If you'd taken it, perhaps I might have let it go. But you didn't, so now it is mine."

"No!"

"You want it back?"

"It is my property. My charge. My duty."

He almost glowed with satisfaction. "So, you *do* have the power. And you have used it, haven't you? How else did you trap an earl?"

Meg stayed still. It was the best she could do. "My marriage was entirely the earl's idea. What do you want, Sir Arthur?"

He smiled, completely relaxed by now. "An interesting question, especially with such power at my command. What do I *want*? Fabulous wealth? To be Prime Minister? To be king, even?"

"Sir Arthur! You cannot—"

"Can I not? Is there a limit to its powers?"

Meg had never imagined this situation. "I don't know. But I do know that it creates havoc rather than benefits. Believe me, Sir Arthur, you do *not* want anything to do with that stone."

"Don't I, indeed?"

"Look at my parents!"

"An interesting speculation. Perhaps they wished for death. Your father was in considerable pain, your mother distraught at the thought of losing him. Perhaps your stone granted exactly what they asked for."

Meg was trying to handle that when he added, "And look at you. Are you not in exceedingly improved circumstances?"

"There is always a sting in the tail, Sir Arthur. Always."

He cocked his head. "Really? Is the earl not to your taste? Poor Meg. I hear they have insanity and debauchery running in that family instead of blood."

"Nonsense. And I repeat, my marriage was entirely the earl's idea. He approached me."

"But what put the idea into his head? No, Meg, you will not persuade me of your innocence. If there are stings, I'm sure you deserve every one. Do you need advice on your marriage bed? You could talk to me, an old family friend. . . ."

Nausea swelled in Meg.

"No? What a pity. I doubt you deserve much sympathy, even if he is a monster in his rutting. Countess of Saxonhurst? A poor little dab like you."

Meg rose and grabbed her muff and gloves.

"Don't forget the stone, my dear."

She froze. A moment later, she knew she would have been wiser to sweep out, to not let him know just how much she cared.

He rose, smiling. "I will consider further on what wish I want to make. That is all for today."

She tried to face him down. "I insist that you return my property."

"It is not yours any longer."

"It is mine by right, and I will have it back! I am not impoverished Meg Gillingham anymore." Now she swept toward the door, but he seized her arm and roughly swung her back.

"High and mighty, are we? You foiled me, Meg. You stole Laura from me."

"Indeed I did!" She tried to wrench her arm free. "And you will never touch her. Never. I promise you that!"

"Even to get the *sheelagh* back?"

She froze, but looked straight into his eyes. "Even for that."

He studied her. "I could put it to her. Such a sweet girl. Wouldn't she make the noble sacrifice?"

"I've warned her never to be alone with you. And I'll tell the earl everything before I let you near her. He'd crush you like the louse you are."

Rage flared in his eyes, and bit through his fingers, but he smiled, too. "So. You're anxious to keep this from your husband, are you?"

Meg cursed herself for hasty words.

Sir Arthur's smile widened. "I'm sure he wouldn't be pleased to think that he'd been the dupe of a magic trick. A mere puppet on a magic string."

The best Meg could do was to stay silent.

He let her go. "You'll pay for my discretion, won't you, Meg?"

She rubbed her bruised arm. "I have very little money."

"I don't want money. Laura would be better, but you'll do."

She stepped back, beginning to shake. "No!"

"No?"

"You won't tell the earl anyway. If you do, you'll never get your wish."

"But you see, my dear, I'm not sure I want the wish. I have money. I don't want political power. I certainly don't want to be king. A tiresome business, that. I want Laura, but you wouldn't ask the magic stone for that.

So," he said, moving toward her, "what else could you magic up for me? Revenge on you for thwarting me? I can get that through telling the earl"—he put out a hand and half-circled her neck—"or in other ways."

Meg swallowed and made herself not show fear. She was sure he fed on fear like a vulture on carrion. "Saxonhurst wouldn't believe you."

"Then why are you so worried?" He let her go and moved back a step. "Go, my dear. Go. And I'll send a letter straight around telling the earl all about your little family secret, and that you used the stone to trap him into marriage."

Meg longed to call his bluff, but she didn't think he was bluffing. "I cannot lie with you. I cannot. Do your worst."

"Lie with me?" He laughed. "Why would I want that?"

"Then what?"

"I have someone for my needs. A pretty young thing. But she's over her first shock and tediously amenable. Laura would have been exciting in her fear and anger. And so deliciously innocent . . . Are you blushing? But you're four days married, my dear."

"That doesn't make me beyond shame. What could you possibly want from me? I'm not young, and I'm not innocent."

"Oh, let me tell you." And his eyes now glittered in a febrile way that made her feel quite sick. "When my young partner is too easy, I find it helps to be punished for my sins. But it's so hard to find someone who will punish me properly. Hattie obliges with the whip sometimes, but her heart isn't in it. You'd be stern with me, wouldn't you, Meg? Angry."

Meg took another step back, coming up against a wall. "You want me to whip you? You're mad."

"Not mad. No. Think of me as a penitent. A flagellant."

"You certainly have much to feel guilty about."

He grinned. "Exactly."

He *was* mad, and in this light she knew that Saxonhurst wasn't. "If I whip you, you will return the stone?"

"Oh no. The whipping will just buy my silence for

twenty-four hours. Until you return tomorrow to hear my wish."

"Or another demand for a whipping."

"Perhaps." His grin said certainly. He fumbled in a drawer, already breathing heavily, and took out a long cane. He swished it through the air so it sang, and his grin widened.

She should refuse. Return to Marlborough Square and tell the earl everything. He'd deal with Sir Arthur.

Yesterday, she could have done it, but now after their terrible scene, she didn't know how he'd react. If he didn't believe her, he'd think her mad. If he did believe her, he'd know she'd tricked him into marriage. It was all very well for Mr. Chancellor to say he only minded about his grandmother, but he minded because his guardian had forced him to bend to her will.

She'd have to do this at least once.

Sir Arthur laughed and rang the bell. For a moment, Meg wondered if it had been some strange kind of joke, a vicious tease. But when the housekeeper came in, he said, "Have Sophie wait in my bedroom, Hattie."

The woman looked at Meg with raised eyebrows, but merely said, "Very well, Sir Arthur," and left.

"Who is Sophie?"

"A maid. More importantly, my convenient of the moment. She's young, just thirteen. So deliciously frightened at first. But she's turned into a willing little bawd. I require some pepper with my pudding."

He eyed Meg for a moment, and she knew exactly what he was thinking and couldn't help but shake her head in rejection.

"No indeed, Meg. You'd be pepper all right, but you're too long in the tooth. And too tough. You wouldn't fear me enough. . . . Ah, Laura. Laura."

He seemed in a trance. She thanked heaven she couldn't see inside his foul mind. Faintly, she heard a door open and shut. Presumably the obliging Sophie had arrived, poor child. Meg wished she could do something for the girl.

She stared at the cane in his limp hand, wondering if she could actually bring herself to use it on him.

Then, as if waking, he looked at her. "Come back tomorrow."

"What?"

He put his hand between his legs and she could see how bloated he was there. "Just the thought . . . enough for now. Come back tomorrow, and we'll talk about . . ." He staggered toward the next room.

As he opened the door, Meg caught a glimpse of a plump blond child who lounged on a big bed, eyes wide. That was willingness . . . ?

The door slammed shut.

Tomorrow?

Never. Rather than that, she'd confess every sin to the world in Hyde Park!

Chapter 15

Meg snatched up her gloves and muff and ran for the door.

Hand on knob, she made herself stop. She was never coming back to this house again. Never. So, this was her one chance to search. Teeth gritted, she fought against panicked flight.

Right. If she was close to the *sheelagh* she could always sense it. She quickly circled the room.

Nothing.

He might keep it in his bedroom.

Then it could stay there! But she made herself press close to the door trying to block the little squeaks and hoarse groans. She didn't think the *sheelagh* was in there.

She ran into the corridor and into the next room. A spare bedroom. Nothing. And the next. And the next.

Having checked every room on the floor, she paused, listening for sounds of servants. The whole house was eerily silent.

With a shrug, she raced up narrow stairs to the attic area, and found servants' rooms and storerooms. But no indication of the *sheelagh*. Anyway, the storage rooms were thick with dust. His servants were sluts and no one had been there in ages.

She slipped down the back stairs to the main floor and went cautiously through into the hall. Still no one. The emptiness of the house was making her skin crawl. Even so, she made herself go through two reception rooms, a dining room, and a well-filled library.

She'd forgotten that he was a scholar, and that he and her father had been good friends. How could a genuine book lover be such a toad?

The *sheelagh* wasn't there, though. It wasn't anywhere! Where would he keep it? Where? She couldn't search the whole of London. She could search the basement, though, and would, even if his servants were there.

Abandoning all caution, she ran toward the back of the house and down more narrow stairs. She opened every door in the cold, gloomy basement, but only found more evidence of poor management. It was hardly surprising, when his housekeeper was little more than a procuress! Sir Arthur Jakes was the epitome of a whited sepulcher.

She flung open another door.

The housekeeper's hot, luxurious parlor! And she was there, still in black bombazine and cap. Meg, however, could only see her back, because she was straddling a man!

The handsome man with dark hair and eyes showed no shock or embarrassment. He just grinned and waggled his brows at her. The housekeeper bounced on, oblivious.

Meg backed out, shaking, and shut the door.

For a moment she just slumped there, felled by the whole experience. It was truly like a horrible, unbelievable dream.

With a cry, she headed for the nearest way out. She staggered through the kitchen, ignoring the handful of servants, who were predictably lolling around drinking ale, and out to gulp fresh air and freedom. The scrap buckets and outhouse by the back door gave off a stink, but the air seemed fresh compared to the foulness within.

Nothing could make her ever return.

She hurried through the garden, and didn't pause until she was out of the back lane, into a street with normal people, and sanity. There, she leaned against a wall, legs too weak to go on.

After a moment, she made herself move, made herself go to find Monk.

"Milady!" He stared at her, perhaps just because she was coming from the wrong direction. "You all right?"

"I'm all right now," she said as steadily as she could. "But I wish to leave."

"Right. Best to walk to Stokes Street. There's a hackney stand there."

They'd only taken a couple of steps, however, when a

shriek made her jump. Meg looked around, but only in curiosity.

Then: "Murder! Murder!"

The screams were faint, but Meg knew they were coming from Sir Arthur's house. She didn't know how or why. She just knew.

She grabbed Monk's sleeve. "Let's get out of here!"

He nodded, wide-eyed. "Don't run. Act normal."

Meg made herself just walk briskly along the street and away from the growing hubbub.

Then a man's voice bellowed, "There she is! The murderess! In the brown cloak. Get her!"

Meg froze in disbelief, half turning back to protest, but Monk grabbed her and broke into a run. "Come *on*, milady!" Seeing the gathering crowd all looking in her direction, Meg picked up her skirts and obeyed. Immediately, a tally-ho sounded. She did her best, but soon Monk was towing her and she was fighting for breath.

Despite the hunting cries behind them, she slowed. "I can't . . ."

Abruptly, he dragged her into an alley, already struggling out of his coat. "Your cloak, milady! Quick now!"

Wheezing for breath, she pulled off her long cloak, and he tossed her his braided jacket, then flung the cloak on, pulling up the hood. "Hide!" he commanded and fled at twice the speed they'd been making before.

Hearing the howling pursuit, Meg tumbled over a low wall and huddled there, shivering with terror and cold. Soon footsteps pounded by in a general chorus of "Stop the murderess!" "Stop her!" "Seize her!" They sounded horribly like hounds in full cry, and she felt like a terrified fox or rabbit.

No, my lord earl, she thought, *being hunted is no fun.*

The pack went on forever because some, like her, hadn't the stamina for long, hard running, and staggered after, already wheezing. They talked more, though.

"Lying in all his blood . . ."

"A doxy with him . . ."

"Jealous lover . . ."

"Housekeeper says . . ."

"A high-born lady . . ."

Sir Arthur! He was dead? How?

And people thought *she'd* done it?

She covered her mouth to stifle a moan. And the housekeeper knew her name. The servants had seen her rush out of the house. The constables would soon be on the earl's doorstep, demanding the countess!

If there'd been a pit at her feet, Meg would have thrown herself down it, even if it led to hell. She certainly never wanted to face her poor husband again. Eccentric? Feckless? Given to destructive rages? No matter what his faults, she was sure he'd never been hunted down for murder.

The mob had passed, however, and she couldn't skulk here forever. For one thing, she'd freeze to death.

She pulled on Monk's coat, but then worried that she'd attract attention in a footman's blue and braided jacket. Poor people wore castoffs, though. She took the jacket off again and rubbed and rolled it on the ground until it looked like a soiled rag. Then she put it on again, discarded her lovely velvet cap and cloth muff, and crept away down the narrow lane, shaking with awareness of danger.

Like a rat sneaking behind the wainscotting, she felt safe in the lane that ran a narrow cart's width between the backyards of the houses. She had to find a place to hide, however. A place where she could think. Away from here, in case the hunt turned back.

That thought gave her courage to sidle into the open street and hurry away. She didn't even think where. Just away.

She tried to look like any poor woman going about her business, but when she paused by a greengrocery to get her bearings, the scrawny man came out and shouted, "Bugger off, you! I'll have the constables on you!"

Meg ran, stopping a few houses away to look back at him, aghast. Even in the days when she had been tempted to steal an apple, no one had ever treated her like this!

He was still watching her, and he shook his fist, shouting "Garn!" exactly as if she were a mangy cat.

Meg turned and staggered on, terrified. She was no longer a respectable member of society. She was vermin.

She began to notice other vermin. Mostly, she could tell them—men, women, and children—by their scruffy, dirty clothes, but she could recognize the looks in their eyes, too.

Did she look like that?

"In trouble, dearie?" asked a kindly voice.

Meg started, and slid a look at the plump, middle-aged woman. She wasn't vermin. Her clothes were clean and respectable, her face kind.

Even so, Meg said, "No," and began to edge away.

"Don't run off, dear," the woman said. "I'll not harm you. Life throws these funny turns at us, doesn't it? My name's Mrs. Goodly and I've suffered through a few of them. If you want it, I've a quiet room nearby, and I can make you a cup of tea. Then I'm sure I can find some way to help you in your predicament."

The soothing run of words held Meg. She didn't think the woman could help with her problem, but refuge of some kind would be pleasant. . . .

Then something in the woman's eyes—a glint of calculation, perhaps—sent a warning down her spine. Mrs. Goodly might be a Good Samaritan, but there were such women who made a business of trapping young women into brothels.

"Come on, dearie." The woman reached for her.

Meg turned and ran. As she stumbled around a corner, she heard laughter and a coarse voice calling, "Lost that one, Connie, eh?"

Dear heaven, she'd been right!

The narrow escape drained the last traces of courage from her. The world now seemed a jungle, hung with poisonous vines, concealing only fanged predators.

She wanted to go home! She wanted none of this to have happened.

After a startled moment, she realized that home now meant Marlborough Square. Home meant the earl. He'd probably toss her back onto the streets after the mess she'd landed in. She leaned against a wall and burst into tears.

Thank God. Monk carried a handkerchief in his pocket, and she was able to dry her tears and blow her nose. The brief burst of weeping seemed to have cleansed her a bit, too. She could think a little.

Seeing curious but indifferent looks all around, she raised her chin and walked on.

Walking to nowhere.

This was ridiculous. She couldn't just wander until she froze to death. Her feet and hands were already icy. She had to go somewhere.

Perhaps she should go home. Part of her reluctance was shame and an illogical hope that she could somehow sort the mess out so that Saxonhurst need never know.

Then, a lad ran to a nearby street corner, a pile of news sheets over his arm. "Latest! Latest!" he cried. "Read all about it! Foul murder of man and mistress. Countess involved!"

Meg just stared at him. The ink must still be wet!

She didn't think everyone around would suddenly turn to her and know her for the countess involved—nothing was less likely—but she was appalled to think the news was already out on every street.

Passersby stopped to give him a penny for one of the sheets, and she heard him saying to each one, "Lady Saxonhurst, they say. Newlywed an' all."

All around her people paused to read, sometimes two or three to a sheet, exclaiming and speculating about the scandalous affair.

She was ruined. Absolutely ruined.

Saxonhurst would never want to see her again.

She hadn't *done* it, but that didn't seem to matter at the moment. What she needed was some kind of rat hole to hide in.

Could she find help among her old neighbors on Mallet Street? She didn't think anyone there would stand against the law for her, and surely that would be the second place the constables would check.

Where, then?

Wearily dragging herself along random streets, hounded by news-criers, some actually shouting her name, Meg felt scoured raw and naked.

Then a refuge occurred to her. A desperate one, but the only possibility. Surely the Dowager Duchess of Daingerfield would not want the scandal of a public arrest in the family. Even though there was no love lost between them, the duchess would have to hide her. Perhaps she could help clear her name.

At the least, it would be sanctuary for a little while.

In fact, once she was there, the duchess could send word to Saxonhurst. This might even be the emergency needed to bring the unhappy family back together! Meg took her bearings and started the long walk to Mayfair and Quiller's Hotel.

Shivering with cold, and weary, she eventually arrived on the busy street. The hotel looked exactly like a gentleman's residence, with only a discreet plaque to identify it. Meg was about to climb the steps, when she noticed the way people were staring and shifting to avoid her. They thought her a beggar.

Looking like this, she was never going to get in to see the duchess. Weakened by shock and exhaustion, Meg would have given up then if there'd been any way to do so. But the only way to give up was to hand herself over to the law and be thrown in prison. She'd heard enough about the inside of London's prisons to want to avoid that.

Knowing she was attracting attention just standing there, she walked on, circling the block, wondering how cautious, staid Meg Gillingham had come to these straits.

And what had happened to poor Monk? He was swift and clever. Surely, he'd got away. Of course, then he'd got straight to his master and tell him the sorry tale.

What would the earl do?

She had no idea. The man was a mystery to her, and a rather frightening one. It was all very well for Mr. Chancellor to say Saxonhurst never hurt people, only things. The earl had never been married to a woman accused of murder before.

A woman who lied to him, and admitted that she kept secrets from him.

A woman, if he ever found out, who'd used Black Arts to trap him into a disastrous marriage.

She stopped with a hand over her mouth. Oh God, this was all the *sheelagh's* fault! This was the sting in the tail.

Look what had happened to her parents, after all.

She sagged against the trunk of a leaf-bare tree, grief

squeezing like a vise at her chest. Her mother would never have wished for her own death. Her love for her husband had been powerful, but she would never have deliberately abandoned her children. So, whatever wish she had framed had gone wrong, or the *sheelagh* had claimed her life as price.

And Meg had brought this evil into the earl's world.

As she made herself stagger on, she decided he and everyone else would be safer if the marriage was annulled. The duchess might know how to achieve that, and she'd certainly be willing. Saxonhurst would be better off, even with Lady Daphne Grigg, than he was with Meg Gillingham!

But first, she had to get into the hotel.

A rough voice curtly told her to "mind her back." She hastily moved out of the way of two men with a barrowful of vegetables, then watched as they turned down a lane. They might be heading toward the hotel!

Cautiously, she followed. One man dragged the two-handled cart, whole the other helped heave it over rough spots. Meg felt around the two keys in her pocket, seeking the few coins she'd possessed on her wedding day. How much did she have? A sixpence and a few pennies.

What a dowry for a countess!

Determined to try, she came up behind the man at the back.

"I have to get in to see a lady in the hotel," she whispered. "I'm desperate. I know she'll help me." She showed him the sixpence.

He nudged the cart over a bump. "So?"

"Let me pretend I'm with you? I'll help unload."

The man who was pulling stopped and turned. "Harry, we've no time now for that!"

"Nah," said Harry. "She just wants to help unload." Meg showed the sixpence again and Harry took it. "No reason for us to complain if she likes to work."

"Half that's mine," said the other man, going back to hauling.

Playing her part, Meg helped push the cart over the next rough bit.

"Pudding in the oven?" Harry asked.

"What? Oh"—Meg blushed—"no. Just in a bit of

trouble. The old lady in the hotel, she knows my husband. I think she'll help me." Even now, Meg found it hard to tell lies.

"Fancy folk don't help the likes of us, ducks, but it's no skin off my back."

Meg pushed the cart again, thinking of backs and skin. One punishment for minor crimes was whipping at the cart's tail. Being dragged around half naked, and whipped until the blood ran. Of course, they wouldn't do that to a countess.

Would they?

For murder, they'd hang her anyway.

Surely the earl could stop that.

Transportation?

She had no idea what powers the nobility had about such things.

But she hadn't done it!

She was so panicked, she kept forgetting. She hadn't done it. Someone else had murdered Sir Arthur. Who? Why?

Little Sophie?

But no. If the gossip was true, she'd died, too, poor child.

The housekeeper?

Perhaps. But why?

They were at the back door to the hotel by then, and the man in front rapped at the door. A manservant opened it.

"Provisions ordered from Samuel Culler."

"You're late."

"Came in from the country late."

"Never mind your excuses, get 'em in that store shed over there." The servant slammed the door.

Meg looked with frustration at the freestanding wooden shed the men were opening. Then she grabbed a net of brussel sprouts and stalked through the door.

She'd expected to walk into a kitchen, and had a number of good lines to try. Instead, she found herself in a deserted, dark corridor. Ahead, a half-open door probably led into the kitchen, judging from the racket and smells.

Almost past caring, she shed her foul coat and dumped it in a corner with the sprouts, then walked boldly past the door and climbed a set of narrow stairs. Nobody stopped her.

At the top of the stairs, before a baize-covered door, she paused to gulp in air and tidy her hair as best she could. Now, in her decent dark gown, she might be taken for a guest, or at least the servant of a guest. That, of course, meant she'd be safer inside the hotel then in the servants' quarters. All the same, she didn't want to go out into the public spaces.

She went up past the main floor to a higher one where the guests would have rooms.

She'd been in a hotel like this once when traveling with the Ramillys, but she had no idea whether they were all the same. That one had dining and reception rooms on the ground floor, and a kind of drawing room on the upper one, where the guests could sit if they wished to, and take tea or other refreshment. The rest of the building had been guest rooms, some suites with private dining rooms, some just bedchambers.

She was sure the Dowager Duchess of Daingerfield had a suite, but that didn't help her find it. She'd never find it skulking here, however. She squared her shoulders, turned the knob, and walked boldly out into the guest part of the building.

A white-haired gentleman strode by briskly, hat at a jaunty angle, cane swinging. He did not so much as glance at her. Meg walked in the opposite direction, trying to look like someone's companion on a busy errand. Or a governess. She'd been that once. It should be easy.

Then a man in shirt sleeves and apron backed out of a room, carrying a tray. He must be a hotel servant.

"Excuse me," Meg said. "I'm afraid I've lost the way to my mistress's rooms. The Dowager Duchess of—"

"That un," he said with a grimace. "Bet she's waiting for you with boiling oil ready! You're on the wrong floor, blossom! Don't know how you got up here."

"Oh."

But he'd already hurried off toward the stairs she'd used. Of course, the invalid duchess would be on the ground floor if there were guest rooms there.

She teetered between going back to the servants' stairs

or using the main ones, and decided it had to be the main.

I belong here, she said to herself as she walked back toward the wide, carpeted stairs. *I am governess to some children staying here, engaged on a legitimate errand. I will not look like a fugitive from the law.*

She walked down the stairs, not acknowledging a fashionable couple going up chattering about theater plans for the night. They ignored her as if she were a ghost. Down below, a porter stood by the door, constantly ready to attend to people coming and going. Close by, a powdered footman hovered, available for any request or errand. This being a quiet moment, they were chatting.

They paid her no attention, but they'd notice her if she looked lost. She slowed as she went down the last few stairs, trying to think what to do.

Where would a private suite be? Surely not at the front. Through one door she could glimpse a front room and it was a dining room.

At the bottom of the stairs, without pause, Meg turned around the carved newel post and headed toward the back. Two servants hurried by, one with a box, the other with a cloak over her arm. Another overtook her from the other direction. None paid her any attention except to swerve around her.

She thought of again claiming to be lost, but there could be so few private rooms down here that it would sound very strange.

She was going to have to open doors.

She picked one, and walked in.

Then walked right out again, the image fixed of two older gentlemen glaring at her through the smoke of their pipes.

Gentlemen's smoking room, and one portly man had taken his shoes off. He must be troubled with corns or bunions!

Tempted to giggle, Meg picked the next one, ready to apologize and back out again.

She walked right in to the hawk-eyed glare of the Dowager Duchess of Daingerfield.

"Get out of here!" snapped the old woman, who was on a chaise, a fur over her legs, a book in her hand.

Meg closed the door behind her and leaned on it, suddenly weak. "You probably don't recognize me, Your Grace. It's . . . it's Lady Saxonhurst."

Color flared in the woman's sallow cheeks. "Why are you here?" The duchess's hands had tightened on her book, and could even be shaking. With rage? Fear? "Are you going to attack me?"

Meg stared at her, suddenly filled with pity. "Of course not, Your Grace."

"Then what do you want?"

Meg wanted to shake the silly earl who wouldn't bend, and who had this belligerent old woman afraid. "You did say I could come to you for help, Your Grace."

The yellow eyes narrowed and the duchess put aside her book, steadier now. "You want help? Then I'll go odds Saxonhurst doesn't know you're here. Sit!"

Meg obeyed the barked command, feeling rather like a puppy.

"Help with what?" the duchess demanded.

It was appallingly difficult to put things into words. "Well, Your Grace, I have landed in a pickle, I'm afraid."

"Don't sidle around things like an ingratiating church-warden. Tell me straight!"

Meg swallowed. "Some people seem to think I've done something . . . that I've committed murder!"

"Whom did you kill?"

"No one! But I think . . . Sir Arthur Jakes is dead, you see. And some people seemed to think I did it. So I ran. Or rather, Monkey did. And when he went, I couldn't think where to go. I don't want to go to jail. So I came here."

"Monkey?"

"A footman."

The duchess rarely blinked. Meg realized that was what made her stare so unnerving. "Who is Sir Arthur Jakes?"

"A friend of my parents, Duchess. And our landlord." Trying to ignore the fixed, hawk's eyes, she went on to tell her story, leaving out the reason for the visit and Sir Arthur's disgusting behavior.

"You took no servants?"

Meg was beginning to realize how thin her story

sounded without the essential details. "I am not used to servants, Duchess. And I was just visiting an old friend."

"You have no business visiting gentlemen without your servants. No lady does."

Feeling like a scolded puppy now, Meg lowered her head. "I'm sorry, Your Grace."

"I have never left a house alone," the old woman declared. "Since becoming Duchess of Daingerfield, I have never gone on foot in a public thoroughfare. I would take a carriage, young lady, to cross the street!"

"But I'm not a duchess, Your Grace." Meg added a silent, thank heavens.

"You are a countess. Learn to act like one. How will the world go on if people do not behave according to their station?"

She was, Meg saw, completely serious. Dangerous laughter teased at her.

"Well?" the duchess demanded.

"I really don't know, Your Grace."

Too late, Meg realized her inner amusement must be showing. The duchess's whole face pinched.

"You have no intention of conforming to your new status, have you?"

"I will try to be a good wife—"

"That is not the same thing at all. I trained Daphne to fill the role of countess adequately. Daphne!"

An adjoining door crept open and Lady Daphne Grigg peeped in. "Duchess . . . ?" She trailed off at the sight of Meg.

"Come in here. You remember Saxonhurst's bride?"

Blotches of color flared in Daphne's sallow cheeks, but she curtsied. "Countess."

"You can dispense with that," the duchess said with a curl of the lip. "She doesn't hold with manners, do you, gal?"

Recognizing war, Meg sat straighter. "I wouldn't say that, Your Grace."

"Then what would you say?"

"That good manners have little to do with rank."

"Idiocy. But I don't suppose it matters. They doubtless aren't high sticklers in the Fleet, or wherever they send murderesses waiting to be hanged."

Daphne gasped, fluttering a pale hand to her flat chest. The hand that wore the emerald ring she had said was her betrothal ring. "Murder . . . ?"

"She is believed to have committed murder." The duchess made the indictment sound like the very epitome of bad manners.

"Not . . . not *Saxonhurst!*"

"Don't be a fool! And sit down before you decide to faint."

Daphne sank into a chair like a rag doll. Meg wondered if someone could actually decide to faint, and whether she should look for smelling salts.

"This is the story, Daphne." The duchess might be enjoying herself in a sour sort of way. "Saxonhurst's new bride decided to visit an old friend—an old *male* friend—without escort or chaperone, and on foot. Shortly after her visit, the man was found dead, and those around leaped to the conclusion that she had struck the blow. Why," she fired at Meg, "would they come to such an unlikely notion?"

Meg knew her cheeks were stained a guilty red, but she was also icy cold inside. It sounded such a sordid tale. If she escaped the gallows, she'd have no reputation left at all.

"Well?" the duchess demanded.

"I suppose because I was the last person to see Sir Arthur."

"If you were the last person, then you killed him."

"The last person *known* to have seen him."

"And you left him in fine fettle?"

"In very fine fettle." Meg hoped she'd suppressed all trace of a grimace.

"Then he can hardly have been murdered in the time it took you to be shown out of the house, could he?"

Meg sighed. "I have not quite told you the whole story, Your Grace."

"That is obvious. I can hardly be expected to help a liar."

"Help!" squeaked Daphne. "But you said—"

"I said I didn't approve of Saxonhurst's bride. However, I do not want a family connection dangling at Tyburn. Well?" she demanded of Meg. "Are you ready to tell me the truth? Was this man your lover?"

"No! He was my father's age."

"What has that to do with anything?"

"Nothing," Meg admitted with a sigh, remembering Laura and the poor girl in Sir Arthur's bed. "But he was not my lover. I didn't even like him."

"Yet you visited him."

"Do you only visit people you like, Duchess?"

The old woman jerked as if hit. "Impertinent child! Tell your story. The true one this time."

Meg reminded herself to try to sweeten the duchess rather than souring her, and contemplated how much she'd have to reveal to make her story make sense.

"Sir Arthur stole something from me," she said at last. "An item of only sentimental value, but one I wanted. I went to ask him to return it. He refused, but said I should go back another day. He was clearly intent on playing games with me, so when he left me to make my own way out, I took the opportunity to search the house."

"Indeed." The duchess's thin brows rose. "Could you not have found a servant for such a distasteful task?"

"I wish I had."

"Why did you not put this matter in Saxonhurst's hands? Despite his shortcomings, I'm sure he could have managed it without embroiling us all in such unpleasantness."

Meg tried not to squirm. It was impossible to make this make sense without mentioning the *sheelagh*. "I didn't want to bother him," she muttered.

The duchess's eyes narrowed. "What is this sentimental item?" she demanded, as Meg had feared she must.

"A stone statue."

"A *garden* ornament?"

"It could be, Your Grace."

"But is not. We are not playing foolish charades here, girl. What is it?"

Meg couldn't help blowing out a resentful breath. "It's an old Irish figure. Very old. It has no particular value except to an antiquarian, but it has been in my mother's family for generations. That's all," she lied firmly.

The duchess's lips pursed. "Why is it so important?"

"As I said, it's been in my mother's family for generations."

"Then why would this Sir Arthur steal it?"

"I don't know." As silence built, she added, "Just out of spite?"

"Spite? Why was he spiteful toward you?"

Meg cursed herself. "I prefer not to say, Duchess. It has nothing to do with this."

"Nonsense! If there was bad blood between the two of you, it gives you a motive for murder."

"I would hardly kill someone over a stone statue!"

The duchess gave a sharp crack of laughter. "Not into pagan sacrifice, I see. But you *could* kill in the right cause?"

Meg thought about Laura. She prayed she would have been able to kill Sir Arthur as a last resort. "Perhaps anyone could."

For a moment, something potent lingered in the silent air, then the duchess nodded. "True enough. There are times that call for killing, and there are people who deserve to die. And there are killers who do not deserve to be punished for it. If you did kill the man, say so now."

Meg did her best to convince. "I did not kill Sir Arthur, Duchess."

The duchess nodded. "Would you like tea?"

Meg was so surprised, she didn't reply for a moment, then she said, "That would be very pleasant. Thank you." Absurd tears stung her eyes at this casual gesture of kindness.

"Go next door. Daphne will arrange it." Daphne shot to her feet and hurried out. Poor Daphne. "I'll send someone to discover the exact events and suspicions. You might be in a panic over nothing."

Meg rose, finding her legs unsteady. "I pray to find it so, Your Grace."

"And then what? Back to Saxonhurst?"

"I suppose so."

"You don't sound sure."

Again, Meg could not speak of her tangled marriage, and, indeed, their misunderstandings all seemed minor problems in comparison to this. She turned the unfamiliar gold band on her finger. "I am married, Your Grace. Where else would I go?"

"There might be a way to set you free. Is it consummated?"

Without considering, Meg lied. "Yes."

The duchess grimaced. "Given his intemperate nature, I needn't have asked. Go." She pointed to the adjoining door, and Meg obeyed, glad enough to escape the Inquisitor General.

It was only then that she remembered her plan to gain an annulment. Given that, why had she lied about the consummation?

The truth was, she didn't want an annulment. She wanted to stay married to the Earl of Saxonhurst, and she very much wanted to complete the sensual journey they had begun yesterday. Her predicament would soon reduce her to tears.

She found herself in a small bedchamber, well appointed, but gloomy because little light came through the one window. When she moved the heavy, ecru lace that covered it, she saw that the window looked out at the side of one of the storage sheds at the back of the hotel. No wonder no light came in. To make matters worse, being on the ground floor, it was barred against intruders. Sensible, no doubt, but not a comforting touch.

A lamp stood on a small table by the bed, and Meg lit it, welcoming the warmer glow.

The few items on view in the room—an embossed Bible, a silver-backed hairbrush, and a wooden traveling desk—suggested this was Daphne's room. There was something rather sad about the bland collection. She felt sorry for the young woman, trapped twenty-four hours a day with the dowager duchess. Any escape would be attractive. Perhaps Daphne would even have been a good wife, once Saxonhurst had worked his magic on her. He could charm a weasel into a tabby cat.

A few tears escaped her then, tears of weariness, fear, and loss. She wiped them away, then gave into temptation and flopped back, arms spread.

Lord, oh lord, what a terrible mess. Truly her wish had carried a sting in the tail. Or not just one. It had opened a wasps' nest of them.

She was only now remembering how serious the earl had sounded when he told her not to go running to Quiller's Hotel. Of course, he couldn't have imagined a situation like this, but she knew he'd be angry. She shivered at the thought of his raging, destructive anger, triggered according to Mr. Chancellor, by his grandmother.

And here she was, asking for the woman's help.

She'd been so determined to be a good wife, how had it come to this?

But then she sat up, and straightened her spine. He simply wasn't right about this, rage or not. Both the earl and the duchess were clearly the type to cut off their nose to spite their face, and she'd put an end to it. Like her bickering charges in the schoolroom, she'd have them shaking hands.

Next she'd find a way to moderate his wild enthusiasms and curb his tendency to take in every stray. Moderation in all things. She'd bring calm and economy into his household, arrange his room in better taste, and then she'd be ready to act the perfect countess, and he'd be happy to seduce her, and all would be roses.

She shook her head. One of the few pieces of advice her mother had given her about marriage was, "Never, ever, think you can change someone, dear. Marry them only if you like them as they are."

Well enough when one had a choice!

However, she reluctantly admitted that she did rather like the earl as he was. His whirling impulses alarmed her, but they were exciting. She was in no position to carp at his generosity to the needy. In fact, she thought she could grow used to a degree of extravagance, and she knew she had no problem with his physical attentions. The only real fly in the ointment was his hatred of his grandmother, and the rages it caused.

If that *was* the only problem, then healing the rift could change everything!

Certainly the duchess was not a pleasant woman, and her manner could rasp on anyone, but it must be possible to put things on a better footing. If the duchess helped Meg out of her pickle, surely the earl would have to be grateful. . . .

The door clicked open and Daphne came in with a

cup and saucer. She handed them over without a word. Meg took them, thanked her, and sipped gratefully at the hot, sweet tea. Perhaps her first step should be to break the ice between herself and Saxonhurst's cousin. She didn't blame Lady Daphne for resenting being made to act the servant.

"Do you and the duchess plan to stay in London long, Lady Daphne?"

"We were to stay until the wedding on Twelfth Night." Daphne stalked to a chest and pulled out a cream silk dress trimmed with lace. "Then Saxonhurst and I were to return to Daingerfield for the honeymoon."

Meg looked from the dress to the woman's unsteady lips, not knowing what to say. "Wouldn't his country home be more suitable for a honeymoon?"

"I'd have been safer at Daingerfield."

Meg sipped her tea, wondering how Lady Daphne could think she'd be safe with Saxonhurst just because of where they were. Did that mean that his destructive rages were well known, however? Did he really restrict them to one house and one room?

Perhaps he'd been like that since a child and the duchess's harsh guardianship had only been an attempt to curb him.

Daphne still stood at the end of the bed, thin and stiff as one of the bedposts. "I wouldn't stay here if I were you."

Meg looked at her, trying to find her true meaning. "You stay here," she parried.

"I'm not you. She won't help you. She'll find a way to use you. And she wants you gone. I'm to be the bride."

"But I *am* the bride, Lady Daphne. It's done. I give you back your own advice. Get out of the duchess's clutches."

"And go where? She's kept me tied to her side all these years with the promise of being Lady Saxonhurst. Now I'm too old to find another husband."

"What of your own family?"

Lady Daphne sniffed. "My brother and his wife would love to have an unpaid housekeeper and children's nurse. No thank you. I want my due.

"Well, you can't have Saxonhurst."

"I can when you dangle on a rope."

"I didn't kill anyone!"

"Do you think only the guilty hang? That's why I say, get out of here."

Meg pushed back a spurt of sheer terror. Surely an innocent countess couldn't be trapped by the law. "You contradict yourself, Lady Daphne. Do you want me to hang or not?"

"I just want my due!"

Meg put her empty cup on a table. "Lady Daphne, truly, Saxonhurst would be no refuge for you. But he will help you if you wish." She vaguely remembered him making some such offer. "He is a very kindhearted man, and has no reason to feel harshly toward you. . . ."

"I want my *due*," Daphne cried, then burst into tears and staggered out into the corridor.

Meg stared after her, shaking her head. She hated to think it, but it was possible that the earl had bad blood on both sides of his family. What that indicated for her future, she dreaded to think. She drained her tea and rose to wander the room, trying to make sense of her situation.

No matter how suspicious the circumstances, surely the law would have to step carefully with a countess.

She wouldn't hang for a murder she did not commit.

How much of the story would have to come out, however, before she was free?

And what then? Would the earl even want to see her again after this? Especially if he found out about the *sheelagh*. He would hate the idea of being manipulated by pagan magic.

She halted, wondering what would become of her family. They must already be worried about her, and she'd abandoned them to the earl's mercy.

She just stopped herself from running out of the room and back to Marlborough Square. If the law was looking for the Countess of Saxonhurst, that *would* put her head in a noose. Better to wait and see what the duchess could do, trusting that her family would be safe.

She paced the room, twisting her hands.

Before Saxonhurst's rage, she wouldn't have felt that her siblings were in danger, but now she simply didn't know. She had to put her faith in Mr. Chancellor, and in the servants. Even if half of them were gallows fodder themselves.

She circled the room, feeling exactly like a poor bear she'd seen once, trapped forever in a small cage. How soon would she hear something? How long would it take for the duchess to find out what was going on?

A sonorous clock chimed in the distance—probably in the hall. A half, then the three quarters, then the hour, the full twelve strokes of noon.

Half a dozen times Meg went toward the adjoining door to burst in on the duchess and demand the news. Each time, she stopped herself, but slowly doubts began to grow.

She became unsure whether the duchess really would do her utmost to sort things out.

Why?

Instinct.

Instinct was telling her something was wrong here. Instinct was urging her to seek help from her husband. He would help, even if only because she was his bride, and she was sure he was able to. More able than an old, crippled woman. He and Mr. Chancellor could probably keep her safe even if she had blood on her hands!

As soon as these thoughts settled, she felt an almost dizzying sense of relief. Yes, she had to get his help, even if she had to tell him all. Telling him the truth about the *sheelagh* had seemed the worst thing possible, but now that wasn't true. Hanging was the worst thing possible!

He'd be furious with her over the *sheelagh*. And because she'd fallen into this mess by sneaking out to visit Sir Arthur. And because she'd come to his grandmother, whom he hated. And yet, despite his destructive rages, and even if he wanted to cast her off, she'd feel safer in his care than anywhere else.

She went toward the door to the corridor, but stopped with her hand on the knob.

Though she ached to, it simply wasn't wise to go to Marlborough Square, and she was determined not to make the situation worse. She wasn't sure even an earl could stop the authorities arresting a suspected murderess, and if she had to hide, this was as good a place as any.

What she should do was send a message, but one cleverly phrased so that it wouldn't give away her location if intercepted.

After a moment's hesitation, she intruded upon Lady Daphne's traveling desk. She needn't have worried. The embossed paper and envelopes sat there in neat piles with no hint of the personal, or of secrets.

She took out a sheet of paper and used scissors to cut off the crest. Then she opened the ink well, checked the pen, and wrote:

> To the Right Honorable the Earl of Saxonhurst,
> My lord,
> The velvet beret you were seeking is now at The Dragon. Please arrange, at your convenience, my lord, for it to be collected.
> I have the honor to be, my lord, your Lordship's most obedient and very humble servant,
> Daphne la Brodiere

If he didn't recognize the other references, surely he would see that La Brodiere meant the embroideress, and Daphne would jolt his mind toward the duchess. Shaking the letter dry, she knew she needn't worry about such things. Mad he might be, but the earl wasn't dull-witted.

Now to sneak out of the room and find a potboy or such who would run over with the message. Was *that* too risky? Would the messenger be questioned . . . ?

It was a pointless debate, because when Meg tried to open the door, she found it was locked. She marched to the door to the duchess's room but that, too, was locked.

From the other side, she heard a chuckle.

Something about that laugh sent a shiver right through her. Now, too late, she realized that her instincts had been right—something was very odd about the situation here.

She should have taken Daphne's advice, and left when she still could.

Chapter 16

"Where the devil is she?" Sax glared around his assembled household. "I ride back into town to hear my name being yelled on every street corner. *Saxonhurst scandal! Man dead in his bed!*"

He turned the news sheet in his hand and read: "At ten of the morning, the housekeeper at a gentleman's residence on Bingham Street discovered a horrible sight. Her master, Sir A——— I——, lay among his bloodstained sheets, his throat cut, a young maid of his house beside him, similarly foully done to death. Upon enquiry, it is discovered that the last person to see the baronet alive was a lady of exalted rank, the Countess of S———." He threw the roughly printed paper on the floor. "Of course, the scandal-criers aren't so discreet, and give the names in full. Where the devil is she?"

His butler stepped forward, ashen though dignified. "Her ladyship left the house this morning quite properly, with Monkey in attendance."

"To go where?"

"She didn't say, milord. She declined the carriage."

For the first time in his life, Sax wished the servants to the devil. He wanted to huddle this to himself in private, but it was far too late for that. The whole hell-ridden world knew!

Marlborough Square was half full of gawkers hoping for some juicy development.

Had she done it? Instinct said no, but what did he really know about his wife except that she had secrets?

Deadly secrets?

"Send word to Bow Street. And to Lord Sidmouth at the Home Office. I want immediate word of any developments with respect to my wife. Immediate. Notify the parish constables, too. All of them. And get the military out to control that mob in the square! Where's Mr. Chancellor?"

"Out, milord," intoned Pringle, already dispatching servants on these errands.

"And where's Monk?"

"Not yet returned, milord."

"I pray to heaven—" Sax broke off as a gasping Monk ran in from the servants' stairs. "Where the devil have you been?"

"Sorry, milord!" Monk gasped, leaning forward to catch his breath.

"I'll give you sorry! What's happened to Lady Saxonhurst, and how in perdition could you let her get into such a mess?"

Monk spoke between wheezes. "She just . . . wanted to visit . . . an old friend, milord!"

"On the other side of London? Without a carriage? You knew damned well she was up to something! You should have stopped her. Unless"—and the demons he'd thought conquered snarled back into life—"you're in league with her, you and Susie both."

"In *league,* milord?" Monkey straightened in astonishment. "About what?"

Susie moved to his side, wide-eyed, hand over mouth. Guilt? Or just surprise?

Sax tried to read their expression. Had it all been a plot? The duchess, Susie, Monk, Minerva . . .

"You took her to Sir Arthur Jakes's house, I assume. Why?"

"Because that's where she wanted to go, milord. It weren't my place to tell her she couldn't!"

"You make it your place to do what you damn well please." Sax tried to hold on to sanity. There could be no connection between this Jakes and the duchess. "Tell me what happened. Everything."

Monk blew out a breath. "She wanted to go there and she didn't want the carriage, milord. I don't know why. We took an 'ackney. When we got there, she 'ad it stop some way from the 'ouse and told me to wait while she went on alone. I protested, milord, I swear I did, but what was I to do?"

Sax rubbed the back of his neck. He'd known Monk for eight years—a scrawny lad whose growth had stopped too soon. Why would be turn traitor? "Nothing, I suppose. So, she went into the house."

"Aye, milord. I just propped up a railing and whistled, waiting for 'er to come out, watching the 'ouse like an 'awk. Gave me a real turn to have her creep up behind me looking like she'd seen a ghost."

Damnation. "Or a dead man, you think?"

Monk shook his head. "She didn't do it, milord. I'd lay me soul on that!"

"What touching faith." Sax scooped up the scandal sheet, checking the details. "Did she have blood on her?"

"Not as I remember, milord."

"That's something. Then what?"

"Then we heard the screaming. Someone from the 'ouse she visited, crying murder. I didn't stop to ask questions, just got 'er out of there at a brisk walk. Next we know there's a regular mob forming, and someone points 'er out as the target. We ran, but to be 'onest, milord, she's not that much of a runner."

"They got her?" Sax felt as if winter air had swirled down his throat, stealing his breath. Torn apart by a bloodthirsty mob?

"Strike a light, milord! You think I'd be back 'ere? I'd cut me own throat and throw myself in the river! I got us down an alley, snatched 'er cloak, tossed 'er me coat, and took to me heels. I'll swear they all followed me, but I had to lose 'em, see, before I could circle back. When I got back to where I left 'er, she'd gone. I've been 'unting the streets for perishing 'ours now without sight nor sound of 'er."

"The paper says the alarm was raised at ten. Has it been that long? Three hours?"

"If that's the time, milord."

" 'Struth!" Sax rubbed a hand over his face. So, she'd escaped the mob, but then what? He was angry at her, yes. And suspicious. But mostly he was terrified by all the things that could happen to a defenseless young woman adrift in London.

He'd returned early, ashamed of himself for running

away. If he'd never left, none of this would have
happened.

"What else could I have done, milord?"

"Kept better watch over her!" But Sax shook his
head. Poor Monk was almost in tears, and he'd shown
wits in a tight spot. "You did the best you could, Monk,
and probably saved her life. A mob like that is dangerous. But why hasn't she come home? Damnation, she
could be . . ." He didn't even want to put his fears
into words.

"She's got sense, milord," said Susie, dabbing at tears.
"And she's used to London."

"Know her well, do you?" he snarled, his monsters
leaping out.

The maid turned white. "No, milord!"

He leashed his wild mind, reminded himself that there
was no logic to it. "She's used to her own small, respectable part of London, not the dangerous whole. Dammit,
I wish she were in the Roundhouse, or even in the Fleet!
I could get her out of those places in a moment. Why
hasn't she come home?"

"If I may, milord," intoned Pringle, "some hours ago,
we had enquiries as to her ladyship's whereabouts. A
gentleman from Bow Street. Of course, I told him
nothing."

"So I would hope. But what does that say to
anything?"

"I am reasonably certain that some of the people in
the square outside are watching for her ladyship's
return."

"They all are, damn them."

"With intent to arrest her, milord."

"If anyone dared lay a finger on my wife, I'd shoot
him!"

"But Lady Saxonhurst may not be aware of that, milord, being . . . er . . . new to her elevated status. And
it is a matter of murder."

"She might fear to return here?"

"Perhaps, milord."

"Cousin Sax . . . ?"

Sax turned to see Laura standing at the bottom of the
stairs, pale-faced, with the twins hovering on either side

of her. "Has something . . . has something happened to Meg?"

Meg.

She hadn't even given him her correct name. Vaguely he remembered the twins calling her that yesterday, but he'd been deafened by lustful anticipation.

Was anything about her honest?

He put that aside. Whatever she was, she was his wife and no one would harm her. And these youngsters were surely innocent.

"To tell the truth, my dear, I don't know. I've only just arrived home."

Then he wondered if perhaps Laura could shed some light on the strange goings-on. Clearly she knew some of her sister's business.

"Come into my study, all of you, and we'll have a council about it." He glanced at the servants. "Not you lot. In fact, get out into the streets and sniff out any trace of my wife."

As the servants scattered, he shepherded the young ones into his study, suddenly aware of his responsibility for these vulnerable almost-strangers. If something had happened to their sister, he couldn't just toss them out, or even farm them off on someone. They'd suffered too many losses as it was.

He'd have to take care of them himself.

By himself.

He definitely needed their sister back.

And where the devil was Owain?

He settled them on seats, pondering how best to approach things.

Laura sat straight, hands tight in lap. "Someone said . . . murder. . . ."

"A wild accusation," Sax assured her. "Unfortunately, your sister seems to have been in a house when murder was committed." He hesitated for a moment, but they had to know. "I'm afraid Sir Arthur Jakes has been killed."

"Sir Arthur!" the twins squeaked in unison, but looking more astonished than upset.

Laura put a hand to her chest, and if anything, looked paler. She definitely knew something. "You know," said

Sax, going over to the twins, "this probably isn't very interesting for you. I promise I'll make sure Minerva—Meg—is safe. Why don't you go down to the kitchens and see if Cook has any cakes for you?"

They rose, but with shrewd looks. The clever children knew they were being sent away from "grown-up matters."

"Was there a lot of blood, sir?" asked Richard.

"I wouldn't know, you ghoulish creature." He eased them toward the door.

"Why would anyone kill Sir Arthur?" asked Rachel.

"I don't know that either. It will all come out in time." He opened the door and pushed them both gently out.

"But—"

"But your sister had no reason to kill anyone, so that's all right." He suddenly wondered if the ten-year-olds were capable of running off into the streets to find their sister, or to go searching for the murder scene. God knew what ten-year-olds were capable of.

"Clarence," he called to the hovering footman. "Take Master Richard and Miss Rachel to the kitchens for cakes. And," he mouthed, "keep and eye on them."

The limping footman winked.

Sax shut the door, aware of too many people to think of at once. He was not used to thinking of anyone but himself. Where the devil was Owain? He turned and found that Laura had risen, looking as if she'd like to leave, too.

"Sit down, Laura. We need to talk."

With a sigh, she obeyed, eyes down.

"You know why your sister went to Sir Arthur's house, don't you?"

Laura nodded.

"You have to tell me."

She looked up, pretty enough in her fear and confusion to drive a man distracted—if the man wasn't already driven distracted by her exasperating sister. "But it's a secret, my lord."

"Not from me. I'm your sister's husband."

"Especially from you!"

Like a canon blast, all his devils burst free, but he fought them. His wife was in danger. This was no time to indulge. Even if she was his grandmother's tool, he'd rescue her for his name's sake. Then he'd deal with her.

He sat down opposite his lovely sister-in-law, doing his best to look calm and kind. "Laura, your loyalty is admirable, but you must tell me what is going on. Minerva could be in great danger, and I can't help her if I am in the dark."

She bit her lip. "She thought . . . she was sure that if you knew you'd not *want* to help her. . . ."

"I promise you," he said steadily, "it doesn't matter what she's done, I will help her."

Laura's fingers tangled in her lap and she looked around, teeth deep in lower lip, as if expecting wisdom to suddenly appear on the paneled walls. But then she spoke. "Last night . . . at the theater . . . Sir Arthur told Meg that he had something of ours. Something we'd left in the house. He said she had to visit him to get it back."

Evidence of the plot? A letter from his grandmother? "What is it?"

It seemed a simple enough question, but it threw her back into confusion. She covered her mouth as if about to cry, feeding his fears like oil on flames.

"Come on, Laura! What can it be that's worth this level of secrecy?"

She stared at him, tears glossing her huge eyes. "It's a magic statue."

"What?" With her hand over her mouth, it had been a mumble and he must have misheard.

She leaped to her feet. "I *knew* you'd never believe me! And if you do, it will be even *worse*!" She burst into a full torrent of tears.

Suppressing curses, Sax put an arm around her and gave her a handkerchief. He eased her back onto the sofa, and stayed by her side. "Now, now, Laura. No need for that. Calm down and explain yourself."

Had she really said "magic statue"? And what part could that play in his grandmother's schemes?

She clutched the white linen and sniffed, blue eyes liquid, but not particularly red. She'd certainly drive some man mad one day. "You won't believe it. I'm not sure I do. It doesn't work for me, you see." She blew her nose twice, then faced him. "We have this stone statue, my lord. It's a wishing stone. A person with the power can make a wish on the stone, and it always comes true."

Sax tried to detect a joke. Or a lie, though he knew she wasn't lying. No, she'd swallowed her sister's lie, silly little fool. "You're quite correct, Laura. I don't believe it. For one thing, a family possessed of that kind of treasure would hardly be in dire poverty, would it?"

"But Meg wouldn't use it, you see! She has the power, but she doesn't like it at all. She's says it's wicked, and that there's always a sting in the tail. And it's true!" she wailed into the handkerchief. "Look what's happened to her!"

"Laura, stop that!" When she gulped and quieted a bit, he said, "Nothing has happened to Meg yet." He hoped. "And think. None of this can be your magic's fault if she never uses it."

Instead of consoling her, that sent her back into the handkerchief, shaking with sobs.

Strongly tempted to slap her, Sax chose instead to wait. He was not without experience with emotional young women. Time was passing, however, and his wife could be in danger. The sobs slowed, then stopped, and she emerged, sniffing cautiously.

"Now," he said, "do I gather she *has* used it? Recently?"

Laura nodded.

"What did she wish for?"

Silence stretched, but he let it.

Eventually, she whispered, "You."

When he just stared, she added, "Not *you,* exactly, my lord. A way out of our predicament! But it turned out . . . to be you."

After a stunned moment, Sax had to laugh. "Jupiter, girl! How foolish can you be? My marrying your sister was part of a strand begun decades ago. How could a wish affect that?"

"It does, though," she said, steadier now. "Or that's what they say. Time has no meaning for the *sheelagh.*"

"The what?"

"It's an old Irish statue. It's called a *sheelagh-ma-ging.* Or gig. Something like that."

He rose, hardly able to believe that even Laura could believe this nonsense. "Whatever it's called, it had nothing to do with my decision to marry your sister. But, if it's so precious to her, why did your sister forget it?"

"She didn't." She cast him a worried glance, then added, "She didn't want you to see it. She went back for it. . . ."

He put his hands on his hips. "You mean to tell me that your harebrained sister left this statue in your old house because she was afraid to let me see it because she *believed* in this faradiddle?"

Laura bounced to her feet, fierce as an angry kitten. "She's *not* harebrained. It's not all folly, my lord, I assure you!"

He ignored that. "Then she crept out of this house before dawn, to try to get it back?"

"Yes, my lord."

"Harebrained." He ignored her glower. "For the moment, I'll accept that your sister believes this idiocy, and wants to get her magic stone back. So, Sir Arthur had already taken it?"

"I suppose so, my lord."

"Don't sulk. Why would he do that?"

"I'm not sulking. I'm *angry* with you. I told you you'd never believe me."

"And you were right, I give you that. But I do believe that you believe it. And that your sister believes it." And he felt like laughing for joy at such a simple, if ridiculous, explanation. "So, why do you think Sir Arthur would steal this stone statue? How big is it, anyway?"

"Not very big. It's flat and carved, and about a foot."

"So he could carry it alone."

"Oh yes. I can, though it is heavy." She seemed to have overcome her anger. Her frown now was thoughtful. "Sir Arthur must have learned about the *sheelagh* from our father when he was sick. If so, perhaps *he* believed in the magic"—a minor glower fluttered his way—"and wanted to try to make a wish. But it only works for women, my lord. I think."

"And only, in fact, for your sister."

He tried to hold back his skepticism, but she glowered

again. "And for our mother. If you don't believe me, my lord, how do you explain the fact that you married a simple woman you first met at the altar?"

He held up a hand and ticked off fingers. "One, I had to marry in a hurry because of a promise made to my grandmother years ago. Two, I chose your sister because one of my servants is sister to one of your old servants, and suggested her. Three, I preferred a woman who would be grateful to me rather than one who would expect me to be grateful to her. You see. Logical and believable. No magic required."

Her shoulders sagged. "I must admit, my lord, it does sound so."

"Good girl. So, Meg—I gather she's always called Meg?"

Laura nodded.

"Meg went to Sir Arthur's house today to get it back. She went alone because she was afraid to tell me because"—he shook his head—"she seriously believed that she'd somehow brought about this marriage with her magic statue. Incredible! And typical of the woman to walk into a murder."

"No, it isn't!" She was back to being a spitting kitten. "Meg is the calmest, most sensible person possible. She never gets into excitement or adventures at all!"

He raised his brows. "Are we talking about the same Meg?"

Laura giggled, hand over mouth. "It's true, though, my lord. She's . . . well, I love her dearly, but she's so very staid. So very practical. She's had to be."

Sax thought of fancifully embroidered underwear and suppressed a smile. Lord, but at the thought of his staid, practical, harebrained wife he was growing hard. He wanted her here with him. He wanted to continue the seduction he'd so foolishly broken off. To explore her—excited, impractical, and as harebrained as possible—naked in his bed. Damn his stupid demons that had driven him away from her last night! How could he ever think her part of his grandmother's web?

"What are we going to do, my lord?"

He snapped out of his heated thoughts. "Find her.

Don't worry about this business of murder. That's easily handled."

Assuming she didn't actually do it. He'd go odds his wife wasn't vicious, but sometimes there was good cause for murder. Had Sir Arthur lured her to his house to rape her?

"I am a little worried about her wandering the streets, though. Do you know where she would go?"

Laura shook her head.

He itched to plunge out into the streets himself, but he made himself stay calm. It was pointless without a destination.

"Where would *you* go?" he asked, pacing restlessly. "In her situation, running from the mob, where would you go?"

But Laura just shook her head again, wide-eyed. "I don't know. I don't know what I'd do. Come back here?"

"Not so stupid an idea, even with the constables outside and a mob—damn their eyes—gathering. Where else?"

"Perhaps Reverend Bilston? Or even Dr. Pierce, Jeremy's tutor?"

Sax went into the hall and called for servants, then sent messages to both places. He didn't have much hope, however. If his wife was at either place, someone would have sent word.

Why hadn't she sent word?

Where could she be that she couldn't or wouldn't send a message?

Injured?

Dead?

He was still in the hall, pondering, when someone rapped on the front door. An urgent yet feeble rap. In a flame of relief, he strode by his butler and swung the door wide, ready to sear the Countess of Saxonhurst with his opinion of her erratic adventures.

He came face-to-face with his cousin Daphne.

"Oh, for pity's sake." He began to shut the door in her face when something in her expression stopped him. Fear? He swung it wide again. "Come in. But if you, too, are accused of murder, I'll let you hang."

Daphne stalked in. "Saxonhurst, you're a swine. I loathe you. I wouldn't marry you if you were the last man on earth."

He slammed the door on the gawking mob. "Then we'll doubtless get along a lot better. Anyway, I'm married."

"Not for long."

"What?"

She looked around. "You may not mind conducting your affairs in front of the lower orders, but I do. Where can we talk?"

He led her briskly to the study.

"A doxy in your own house?" Daphne sneered as soon as the door was shut.

"Frequently, before I was married. This, however, is my wife's sister. I doubt introductions are important at the moment. So, Daphne, what is going on?"

"Scandal is what is going on, Saxonhurst, and look what's come of your folly! That . . . that crowd out there! They were pressing against the hackney, staring in at me as if they'd like to eat me!"

"Don't worry. It's my wife they want to eat, and they wouldn't know her if they saw her. In fact," he added, "you're probably lucky they didn't assume you were she. Oh, for Jupiter's sake, if you faint, I'll slap you."

Daphne sat up straight again. "You really are—"

"We've done that bit. Now—"

A tap on the door interrupted. Pringle entered, bearing a grubby bit of paper on a large silver tray. "A message for you, my lord."

Sax grabbed it and unscrewed it. After a quick glance, his heart pounded with relief and the drive for action. "Who brought it?"

"A potboy from Quiller's Hotel. I have detained him."

"Good man. I'll be with you in a moment." As soon as the door shut, he turned to Daphne. "Speak."

She, however, had slumped as if all the starch had been rinsed out of her. "She got a message out."

"Foiled your plans?"

She looked up and he recognized again the fear in

her. "I don't suppose you'll ever believe me, but I came here to help."

"Why?"

Her lips trembled between disapproval and anxiety. "Because it's too much! I'm no longer sure what the duchess is capable of. She seems to *want* your wife to hang."

It confirmed his fears, but he stayed calm. "It's a neat way of ending a marriage."

"But think of the scandal!"

The woman was pathetic, but he couldn't help feeling sorry for her. She'd been in the dragon's claws all her life and lacked his own rebellious streak. And it was more than that. For the first time he realized that he had always known relief would come. Once he was of age, he would have his fortune and his freedom. Daphne had faced a life sentence unless she married.

He was gentle, therefore, when he said, "Thank you for your kind efforts, even if they were in a strange cause. Do you require a carriage to take you back?"

She shrank away. "You can't send me back! Please, Saxonhurst!" She pressed her lips hard together before saying, "I hoped that if I helped you, you would help me. We *were* promised in the cradle. We were. You owe me something!"

A lifetime spurred him to throw her out, but something in Laura's face, an appalled pity, demanded another way.

He went to take his cousin's gloved hand, startled to realize that through the years he had never touched her skin. She'd worn gloves, even in the schoolroom. "Daphne, calm down. I'll help you because we're cousins. I've always been willing to help you on that basis. You don't have to go back to her. All right?"

She nodded, but her face stayed pinched. She'd never transform into a sweet, loving person. Perhaps it wasn't her fault, but it was too late. He let her go, and she tucked her hand protectively beneath the other.

"I'm off now to sort out my wife's affairs, but Laura will settle you into a room."

"That little nobody!"

"She lives here. You don't." He smiled at Laura, who

looked very young and uncertain. "If you don't mind, sister."

She blushed at that, and some of her spirit returned. "Of course not . . . brother."

He winked at her and turned back to his cousin. "Is there anything special I should know about the situation?"

"I don't think so. Grandmother has a train of servants with her, of course, including a man I don't much care for. He's estate manager at Crickstone, but she sometimes calls him her bodyguard. He's big enough."

"I hope so. I'm ready to beat up someone."

Chapter 17

Sax went into the hall, and almost collided with Owain.

"What the devil is going on?" his friend asked.

"Trust you to be out when you're needed."

"I had appointments in the City."

"Never mind that." Sax headed for the butler's pantry, giving a quick account of the significant facts.

"Magic?" Owain asked.

Sax stopped to look at him. "What a brain you have for nonessentials! The important detail is that my wife is in distress and danger. I'm off to talk to a potboy, then on to rescue my maiden—alas, that she's still a maiden—from the dragon. Come on."

The nervous lad could only tell them that he'd been passed the note and tuppence through the grille on a lower window at Quiller's, with instructions to bring it here.

Sax asked a few questions, then turned to Owain. "Don't we have a man here to fix things?"

"Seth Pocock, yes."

"Give this lad a florin and have someone find Mr. Pocock."

In moments a wide-eyed, strapping young man was being interrogated about grilles and windows.

Eventually Sax turned back to the boy. "You can guide me to this window. Pocock, find me one of those driver things. Pringle, my greatcoat!"

Pocock ran to obey, Pringle turned to pass on the order, but Owain said, "You'll be mobbed. And if you aren't, you'll be followed."

"Damnation." Sax was tempted to arm his servants and make a battle of it, but then he grinned. "Disguise! Pringle, find me some grubby clothes!"

As the butler stalked off, Sax followed him into the servants' hall to give general instructions to the few left there.

"Owain, you stay here and guard the castle. I've sent word to Sidmouth and Bow Street. The army should be here soon, too, to disperse that mob."

He began to strip off his outer clothes, but Owain pulled him aside. "Sax, what if she really did kill this man?"

"I'll get her off."

"But what then? You can't live with a murderess."

He peeled off his jacket and tossed it onto a chair. Nims had appeared, and stumped over to take loving charge of it.

"We'll face that later. I don't believe she's capable of violence."

"Anyone is, given the right circumstances."

Sax knew that. He'd deal with that problem only when he had to. He tossed his embroidered waistcoat straight to his valet, and stripped out of his pantaloons just as a well-built groom ran in with a bundle.

"Me Sunday best, milord!"

Sax flashed him a smile. "I'll replace it with new."

Soon he was dressed in old-fashioned and well-worn knee breeches and jacket, with a colorful cotton neckerchief instead of a cravat. He smeared soot on his own snowy white stockings and to Nims's horror, attacked his perfect leather boots with cinders until the finish was ruined.

"Just be glad I didn't order you to do it," he said to his cringing valet. Then he spread his scratched and blackened hands. "Gets rid of the gentleman's hands, too."

Pringle entered at the moment, bearing his silver tray, and almost recoiled at the sight, causing Sax to grin. The situation was serious, but he was rather enjoying this part of it. He plucked another message off the tray, this time expensive paper, properly sealed with a crest. Sidmouth at the Home Office.

He read it, pulled a face, then tossed it to Owain. "Best he can offer if they find her is excellent accommodations in the Tower. Couldn't be seen to be favoring wealth and privilege these days, etc. Someone get me something to carry out of here. A carpet. A bundle. Anything to lessen suspicion." He spoke to Owain again. "When I find her, we'll have to lie low while you sort this out."

"Me?"

"What else do I pay you for?"

"I demand a bonus."

"Of course." Sax squinted into a small mirror and pulled on the groom's slouch-brimmed hat, then rubbed his dirty hands over his face. "I'll find a way to get word of where we are, but I'll only know you've done your bit when the scandal sheets announce the capture of the real murderer."

"How on earth am I supposed to—"

"I have infinite trust in your abilities, my friend."

"Where are you going to hide? In the country?"

"I have no idea."

"Sax, this isn't going to work."

But Sax could only think of his wife alone and frightened in the dragon's lair.

"Make it work." He hoisted a rough bundle of cloth on his shoulder, and with the wide-eyed potboy trotting alongside, headed out the back door to be a knight in musty fustian.

A few enterprising gawkers were hovering in the back lane. He swore at them in a thick accent and trudged by. They hardly gave him a glance.

He didn't think he'd be followed, but he wandered around a bit just in case. Then he tossed the bundle to an old woman who looked in need of help, hoping it contained something she could use, and let the lad lead him to Quiller's.

He hadn't thought he lived a particularly protected life, but he soon realized that he'd never been out in the streets as an ordinary man. No one paid any attention to him, which was disconcerting, but quite pleasant. He was almost invisible.

However, he was used to people moving out of his way. After a few unpleasant collisions, he had to learn how to weave along a crowded street.

Women gave him the eye—all ages and types—but

they weren't whores looking for guineas, just ordinary women having a bit of fun. Most of them would have had a fit if he took them up on it. His sense of mischief tempted him, but he remembered his purpose here.

He was familiar with Quiller's, but not with the back area. He followed the potboy down a lane and into the hotel's yard. There, the lad pointed to the window. It was off to one side, in a narrow space between a shed and the hotel wall, which would help him hide, but hotel servants were in and out of store sheds and outhouses all the time.

He looked at the lad, who was probably a scrawny fourteen or so. "You've done me a service today."

"Just carried a message, milord."

"Would you rather work for me than here?"

The keen eyes sharpened, but warily. "Doing what?"

"What do you want to do?"

The boy hesitated, then said rather wistfully, "I wants to be a cook."

"Very well. Go back to Marlborough Square and sign on to learn the cooking trade." Sax had no idea what was involved in this, but it had to be possible. After all, people did learn to cook, and chefs were becoming quite fashionable.

The lad was staring at him. "Really? Me?"

Perhaps it wasn't that easy. "Go. It might take awhile, but we'll do it."

A flush and a glitter in his eyes made Sax think of someone in love, then the lad turned and ran off as if fearing the chance would disappear. Sax watched him, hoping he hadn't promised more than could be done. Of course not. With money and power anything was possible—except, maybe, saving a true murderess from the gallows.

Devil take it, at the worst, he'd get her out of the country.

He slipped into the space between shed and window, and keeping a wary eye out, rapped. "Meg?"

After a moment the window rose an inch. "Who is it?"

"Who else but your noble hero, galloping to the rescue?"

The curtain went up, and her face stared out at him through grille and glass. *"Saxonhurst?"*

"You have other noble heroes?"

She turned a delightful pink. "Of course not. I mean—"

"Good. This space could get a bit crowded." He'd never known a woman who blushed as bewitchingly as his wife. He cursed the dusty glass that lay between them, preventing a kiss.

She also frowned bewitchingly. "Be serious, Saxonhurst! I'm locked in, and I don't know—"

"Hold on a moment." He ducked around the corner as a couple of women servants strolled toward the closest shed. They unlocked the door and took out two baskets, then tarried a moment, chatting about a rather unpleasant-sounding female itch.

When they'd gone, he returned to the window. "Still there?"

The curtain rose again, surrounding her disgruntled face. "Where else would I be?"

He grinned, astonished by the pleasure he found in her in all her moods. "I don't suppose you'd care to describe your underwear."

"What?"

"You could whet my appetite for later. What is it? Flowers? Fruit? Lightning bolts?"

"You describe your underwear, my lord, and I'll describe mine."

"Now Meg, you should know better than to throw out a challenge like that. I'm wearing—"

"Oh do stop!" But he saw the laughter fighting to get out. He'd seen her laugh too rarely, but he'd always known it was in her. Lovely Meg. Delicious Meg. Then she sobered, and he saw real fear. "I'm in a terrible predicament. Perhaps you don't know—"

"Of course I do, and I'll scold you later over it. You can't imagine I'd let anyone hang my countess, can you? And if they do arrest you," he teased, "I've arranged for the best accommodation the Tower can provide."

"The *Tower!*"

Her terror stabbed him with guilt.

"They don't behead people on the mound there anymore. You'd be quite safe, and they'd doubtless let me have long visits. Actually," he added, "given the trouble we've had so far in finding peace and quiet, it sounds quite tempting. . . ."

Silence can be very eloquent, and this one, reinforced by a glare, carried heavy recrimination.

He grinned at her. "You look fetching in that lace mantilla, my dear. Slightly nunlike. You can hardly be displeased to know you tempt me." He put a finger on the glass that screened her nose.

"You tempt me, too," she said, but more as a complaint than a compliment.

"This will be a lot more fun without iron bars between us. Listen, this grille is to keep people out, not in, so it's on the inside. Is it held in place with nails, or screws?"

She inspected the edges out of his sight. "I don't know. There's a slot in the top."

"Screws. Good." He pulled out the tool he'd brought after Pocock's advice. "This thing is a screwdriver. I'm told that if you put the tip in the slot and turn, you should be able to work the screw out."

"There's about ten of them!"

"Then you have a lot of work to do. Go to it."

"I'm going to close the window. It's freezing, and if anyone comes, it'll be less obvious." She dropped the curtain, too, so he couldn't see what was going on.

Though it went against his nature, he resigned himself to waiting.

He wasn't familiar with tools, and hadn't even known about screws until Pocock had explained them. He hadn't really known about Seth Pocock, his handyman, in any clear way.

He was beginning to be disturbed about the number of things he didn't know.

He'd tried out the screwdriver—screwundriver?—and knew it took a fair amount of strength to make it work. He wasn't entirely sure his countess would be able to use it, especially ten times. He was afraid it would hurt her delicate hands. He couldn't get in to do it for her, though, so she'd have to.

"Well?" he asked after an anxious minute or so.

Muffled by the window, she said, "It's working, but slowly."

"More servants!" he hissed and ducked away again.

As he waited for a man and woman to complete their errands and a bit of flirtation, he gritted his teeth in frustration. St. George didn't have to hover around while his maiden unscrewed herself from the dragon's clutches.

Perhaps she'd been thinking the same thing. When he went back to the window, she opened it a crack, and asked, "Why haven't you just confronted the duchess and demanded my release?"

At least part of the answer was because he'd wanted an adventure. Another part was because he didn't want to be in the same room as the dragon. But he did have better reasons to offer.

"Because I'm not sure what she's up to, and I don't want the slightest risk of you ending up in jail, even in select quarters. Owain's looking into it, working with Bow Street, the Home Secretary and such. As soon as we know the whole situation, we'll deal with it, but from a position of power. How are you doing?"

"Two screws left at the top. My hands hurt."

He winced, but kept his voice light. "I'll kiss them better. In fact, rest a moment and let me work my magic."

"Magic?" Her nervous tone made him grin. Her and her harebrained belief in magic statues.

"Push a hand out here."

After a moment, her right hand eased through the grille and between the small gap at the bottom of the window.

He hunkered down and kissed her chilly knuckles. He rubbed her fingers between his own cold hands and breathed on them to warm them up. "Don't you have a fire in there?"

"Yes, but it's small. And I'm here by the open window."

He turned her hand and saw the reddened grooves made by the tool. "Damnation. I wish I could get in there to do the work."

As he kissed the marks, he heard her chuckle, and she pushed her way up under the lace curtain like a puppy coming out from under a blanket. "I suspect my hands are more accustomed to work than yours, my lord earl."

Tussled and grinning, she looked absolutely delicious. He nipped her thumb. "Impudent wench. Mine at least are bigger and stronger." He spread his hand over hers, palm to palm, showing how much bigger it was. Then he folded his fingers in with hers. "We match well, though."

"Do we?" Even through dingy glass, he could tell by her widened eyes that she felt it, too, that sudden joining as if skin had meshed and life blood flowed between them. He thought for a moment quite seriously of smashing the glass that stood in their way—

"You do know I didn't kill him, don't you?"

He looked into her worried eyes. "I know." And he did. She doubtless *was* capable of killing someone, but not of being so unshadowed by it.

Her nose wobbled, and that hint of tears made him want to tear the wall down with his bare hands. He'd never felt so powerless in his life. He pulled their hands apart and stood. "Come on, Meg. Let's get you out of there."

The curtain dropped between them again and he heard vague sounds as she worked on the last screws.

Her hands were probably tougher than his, but he was going to make sure that they never had to work again. He was going to pamper her, and fill her days with undiluted carefree joy, and reap the reward of her company. Hers and that of her whole, wonderful family—

He saw the grille shift, and put out a hand uselessly to steady it. "Be careful it doesn't fall on you!"

She didn't respond. It had been a silly thing to say.

He was rather surprised by her silence. He'd think she'd have all sorts of questions about the murder, and about what he knew of her adventures. Then he shook his head. Still trying to keep her secrets. She didn't know he'd had a long talk with her sister.

"So," he said, mostly just to tease, "why did you go to visit Sir Arthur in the first place?"

"He asked me to." The grille shifted a bit more.

"If you open the window wide, I could help hold it."

"I can't now. I have my hands full."

After a moment, he said, "You could have taken a carriage."

"I took Monk."

"And a hackney."

"Is he all right?"

"Who?"

"Monk."

"Perfectly. Why, Meg? Why go that way?"

He thought she wasn't going to answer, but she said, rather breathlessly, "I didn't want you to know. That's the last. I'm holding the grille on."

"Well, don't. Or rather, move it carefully away. I assume it's not too heavy for you." Damned if he knew what he could do if it was.

Useless sort of noble hero he was turning out to be.

"I can manage." He heard a faint *clunk* and then the window was pushed all the way up. A moment later one white stockinged leg appeared, interestingly exposed nearly to the garters, followed by the other, then the whole of his idiotic, delightful, capable wife. He helped her through, but she pulled away to brush herself down and fuss with her skirts.

Then she faced him as if expecting an inquisition.

Here? He didn't think so. Anyway, her eyes had widened at his full appearance.

"See what I'm willing to sink to for you? Let it not be for nothing." He pulled down the window, took her hand, and they walked briskly out into the yard and away. "It's as well I'm dressed like this. Anyone will take us for servants."

"I was a servant," she pointed out.

"A legion of governesses would probably disagree with you, but in any case, I don't mind."

"Good. I don't mind your being an earl, either."

He flashed her an appreciative grin. He liked her saucy.

In fact, he liked his wife in all her extraordinary aspects. Even if she'd committed murder, she would have had excellent reasons.

In moments, they were blending with the people on the street. People dressed mostly in heavy coats and cloaks, hurrying because of the biting wind. That was when he realized her teeth were chattering, that she was only wearing a light woolen dress.

He wrapped an arm around her. "Why didn't you bring your cloak?"

Instead of answering, she tried to pull free. "My lord!"

"Hush. We're just Meg and Sax, out for a stroll. And being common folk, we can stroll down the street entwined if we want. Your cloak?"

She gave in and snuggled closer. "Monk took it to lead the hunt away from me."

"Ah, yes."

"He gave me his coat, but I discarded it when I slipped into the hotel. In my dress I'd look like an upper servant, but in a castoff footman's coat, I'd never get past the door."

"Castoff? I assure you I clothe my servants extremely well."

"I'm sure. But I thought I'd blend in better if it was messed up a bit."

"Oh dear. Monk will not be pleased."

"Then you'll have to save me, my noble hero, by buying him new."

"No point. He's off to be an innkeeper."

"Oh. True."

They hurried along, though he realized now that he had no idea where to take her. And his demons were still lurking, damn them. Deep down and dormant, but still there. He had to get something out of the way before he could think about everything else. "Why did you go to the duchess for help?"

She looked up wide-eyed, and perhaps all her trembling wasn't from the chilly wind. "I couldn't think what else to do. I know the duchess doesn't like me, or our marriage, but I felt sure she wouldn't want a scandal. I did think she was going to help me, but then they locked me in!"

The demons whimpered and died. He held her closer and rubbed her arms. "We have to get you a cloak or something. I know a mantua-maker near here. . . ."

He tried to steer her down a side street, but she pulled back.

"What?"

"You can't go into a fashionable shop looking like that."

"The Earl of Saxonhurst can look any way he wishes."

She rolled her eyes. "Even if they know you well enough to recognize you, I thought we were evading the law."

"Damnation."

"Quite. There's probably a second-hand place somewhere around here. How much money do you have?"

With a sinking feeling, Sax patted the groom's pockets, grimacing when he came up empty. "I never carry money."

"You never . . ."

Her astonishment was almost funny, except that he was feeling like a damned fool. "You?"

She shook her head. "I've spent my last few pennies."

Suddenly, she looked terrified. Penniless. It didn't signal disaster to him, but it did to her, poor thing. He took off his jacket and wrapped it around her shoulders.

"Now you'll freeze to death," she said, but she huddled into it anyway. He could see her shivers, and he suspected they were as much from terror as cold.

"We can switch around from time to time. But what we really need is some safe quarters while we work out what to do. We could go to Iverton's."

They had paused on a corner where a wall offered a bit of shelter. The wind still cut through his shirt like blades of ice. Had he ever truly been cold before? He didn't think so. It was singularly unpleasant, and seemed likely to steal his ability to think clearly.

All around people hurried home to warm fires and waiting dinners. A chestnut seller wheeled by, pausing to sell a warm paperful to a cheerful couple. The aroma made Sax long for a few pennies to buy some, and frustration made him want to rage. Never before in his adult life had he not been able to satisfy his hunger. Never.

For anything.

Now he had three hungers—for warmth, for chestnuts and for the woman in his arms—and due to his folly, none was likely to be satisfied soon. Doubtless some would say it was good for his soul, that deprivation and discomfort would elevate his mind. It wasn't working. He was cold, miserable, frustrated, and angry.

Then, on a corner, a news-seller started a new cry, "Latest on the Saxonhurst murder! Latest! Countess's lover lies in his blood!"

"Oh, sweet lord!" Meg whispered. "He *wasn't*!"

"Your lover?" He crushed her into his arms. "I know."

She stared up. "How?"

Despite the cold, there was a sparkle of perfection to the moment. "How do we know spring will come?"

"You trust me?" Before he could say yes, she shook her head. "You shouldn't. You don't know—"

The demons tried to revive, but they were husks by now. He slid his hands under the coat, to rub her back, to feel the warmth. "I know about your magic stone."

She actually turned paler, foolish woman. "How?"

"I made Laura tell me why you'd gone to Sir Arthur's."

"Made? How?"

"Thumbscrews." He laughed. "Now it's time for you to trust me."

Tears swelled in her eyes. "I'm sorry. I trust you, too. I'm sorry. I'm just so scared. Cold and scared."

She stared to shiver again, and he held her closer, cursing his absurd powerlessness, wondering how cold a person had to be before they died of it. It happened sometimes to the outside passengers on a coach, and his groom's shirt, though of thick, warm cloth, seemed unable to block the cold at all.

He kissed her unruly hair. "Look, love, we have to find shelter of some kind, somewhere the authorities won't find us. I'd rather not put my friends under the obligation of hiding us, except as a last resort. Can you think of anywhere?"

"The workhouse?"

"I'm on the Board of Governors of one. Would that give us special entree?"

He was rewarded with a chuckle. "They'd separate us anyway, so we'd have no chance to make plans. We can't go to your home?"

"To *our* home? The law's hovering, and the mob has

gathered, hoping to see you and your bloodstained hands." He felt her trembling. "In my grandfather's day, the law would never have dared touch you, but I'm not sure I can stop them now. Damned democrats."

Cold, he was discovering, was invincible. It was devilishly tempting to ask for some time in the jacket. He wouldn't, but there wasn't much point in freezing to death, either. "Let's move. It'll keep us a bit warmer."

"Marlborough Square is probably too far anyway," she said as they marched on, huddled as close as two people could be. "You're very cold. If we keep switching the coat, it will slow things a bit, but we'll both soon be frozen. My feet already feel like blocks of ice."

He glanced down at her cloth half-boots. Foolish things. "My boots are doing a tolerable job, but I'm afraid there's no way for us to swap footwear. Strange predicament, isn't it?"

"Do they keep the prisons warm?"

He laughed. "I doubt it, or I'd be tempted, too! Do churches stand open for homeless waifs?"

"No."

"What happened to Christian charity? Here we are, looking for a bed for the night, and no one is even offering us a stable."

"Perhaps they would if I were pregnant."

"No. They'd be worried your baby would be a charge on the parish."

"True. Perhaps Christ would not consider us Christians at all these days. Oh!"

"What?"

She fumbled in her skirt pocket and pulled out a key. "Mallett Street!"

"That's a key to your old home?"

"Yes, and we're only streets away. Come on! And faster." She took his hand and tugged at him, showing that he must have begun to slow with the cold. "You'll be warmer if we hurry, and I left some wood there. We can make a fire."

That thought was enough to spur him on. Fire. Warmth. Shelter.

They stumbled along the darkening street, breath puffing white before them, then down a back lane, the rutted ground made rock hard by frost. She stopped and gingerly opened a gate. It squeaked. "I hope no one hears. They should all be preparing dinner, or eating it."

The idea of food, any kind of food, was almost painful. His teeth were chattering.

At the back door, she inserted the key, fumbling, probably because her hands were as icy as his. Then she turned the lock, opened the door, and dragged him in.

As she closed the door behind them, he slumped against a wall. "Thank God." Then he said, "It's as cold inside as out!"

"Of course. There's been no fire here for days." She turned and pressed herself to him, rubbing his arms. "Have you *never* been in an unwarmed house?"

"I don't think so. Warm me, Meg?"

Chapter 18

He didn't intend it to be flirtatious, but she turned coy and flustered. Lord knew, the last thing on his mind at the moment was sex. And that was a first, too.

Perhaps she realized it. She shook her head, probably at herself. "Come on then." She pulled him down a corridor to the front hall of the house, then upstairs.

He couldn't imagine that it would be warmer on the upper floors, but he followed, rubbing himself and astonished by how very cold it could be inside a building. The only improvement was escape from the wind.

She went into a bedroom and stripped an eiderdown off the bed. "Here."

He snatched it and wrapped it around his shoulders. Not instant warmth, but better. Better. She dragged a woolen blanket off the bed, and huddled into it herself, then went to the next room where she repeated the process.

Now they each had a fluffy eiderdown and a blanket, and he was beginning to think he might be human again in time. A few feathers escaped and fluttered to the floor. These coverings were old and worn, but never had anything seemed more precious.

"Better?" she asked anxiously.

"Much. But my breath's still puffing in here."

"Let's go to the kitchen and see if the wood's still there. With a fire we can even boil water."

As he followed her, he said, "Brandy would help."

She paused to cast him a look.

He sighed. He supposed it was too much to expect.

In the kitchen she went straight to a box near the old-fashioned stove. "Yes. There's wood still here. The tinderbox should be in that drawer, there."

He found it. "I'll do this." He prayed he was able. He had struck a light for himself a time or two. He'd never built a fire. He checked that there was tinder in the box, pondering the fact that he'd only ever used a tinderbox as a boy in play. Fire was something he took for granted.

Like everything else.

He watched Meg competently layer twigs and pieces of almost shredded wood with larger sticks. No logs here, brought in from the estate. In fact, no proper firewood. Ends of planks, broken branches, even a piece of a chair leg.

Scavenger's wood.

He hadn't realized just what straits she and her family had been in. He'd had no idea what poverty truly meant. Perhaps he still didn't, but he was learning.

She glanced over at him. "Time to start a light."

It suddenly seemed the most important feat possible, to be able to create fire. He knelt by the grate and flicked flint against steel, clumsy because of the cold, and because of wretched inexperience.

Sparks flew, but feebly, and the tinder wouldn't catch.

"Perhaps I should do away with my servants and learn to cope for myself."

"They'd hate that."

He smiled at her. "True."

Determined to prove he could do something useful, he flicked harder and harder. At last, a spark caught and the tinder flared. Hastily, before it could burn out, he put the flame to her smallest pieces of wood and watched with delight as the fire caught.

It was good, dry wood, and the flame crackled through, bringing light and heat. Not significant heat yet, but it warmed and brightened his heart. He leaned forward and kissed her firmly on her parted lips.

She accepted it as it was meant, smiling brilliantly at their improved circumstances.

They both stayed there, feeding wood to the fire, holding out hands to the fledgling warmth as heat danced on their cheeks. Eventually, he rose, bringing her to her feet with him, sensual thoughts stirring. Oh yes, he was recovering fast.

She, however, pulled away. "I think we left some vegetables. Why don't you check the larder over there? We only threw out the things that would rot. It seemed wrong to waste food."

He wondered wryly about just how much food was wasted in his household every day. He also noted that she had not pulled away from him in coyness, but simply because she had her mind on practical matters.

Sensible Meg.

Silly Meg.

He rather thought they'd have to spend the night here. If so, he had plans. What better way to keep warm?

Obediently, however, he hunted through the larder, keen on the idea of food of any sort. Soon he was aware again of the extent of their poverty. Perhaps they'd had plenty of milk, butter, fruit, and other such perishable food, but he doubted it. All he came up with was a small sack of dried peas, an inch of oats in the bottom of a crock, and some bunches of dry green-gray plants that were doubtless herbs. A box contained some salt, and a shaker some pepper. In a screw of blue paper, he found a small nugget of sugar.

As he put the sorry collection on the plain wooden table, he wondered if this had really been all that stood between a family of five and starvation.

He looked up to see her watching him, looking rather stiff. "We bought food day by day."

"Of course." With the few coins she had. He remembered the twins' enthusiasm for food. He'd known they were getting treats, and had been delighted to provide them, but he'd not understood.

Not at all.

"No vegetables?" he said, noting her empty hands.

"I'm afraid not. I was hoping to make soup. . . ." She went to feed the dying fire a few more pieces of wood. "The wood won't last for long. What are we to do?"

So the wood wouldn't have lasted them long when she'd left for their wedding. And she'd almost turned back in the church.

Why?

Surely she must have been desperate enough to accept almost any aid.

Though his monsters were dead, he had to wonder

what a woman in these dire straits would do to save herself and her loved ones. However, he no longer minded, even if she had been the dragon's tool.

He understood.

And he trusted her now.

He even smiled. If that was the way of it, it would be quite a pleasant twist on the duchess's plan, to take her scheme and make a good marriage out of it.

"Do?" he said. "I think we might as well stay here for the night. With any luck, by morning Owain will have sorted everything out."

"And if he hasn't?"

"Cross each bridge as we come to it."

She came over to the table and poked at his collection. "I could cook the peas, but they'll take hours to soften, and they won't make exciting eating. There's always porridge, but that takes time, too—"

"We need to go to bed."

Her eyes flicked up, startled. Wary.

"Think, Meg. In a bed together, with lots of covers, we can stay warm until morning. We can talk there as well as here, and decide what's best to do."

"Talk?"

The table divided them. "Or other things. If you want."

"I don't."

"Don't you?"

Her steady gaze flickered away, brightening his hopes. "We should keep our minds on the problems."

"All night?"

"Or sleep." She looked back at him, but it was no longer steady, and in the dying light of the fire, he thought he saw a blush.

"I won't do more than you want, Meg." How to persuade her to want it? "Look at it another way. If we can't think of anything else, we may have to surrender you to the law. This might be our last chance for a while."

She bit her lip.

"I'm sorry if that frightens you, but it's the truth. I'm used to thinking myself a pretty omnipotent fellow, but

I can't perform miracles. I will, however, keep you from the noose."

She put her hand to her throat, and he went quickly to hold her. "Stop it, silly."

"But I was there!" She clutched him to her. "It could be made to look bad. I saw that when the duchess was questioning me. My story sounds so strange!"

"You're still the Countess of Saxonhurst. That means a lot."

She looked up at that, chin firm. "It shouldn't. Justice should be fair for Meg Gillingham as well."

"One battle at a time. Bed?"

After a moment, she said, "Very well." But at the door, she stopped dead. He thought she was balking, but she turned and ran back to the big Dutch sideboard, set with plates and dishes.

She pulled over a chair and stood on it, reaching up to the very top, letting her covers fall away. He hurried over. "What is it? Don't fall."

She seized a big, earthenware pot and clutched it to her. He steadied the chair as she clambered down.

"I just remembered!" she declared, eyes bright.

He gathered her eiderdown, and put it around her shoulders again. "What? More magic?"

She didn't take offense. "Almost as good!" She raised the lid and taking out a cloth-wrapped bundle, she peeled back the cloth to reveal a brown lump.

"What is it?" he asked, extremely dubiously.

"It's Christmas pudding, of course! My mother made one in the summer, so we had a little bit of traditional Christmas. And since we wouldn't have a Twelfth Night cake, I saved this for then. It's not Twelfth Night, but I think our need is greater than tradition." She broke off a piece and popped it in his mouth.

He accepted it warily. Christmas pudding always came hot and soaked in flaming brandy. This was cold, solid, and had an unpleasant fatty film to it. But a moment later, the sweetness of raisins burst in his hungry mouth, and he could cheerfully have grabbed it all.

She broke a small piece for herself, but paused. "You're supposed to make a wish."

"I thought that was when stirring the pudding."

"Do you still do that? Stir the pudding?"

"Of course. Cook makes it, then we all tramp through the kitchen in order of rank to give it a stir and make our wish."

"And what did you wish for this year?"

"I don't remember. This was back in August. A good pudding has to stand."

"True."

He saw her sadness at memories and wanted to gather her into his arms, but instinct said this wasn't the moment. "Do you remember your wish."

"I wasn't here. I was at the Ramillys'."

"But your family makes a wish when eating it, too? What was that?"

"I only had one wish then. A wish for help."

"For me."

She smiled and looked down. "I didn't even know to dream of you then."

He took the piece of the pudding and put it to her lips. "What are you wishing for now?"

"We're not supposed to tell." But after a moment, she said, "I'm going to wish that when this nightmare is over, I'll be the countess you deserve." She took the piece of pudding.

"You're already more than I deserve."

She laughed and shook her head, then put a piece to his lips. "So, what is your wish?"

He chewed and swallowed. "That you come and enjoy pudding in bed with me."

And she blushed, showing she knew the other meaning of pudding. His magical, perfect wife.

Meg clutched her blanket and eiderdown around her, feeling like a ship on the waves again, with a gale building. She didn't know what to say. Something swirled in her that longed for what he offered. "It would be warmer in bed," she offered as a halfway step.

"True."

She led the way back upstairs on weakening legs, aware, aware of him following, and not only by the flickering light of the candle he carried.

She'd never been in such a tangle of emotions in her life. Fear of the law lay in her like cold stone, and his

confidence only chipped at the surface of it. Though she
and her family had always been respectable and law-
abiding, she knew that the legal system could be a
monster.

Wrapped around that fear was guilt. He still didn't
realize that this was all her fault. He was cold and hungry because of her use of the *sheelagh*. Sir Arthur was
probably dead from the same cause.

Could she honestly let him make love to her in
ignorance?

A silly problem, but still there, was a feeling that a
marriage should not be consummated in an abandoned
house with everything so perilously unsettled around
them.

It felt illicit.

Forbidden.

When she thought about which bed to use, she considered briefly her parents' big bed. But that was unthink-
able. It would have to be the smaller one she and Laura
had shared. In her mind, however, that bed was as virginal as an altar, and despite their marriage vows, she
felt as if she was contemplating a terrible sin.

And she was contemplating it. Over all her fear, anxiety, and guilt ran a feverish hum that she recognized
as desire.

She paused at her bedroom door, facing the wood. "I
did say that I wouldn't, as long as you weren't reconciled
with your grandmother."

He leaned against her back, wrapping his eiderdown
around them both, like fluffy angel wings. "Do you still
feel like that?"

Mouth dry, she whispered, "I should. She's just an old
woman. A cold one, but not worthy of hate."

He rested his head against hers. Just rested it there.
"I can't talk about it now, Meg, but I can't change either. Ever. It is your decision."

Meg tested that moral outrage. It had gone, perhaps
because of her encounter with the duchess, who was certainly not a kind woman. Perhaps simply through cold,
fear, and need. "It doesn't matter," she said.

He kissed her neck, startlingly warm against the chill
there. "Oh, it matters, lovely one, but not in this." He

pushed open the room and steered her in. "Your room?"

She nodded, seeing it with his eyes. The plain iron bed had only a white sheet over it since they'd taken the blanket and eiderdown. No carpet here. Just homemade knotted rugs. The wall mirror was marred by fly-specks.

"It's not very grand," she said.

He turned to her, eyes sparkling in that way they had. "It's a rake's fantasy! To seduce a blushing maiden in her virginal bower."

Meg felt as if the gates of hell were opening before her. "That's what I'm afraid of."

"What?"

"That it will feel sinful. In fact, it does. Anyway"—she found the strength to step away from him—"we need to talk about what to do."

"Of course." He didn't look at all daunted. He looked like a predatory rake on close trail of his quarry. "It has to be in bed, however, if we're to keep warm enough to think."

She knew that almost certainly spelled defeat, and yet anything else would be idiocy. And desire was seething in her, fighting all the time with her well-honed conscience, and her floundering common sense.

You're married, said desire.

Wait, wait, cried conscience.

This isn't wise! warned common sense.

She looked between her bed and her probable ravisher, dizzied by a sensation frightening close to the panicky weakness that came from the *sheelagh.*

Magic.

Pagan magic.

Oh yes.

Pagan fire.

"Oh."

"Oh?" he queried. When she didn't explain the unexplainable, he said, "May I ask you to play servant? I have no idea how to get out of my boots without help."

Everything fell back to earth. Desire didn't flee, but it was normal now. And he was just a man. A special man, but a man. A nobleman. A pampered, self-indulgent nobleman who couldn't get out of his own boots. She was suddenly very, very fond of him.

"You, my lord earl, are as helpless as a babe without your devoted minions." She put her hand on his chest and pushed. Obligingly, he fell into the chair behind him.

"I admit it. Except in one thing. There's one thing I always do for myself."

Glossily confident. She remembered when that had seemed a fault. "We are getting into bed to keep *warm*. Once there, we are going to talk about my perilous situation."

"Yes, ma'am."

With a shake of her head, she shed her covers, raised his foot, and struggled with his boot. There was almost no ease around the ankle, and she could hardly move them. "Fashionable folly!" she gasped after a while. "You'll have to keep them on."

"And you're only a countess, not a duchess."

"What?" She knew it was something risqué, though. A wicked corner to his mouth told her so.

"I'll explain later, when you're not so innocent."

Her face heated, but she met his eyes as she gathered her covers around herself again. "Talk, remember."

It was a contest this, a hunt. She would put up a good fight, even if she expected to lose in the end. "How can you even think of such things when my neck might be in danger!"

"Imminent death tends to focus the mind on life's essentials."

"Like food. My stomach's growling."

"I'm hungry, too."

Sax watched to see what she'd do with that hot chestnut, but the wise woman knew when to ignore temptation. He hoped she wasn't too good at it.

He stuck his foot out again, eyeing his intractable boot. "I assume you've never shared a bed with a man in boots."

"I've never—"

"Quite. No offense intended. Nor have I, of course, but I imagine it will be dashed uncomfortable. I gather I'm a restless sleeper."

"Then you'll have to sleep in another bed." A gleam

in her eye showed that she recognized a powerful move in their game.

"We won't be able to share our warmth that way," he countered, standing up. "We'll just have to hope you have tough shins, duchess."

She put a hand on his chest to stop him. Did she recognize how easy she was about touching him? What it meant? "Explain this matter of duchesses to me."

"Later."

At that innocent word, her color rose.

Loving the feel of her hand, even through the eiderdown, he said, "I'll give you a hint. Duchess of Marlborough."

She pondered it. "Blenheim and such?"

"Right. The famous duke, rushing home victorious from battle. I'll take you to Blenheim one day, and perhaps I'll duchess you there. If we ever progress beyond innocent."

With a glare—but a laughing one—she shoved him back into his chair so hard that it teetered backward.

"How does your valet get your boots off?"

"He doesn't. I have a boot boy specifically for that task."

"*That's* a full-time job?"

"I change them three or four times a day," he said meekly. "And he cleans them."

With a roll of the eyes, she asked, "So, how does he get them off?"

"He straddles my leg with his back to me. It seems to give a better angle."

She eyed him suspiciously, but then shed her covers and swung her leg over his ankle. Raising his foot, she took a strong grip on the heel of his right boot. Her skirts were raised a bit, giving a glimpse of trim ankles and shapely calves. Her right stocking had a very neat darn above the heel.

Darns could be astonishingly erotic.

Her bottom seemed presented to him, emphasized by the fact that she was bent forward a little. Smiling, he raised his booted left foot and placed it there.

She dropped his foot and straightened, twisting to glare at him.

"I'm just bracing you. I always do that with Crab."

"I warn you, Saxonhurst"—she actually waggled her finger at him like a stern governess—"when we get home, I'm going to interrogate your boot boy, and if his tale doesn't accord with yours, there will be dire consequences."

"My dear countess, you make me regret that I'm telling the honest truth."

"Oh, you're impossible!"

"Impossible to resist?"

"No." She turned back, seized his ankle and began to force his boot off. When he returned his foot to her back, she only twitched.

Would she successfully resist? Devil take it, he hoped not. He was already hard and being delightfully stimulated by the sight of her bottom wriggling as she worked. Even the movements felt by his left foot as she pushed back against it seemed to travel up his leg like flames.

And to think he went through this sometimes four or five times a day, and found it only a bore. Crab, however, was a sinewy man in his forties, not a luscious lady who happened to be his virgin wife.

With a huff, she hauled off his boot and tossed it to the floor. Blowing a stray tendril of hair off her rosy face, she moved to straddle his left leg.

"You look wonderfully warm," he remarked, putting his liberated stockinged foot on her back.

"Then if you're cold, you can do some energetic work."

"But my dear, that's exactly what I have in mind."

He knew she was rolling her eyes as she ferociously attacked his other boot.

For his part, he was almost purring at the more subtle feel of her through only wool and her layers of clothing. He curled his toes against the base of her spine and flexed his heel into the cleft that led down between her legs.

She wriggled in a way that had nothing to do with pulling off his boot. When she pulled up on his heel even more strongly, he let his leg rise between hers.

She stiffened and went still.

"Go on," he said softly. It was a risky move with a

virgin, but he didn't think his countess was any ordinary sort of virgin.

Proving him right, she tugged on his heel as strongly as before, as if each tug didn't jerk his leg against her. When it was off, however, she would have moved away if he hadn't seized her waist and drawn her back onto his knees.

"We should get into bed," she said breathlessly. Her cheeks were rosy red, with exertion he was sure, but with other things, too.

"Oh quite," he murmured by her ear, "but you still have your shoes on. Hold the eiderdown."

When she was clutching the cover down around them both, he raised her left leg in such a way that her skirts fell back, exposing the whole of her white stocking up to a racy garter worked in red and black. He wondered if she would resist that being seen, that small symbol of her inner wickedness, but she stayed passive in his hands.

Testing her, seeing what she would permit and when she would rebel, was the best amorous fun he could remember. Because she would rebel if she wanted to. He knew that. He loved that. He adored his unpredictable, strong-minded bride.

He untied her half boot, noting that the lace was frayed and that the boots were almost worn through.

"I'll have to give Susie a bonus."

She didn't move. "Why?"

"Because everything about my wife delights me."

She turned her head then. "Everything? I've turned your life into mayhem."

"At this moment, I am as happy as I can ever remember being."

She blushed. "I, on the other hand, am cold."

He tugged off her flimsy boot, and rubbed her toes. "You're icy!"

"I try not to lie."

That came close to significant issues, but he had no intention of getting into those until he'd dealt with other, more important matters. He let her leg lower, sliding it through his hands. It was tempting to run his hands on up to her bare thigh, up to where they desperately wanted to be, but she *was* cold, and he wasn't a fool.

He raised her other leg and completed the process quickly, then stood, setting her on her feet. "Do you want to take off any other clothes?"

She flashed him a surprised glance—had she really thought he'd try to strip her?—then shed his groom's heavy jacket. "If I take off any more, it'll be under the covers." She flung her blanket and eiderdown over the bed, then scrambled into it.

He thought for a moment of taking off his breeches, but then threw conventionality to the wind and rushed to join her, only stopping to spread his covers over, and roughly tuck them in.

Chapter 19

The bed was cold.

"Who the devil did I think had run a bedwarmer through it?"

She chuckled, scuttling closer. "Fairies, perhaps? It will warm quickly with our own heat."

He pulled her into his arms, as much to share warmth as from any other motive. After a tense moment, she settled there, head on his chest, arm around him. He was struck almost to tears by the perfection of the simple moment, here in a lumpy bed, fully dressed, and still chilly.

What on earth was happening to him?

"We've forgotten to extinguish the candle," she said.

"Toss you for who gets out to deal with it."

"No money, remember."

"Perdition." But it was all in teasing. "The candle's in a solid holder. It should be safe. And I like the light. I like to be able to see you."

"If it wasn't for needing to breathe, there'd be none of me to see." True. Only the top of her head stuck out. "That stub won't last for long, anyway."

He had a taste for making love in the light, but he wouldn't rush for that reason. Meg would be just as sweet in the dark.

"Warmer?" he asked.

"A bit. My feet are still cold."

He shifted slightly. "Put them between my thighs."

"What?"

"It'll be nice and warm there." It certainly felt it.

After a moment, she wriggled away slightly and brought her knees up. Then he felt her even through his breeches. "Christ!" But he trapped her there with hand and thighs. "I hope ice can't do me permanent damage."

She giggled, but still tried to escape.

"Stay. It's all right." He rubbed her calves. When she seemed warmer, he circled an ankle and guided a foot out and along the swell of his erection. "Cold is supposed to soften a man's ardor. I now have scientific proof that cold feet do not have the same effect."

Curious as to when, if, she would balk, he undid his buttons and slid her chilly toes inside. Through just the cotton of his drawers, he teased himself with her.

She had her head tucked down and he couldn't see her expression at all.

"Warmer?" he asked again.

"Yes, thank you."

It was so demure, he wanted to eat her.

After a while, he worked her toes through the split in his drawers so she came at last against his flesh. Still slightly chilly. Fascinating.

Her breathing had changed. He registered that, and the fact that she still wasn't resisting.

He was.

He couldn't quite understand what was happening here, and he loved that. His life had become far too predictable. Now, he was hard and ready for a woman, but he wasn't quite ready yet for Meg. For his first time with Meg.

He realized with astonishment, and with a hint of disquiet, that he had never in his life lain with a woman whom he really cared about. Oh, he cared about his bedpartners in a general way. It seemed only courteous. He tried to make sure that they found in the encounter whatever they sought there.

He had never before felt this almost frightening need to have it be right, be perfect, for an unpredictable, vulnerable, inexperienced lover.

He slid her away from his skin, rubbing her toes. "Better?"

As if she knew how he was reacting, she straightened her legs and settled back against him.

"The bed is warmer, isn't it?" he said. Parts of him felt almost feverish.

"Yes. For the last little while, Rachel had been sleeping in here with Laura and me. For the warmth. And Richard in with Jeremy. I do want to thank you for rescuing us. I think you can see that we were in a bad way."

He rubbed gently at her back. "I feel blessed to have been given the chance. Is that why you seem so relaxed to be here with me, because you're used to sleeping with your sisters?"

She tilted her head up at last, looking at him thoughtfully. "Perhaps it's just that I'm comfortable with you."

"Even though I'm going to try to seduce you?"

She didn't balk. "Yes. Because you won't do anything I don't want."

He kissed her for her honesty. And for her trust. He still wasn't ready for the momentous step, but he desperately wanted to kiss her. How rare it was, he realized almost with a groan, for him to kiss a woman simply because he wanted to honor and enjoy her.

He wanted to kiss Meg for a long, long time.

She moved into him, in subtle ways growing closer, and then her hand touched his nape, his hair, and he decided this lumpy bed in this frigid house was heaven.

In time, however, his restless hand on her body found a hard edge and he drew back. "I forgot your corset. You can't be comfortable like that."

Her look showed that she thought it was a hunter's move, but she said, "I'd rather be out of it, but not at the cost of leaving this warm spot."

"Let's see what we can do under the covers."

He turned her, and she moved as he directed, trustingly. By feel, he undid the buttons down the back of her gown, finding her stay laces beneath. The knot alone would make her uncomfortable. "Do they hook at the front, or is there just the laces?"

"Just the laces, I'm afraid."

He worked the double bow loose, astonished at how patient he felt, how content with the leisurely pace of this. Despite an almost painfully urgent lust, he was enjoying loosening his wife's stays, brushing against her relaxed body, and breathing her warm, simple smell.

He was quite familiar with the way a man's mind

could split itself between his cock and the rest of the universe, but he'd never before had the balance tilt so sharply the other way. For the moment at least, the sweet presence of Meg in the bed, the way her unkempt hair was escaping to straggle down her back, the feel of her spine behind the awkward laces, was enough to sate her appetite.

"Do you want to take your dress off?" he asked.

"No."

No explanation, but he understood. It was part warmth, part armor. Perhaps it was even her hidden underwear. He remembered wanting to strip her slowly in the light of many candles, and to find every one of her secrets. He still did, but all the competitive edge had melted out of it.

So he undid the knot, and worked the laces very loose so that the bones would not dig at her. Her simple gown had a drawstring at the high waist, so he loosened that, too.

Then he couldn't resist sliding his hand under the stiff corset and forward over the cotton of her shift to cup a breast.

The soft weight and heat of a woman's breast. One of the most perfect objects in the world. He rested his head in the curve of her neck, in warm skin and ticklish hair, and surrendered to the wonder of his wife's left breast.

Eventually, she turned. Turned within his arms to look up at him. He wondered just what she saw. He didn't care.

"We have to talk," she said. "But not yet."

Then Meg almost wished her words unsaid. He looked so raw. No, that wasn't the right word. Unguarded. Vulnerable.

Wondrous.

More dangerous by far than the glossy, skillful hunter.

"I'm certainly incapable of being coherent," he said. "Is it warm enough . . . ? No."

"No what?"

"You don't want to take your gown off."

And she didn't. She wasn't sure why, because the bed

was warming, and she'd be more comfortable. And she was under the covers. But she didn't.

"Will that make it difficult?"

"No, duchess."

He wasn't that much changed, and getting glossier by the moment. "Tell me about the Duchess of Marlborough."

"Later. I want my breeches off, though. Take them off for me?"

She could see that he expected her to refuse. Perhaps that was why she didn't. Surprised at how little embarrassment she felt, Meg worked her hands down his firm body until she found his buttons. They were undone, which reminded her of what he'd done before, and a touch of embarrassment did flare in her, along with a great deal of another kind of heat. Her hand brushed his manly parts. How extraordinarily hard he was.

She felt her own body twitch in recognition.

Clearly, bodies had their own knowledge, and, of course he'd taught her body some of what to expect.

She swallowed a temptation to beg him to be quicker about this, to take her sooner to that magical place.

Instead, head lowered so he couldn't see her expression, she unfastened the waistband and began to work his breeches down over his hips. He raised himself, but otherwise did nothing to help. Eventually, she couldn't reach any farther.

In a spirit of mischief, she plunged under the covers to wriggle them all the way down and off his feet. She'd played undercover games as a child, deep down under the covers in the mysterious world of bed. Though she was much bigger now and thus the bed seemed smaller, she felt the same kind of mystery. The same sense of being in another, dark and mysterious world.

The dark, mysterious world of Sax and sex and marriage.

She worked back up his muscular legs, beginning to gasp for lack of air, and unfastened his drawers.

His male part sprang free, brushing against her cheek.

She shot out from under the covers and sucked in fresh, icy air.

His eyes were bright with amusement and a hundred

other things. "Fun down there, is it?" he said, and dove under the covers.

Meg lay there, head in ice, body in fire, as he found her ankles then worked up—under her skirts!—to untie her garters.

Far too late she remembered that her garters were vividly embroidered. Then she couldn't think why it should matter.

He was pushing her skirts up higher.

Oh dear.

She felt his hands find the frilly edge of her wicked drawers. Was that a growl she heard? Despite the icy air, her cheeks were burning. A hand worked between her thighs, and a finger, one long finger, investigated the split between the two halves of her daring underwear. It slid in, and a jolt made her actually bounce in the bed.

A chuckle. That was definitely a chuckle.

Then he was back down and stripping off her stockings.

He struggled up and out, flushed, disheveled, bearing her old white stockings and her gaudy garters like battle trophies.

Without thinking, she dove down to mirror the performance on him, untying his garters, and peeling down his stockings of fine wool. On the way back up, she hesitated. . . .

Then she found the long hard shape—so very hard, yet smooth like silk velvet, and hot. Very hot.

It was close to her face, and before she'd had time to be logical, to even think of anything as absurd as propriety, she laid it against her cheek as she wanted to, sliding her skin up and down his, smelling a musty, spicy odor that was frighteningly personal and wickedly delicious.

A touch of moisture startled her. Hands grasped beneath her arms and hauled her up into the light.

"Not that I mind," he said unsteadily, "but I was afraid you'd suffocate."

She kissed him then because his darkened eyes called for it, dimly wondering just where sensible, staid Meg Gillingham had vanished to.

He was touching her between her thighs again, bringing that jolt. And more.

Mouth still blended with hers, he rolled over her, pushed up her skirts, and settled between her legs.

She spread them, but when their lips parted for air, she gasped, "My drawers?"

"Are wonderful."

And she felt him part the soft cotton and slide between. Felt him against her. That hard shape. He stroked her with himself, and she felt moisture again.

Hers.

His.

She felt more.

She closed her eyes and lingered on wondrous sensations. His silky hardness stroking places where she seemed so very sensitive, so very wanting.

She was a good girl, a good woman. Except for the necessary brief touches of cleaning, she had obeyed instructions not to touch herself. She'd felt things, but had ignored them as improper.

Where had proper Meg Gillingham gone?

With a laugh, she remembered the *sheelagh,* and how it had made her feel. Like this, in a way. Tingling everywhere. Aching and throbbing, especially down where he touched.

He kissed an eyelid and she opened her eyes, startled.

"Like it?" he asked.

"Enormously."

Delight flashed in his eyes. "Good."

He let himself rest there, hard against her, and used one hand to work down her loosened bodice and stays to expose her breasts to the chilly air. She didn't mind. She was overheated anyway.

Sweet memories of the time he'd put his mouth to her breasts sent a little shiver through her.

"You truly are the most delightful creature," he whispered against her skin and gently suckled first one breast then the other. "Do you think Susie would like rubies, emeralds, or diamonds?"

"Tankards and pots," Meg said unsteadily. Would it be completely outrageous to beg him to go faster?

"Tush, tush. How can you be so prosaic at a time like this. Which do you prefer, my lovely wife? Rubies, emeralds, or diamonds?"

As his lips settled to delighting her again, she said, "I don't know. I don't care. . . ."

"Well?" he asked after a dizzy while.

"Well, what?" Nothing seemed important except her own astonishing body.

"Jewels."

"Surprise me."

And he laughed, shifted, and guiding himself with one hand, pushed into her.

She held her breath. She only realized that when she gasped at the pain. For the first time she wondered at the inconvenient design of woman. Head nestled against her neck, he lifted and spread her, then conquered her.

Meg lay frozen, impaled.

He shifted again, rising up on his arms to look at her.

Answering an unspoken concern, she whispered, "It's all right." She smiled for him, raising a hand to touch his cheek, and the smile became true. "It's all right," she repeated, strongly.

He turned his head to kiss her hand, and began to move, still reared above her, watching her, something more than a smile in his intent face.

And she watched him, mind split between sight—how wonderful he looked when not glossy at all—and sensation down below—the powerful joining, and a stirring desire similar to what he had done before, similar to the *sheelagh*.

Yet different.

Wonderful.

He didn't speak and nor did she. She suspected he could tell how she felt. Certainly, concealing anything was the last thing on her mind. She spoke with her hands, perhaps, restlessly rubbing them up and down his taut arms.

She did recognize, however, with a part of her mind that stayed crystal clear, that this was the power of sex, the danger of it, this complete openness of body and mind, one to the other.

And that more was needed.

She was supposed to surrender herself. To let go of even that last, fragile bit of reason, the bit that still watched and thought.

And she couldn't.

It was too like the *sheelagh,* like death.

She bit her lip, tensing, fighting even, staring into his eyes as if he were an opponent.

"Let it," he whispered, and she suddenly realized that he was hovering desperately in the same dangerous place, holding back only for her. "Trust me, Meg. Let go. Come with me. . . ."

So she closed her eyes and fell, tumbled down and down with him, whirling together like straw figures in an ecstatic hurricane. . . .

Back down to the lumpy, oven-hot bed.

He rolled to his side, still in her, arms tight, then kissed her in a way she had never imagined being kissed, a continuation of the bonding of that perilous wonder.

Eventually, she had to break free. "Believe it or not, I'm too hot!"

And they laughed together as they wrestled her out of her outer clothing, stripping her down to her shift. When he would have thrown them out onto the floor, however, she seized them and tucked them between blanket and eiderdown. "They'll be warm in the morning," she explained.

"My, the things I don't know." And he leaned out of the bed enough to grasp his clothing and pop it under the covers.

Then, he in his shirt, she in shift and drawers, they cuddled together beneath the mound of covers, and kissed each other to sleep.

"I did what you wanted. As always."

The Dowager Duchess of Daingerfield glared at the big man in front of her. He was useful. He was dangerous. "I wanted the chit behind bars."

He leaned insolently against the fireplace. "If we'd been lucky, the mob would've grabbed her, and that would have been that. Didn't think she'd be so nippy. The law'll find her sooner or later, Duchess. Dead or alive. Likely dead. It's bloody perishing out there, and you said she didn't have a cloak."

"Don't use coarse language in my presence, Stafford."

He just grinned. " 'Course," he added, "it would have been better if you'd kept her here once you had her."

Fifteen years. Fifteen years she'd put up with this man because she couldn't have him speak of certain things. And because he was clever, clever enough not to be intolerable.

"She had help to escape here, Stafford. Who?"

"Best I can tell, a potboy took a note for her to the earl's house. The boy's disappeared. The earl probably sent a servant to get her out, but she's not gone back there. I've had people watching the house since before she slipped your leash."

"If you hadn't acted on impulse, we would have been better prepared!"

He shrugged. "You sent me there to find out what I could. Was I supposed to miss a chance like that? Her in the house without an escort? Him tupping that silly little maid. It was perfect."

"Not unless she's caught."

"Or freezes to death. Or flees the country."

"No, not that! Saxonhurst must be *free* of her." She thumped at her knee, then winced as her gnarled hand complained. How had she grown old? How dare her body betray her? "He must be free to marry Daphne. I will have my plan."

"And there's Lady Daphne run off, too," he said in spurious sympathy. "Losing your touch, Your Grace?"

"One day, Stafford, you will push me too far." He just quirked a brow, so she added, "I could turn you in for this murder."

"And lose your chance at the earl's bride?"

Anger was building in her, like a flow of fire, but she didn't let it loose. Her doctors had warned her against it, and she had to live. Had to live to see her plan work. Had to win Helen back.

"Could Saxonhurst get his wife off at a trial?" she asked.

"It'd be touch and go. After a talk with me, the servants are convinced she did it. They even remember blood on her hands. The housekeeper's sure I didn't have time to kill them. She doesn't realize how quick and easy it can be. And anyway, Hattie's not about to tell the world what we were up to, is she? She'll even say that she heard screams back before the countess left the house. People come to believe what they're told to believe, Duchess, especially if it suits them."

"Some people do." Her damnable, intractable grandson hadn't. How could she have imagined such a pale, sad child would fight so hard, resist so adamantly?

He was like her.

It came to her now and then these days, in the sleepless nights that seemed all she had, that she might have made a wrong move somewhere.

"So," she demanded, pushing weakness aside, "where is she? None of this will do me any good if she can't be found and hanged! She has family, doesn't she?"

"Two sisters, two brothers."

"Ages?"

"A brother and sister are young. The sister's about sixteen. Pretty thing, too. According to Hattie, old Sir Arthur had his eyes on her, the miserable lecher. The brother's a bit older. Goes to a tutor every day."

"They might know where she is."

"They might, but they're not likely to tell, are they?"

"There are ways." She glared up at the man. "Never threaten directly. Threaten something they love. What do they love?"

"Their sister, likely. Look, Duchess, be patient. We won't get our hands on the young ones now. They won't be going anywhere these days without an army of servants—"

"I don't have time to be patient. I want it now!"

She choked back other words, hearing how childish she sounded. She'd seen other old people become like peevish children. She wouldn't. She *wouldn't*. She was the Dowager Duchess of Daingerfield. All her life, she'd had her way. Nearly all her life . . .

She would have her plan!

She shouldn't have waited the five years, but she'd had his promise, so she'd been sure of success in the end. Sweet success, gained through his feckless inattention to details.

She shouldn't have waited ten years the other time, either. She should have acted immediately, but she'd hoped. She'd hoped her daughter would realize her folly on her own.

Damn the Torrances and their evil charm. Bewitched her, he had. Stolen her daughter. He deserved to die. But not—

"Find her," she commanded. "Kill her." She wouldn't delay this time. She was old, and panicked urgency beat in her like a drum. "Did you hear me?" Why was he looking at her like that? He was nothing. A hired ruffian she'd had to keep around.

"You're an old woman, Duchess. Perhaps your reign has ended."

"How dare you!" The fires started licking in her again. Anger. Dangerous anger. "You're scum, Stafford. Gallows bait."

"Then you want me to go? Tell the world about our long association . . ."

"You wouldn't dare!"

He grinned. "Wouldn't I? Truth is, Duchess, you're on your last legs, and a man has to look to his future. I'm thinking the little Countess of Saxonhurst might offer a better future. So I will find her. Whether I kill her or not, though, that depends."

"I'll see you out," she snarled. "I'll see you hang! I'm the Duchess of Daingerfield, damn your black heart. . . ." What was that sneering threat in his eyes? What was building in her? She fumbled for her golden bell.

He calmly moved it out of reach.

Chapter 20

The twins had gone to bed, but Laura and Jeremy were still up, waiting desperately for word of Meg. Laura looked over to where her brother sat reading, wishing she could concentrate enough to disappear into a book. Instead, she was playing Casino with Lady Daphne.

In silence.

At least Lady Daphne was someone who knew when everything possible had been said. She'd spoken more earlier, however, and Laura did feel sorry for her. Though Daphne was too polite to say much about her personal affairs, it was clear that her home life had not been pleasant, and that the duchess was a tyrant. It was clear, too, that Daphne was one of those people who was deeply unhappy without any idea of how to break the pattern of her life.

Laura played her last card, gathered the ones on the table, and tallied up her score. As Daphne began to deal the next hand, Laura wondered if something could be done for her. Though she was thin and pale, perhaps she would plump up a little if less put upon. Her skin was excellent, her features even, and her pale blond hair could be pretty if styled.

She played a card. Back before her parents' deaths, the Gillingham household had been a healing place. People had enjoyed it and seemed cheered by it. Perhaps the remaining Gillinghams could create the same magic for Daphne.

And Saxonhurst. Laura adored her brother-in-law, but she didn't think he was truly happy. Look at that silly business of smashing things in his room. She'd had the whole story from the servants, who seemed to think it just an amusing foible.

It didn't amuse her.

It worried her. It needed dealing with.

If, that was, Meg came home safe, and this ghastly business about Sir Arthur's death was sorted out. She glanced at the mantel clock. Nearly ten, and no news.

The door opened, and they all looked up. It was only Pringle, but he was bearing his heavy silver platter with a note upon it. Brak pushed in behind and went whining to Jeremy.

"What's the matter with the dog?" Jeremy asked.

The butler just shrugged. "The animal is often distressed if his lordship is absent for any length of time." He presented his tray to Lady Daphne.

"For me?" She dropped her cards, some spilling onto the floor, and grabbed the folded, sealed paper.

"From Cousin Sax?" Laura asked, but realized immediately that he wouldn't send a message to Daphne.

Daphne was studying the folded paper. "It doesn't say. Where did it come from, Pringle?"

"From Quiller's Hotel, my lady."

Daphne dropped the letter as if it were red hot. "I won't read it!"

Laura seized it and offered it back. "Daphne! It could be important."

"It's the duchess. I know it is."

"Even if it is, she can't do you any harm here. Open it. What if it's about Meg?"

Jeremy had come over. He took the letter from Laura, then thrust it at Daphne. Laura was startled and impressed by this hint of manly authority from her scholarly brother. Daphne responded. Though her lips quivered, she took it and broke the seal. After a moment, she put her hand to her mouth.

"What?" Laura almost shrieked, fighting not to snatch the letter from her limp hand.

"The duchess," Daphne whispered. "She's . . . she's dying!"

"What?" Daphne ended Laura's dilemma by giving the letter to Jeremy who, being a good brother, brought it around to Laura so they could both read it.

It was signed "Waterman."

"Who's Waterman?" Laura demanded.

Daphne had found a small handkerchief and was dabbing her eyes. "The duchess's dresser."

"I regret to inform you," Jeremy read aloud, "that Her Grace, plagued and put upon by alarms and undutiful behavior, has suffered another of her seizures, this time a most grievous one. The doctor is in attendance, but holds out little hope. Her Grace's speech is weak, but she has managed to make clear that she wishes her family, no matter how ungrateful they have been, to be beside her at the last. The duke and his family have been sent for. It is her dearest wish that the two grandchildren who are in London at this time, will put aside their cruelty and come to her."

"I wasn't cruel," Daphne whispered. "Not really. It was she . . . Oh!" She fell into deep tears.

Laura went to hold her. "Don't! I'm sure you had reason to leave her. Just because she's dying doesn't make her a saint."

Daphne looked up at that, tears fading. "She's isn't a kind-hearted woman."

"But she's dying, and—"

"And she has been kind to me from time to time. . . ." She blew her nose.

"So you want to go to her now. That's understandable."

"Wait," said Jeremy. "What if it's a trap?"

Laura and Daphne turned to him. "Trap?" Laura asked.

"Suppose she wanted to get Daphne back. Might she not try something like this?"

"Oh, surely not!"

"She might," said Daphne, torturing her handkerchief. "Nothing is beyond her."

The butler cleared his throat. "If I may be so bold, perhaps a servant might be sent to Quiller's to ascertain the exact situation."

"Perfect," said Jeremy. As Pringle left, he added, "I'll bet it does all turn out to be a ruse. Won't she be furious that you didn't fall for it, Lady Daphne!"

"Then she probably will have a seizure. She's had two already. And it will all be my fault."

"Nonsense. I think we all need tea. Ring the bell, Laura."

Laura did so, thinking how wonderful it was to have a bell, servants, and tea. If only . . . "I do wish we would hear something from Cousin Sax or Meg, though."

Jeremy gave her a firm hug. "We will. And Cousin Sax is up to anything. After all, that potboy took Sax there, so he must have rescued her."

Meg awoke to warm, cocoony darkness. She was in her own bed, with Laura close beside, and she had had some most extraordinary dreams.

Then she realized she was half off the edge of the bed, because Laura had taken the center. Annoyed, she wriggled and pushed, trying to ease her sister back onto her own side—

That leg didn't belong to Laura!

She froze. She hadn't been dreaming. A new smell all around, a sensitivity between her legs—not exactly soreness, but close to that—all reminded her of who was in her bed, and what had happened.

Typical of the Earl of Saxonhurst to treat the whole bed as his territory! She wriggled a bit more toward the center, trying to get away from the chill seeping under the covers. Under pressure, his leg moved a bit, but then her progress brought her closer to his big, hot body sprawled majestically in the very middle of the bed.

Meg smothered a laugh. How romantic! She was very tempted to jab him with her elbow and make him move, but she also wanted a bit of time to think. After all, this symbolized her life. He'd taken it over, taken her over, so that only a narrow strip of Meg Gillingham remained.

She'd taken over his life, however, in a far more absolute way, using the *sheelagh* to command. And despite the terrible stings in the magic's tail, she wasn't the tiniest bit sorry. She could no longer imagine life without this big, impossible, demanding, wonderful man.

Tentatively, she worked a hand across the small expanse of sheet between them, aware inch by inch of a growing heat. Then, with just a fingertip, she touched his body. One body dressed in cotton should feel much like another, and yet this could never be Laura. Perhaps it was not touch, but other senses. Smell, sound, the quiet but firm exhalation of each breath.

What a torrent of emotions and dramas she'd swirled through these past days. And despite the delicious wonder of Sax, of Sax and her, the dramas weren't over yet. She was still accused of murder. And somewhere, the *sheelagh* was beyond her control, perhaps able to be used for evil by others.

But, incredibly, here was the scintillating Earl of Saxonhurst, glossy ruler of his exalted world, endearingly confused about day-to-day life, here beside her, trustingly asleep.

Recently inside her, creating magic.

Hers.

Astonishingly, wonderfully, hers.

Irresistibly, her hand crept out again, and she dared to stroke him—his bare arm. She was Sax's bride. Sax's lover. She might, at this very moment, be carrying his child within her, which meant—

He said quietly, "You awake?"

She snatched her hand back. "Yes."

"What's the matter?"

"Nothing."

He drew her against his body. "Sorry we made love?"

At just this closeness, desire leaped. "The very opposite."

"Wonderful lady." He nuzzled warmly at her neck. "So, why did you sound as if something was the matter?"

After a moment, she said, "I was thinking I might already be with child. And that they don't hang pregnant women."

He nipped her neck, making her start. "Don't be foolish. No one will touch the Countess of Saxonhurst."

She knew better than to suggest that some things might be beyond the power of rank.

He settled her more comfortably against him—against his strength and heat. "All right. Time to talk."

"You just said no one would—"

"I need to know the whole tale. Start with the magic statue."

"I don't think that's a good place to start."

"Silly Meg. Where then?"

"Believe me, there's nothing silly about the *sheelagh*."

"When we get it back, you can show me how it works. Then I'll believe you."

"They should have called you Thomas. And I'm never using the *sheelagh* again. Why don't I tell you what went on at Sir Arthur's?"

"Very well. But you went there to find the magic statue."

Meg sighed. He was right. She couldn't leave the *sheelagh* out of this entirely and still tell the true story. She stirred uneasily against him. "Promise not to be too angry with me?"

He kissed her temple. "I won't be angry with you. Even if you killed Sir Arthur."

"I didn't!"

"I'm sure he deserved to die. A very slimy customer. So I won't be angry, no matter what you've done."

"Ha! You turn into a monster every time you're crossed. You tear rooms apart."

He shifted slightly and kissed her lips. "No, Meg, no. Don't think that of me. I'd never hurt you. I've never hurt anyone. I don't even box. For sport I fence and aim my pistols at targets." After a moment, he added, "I suppose I'd better explain."

He'd never hurt anyone? She remember someone saying he only broke things. She put her hand to the side of his face, feeling the roughness of whiskers there. What did he look like, unkempt and unshaven? Wonderful, she was sure. "Go on, then."

He kissed her palm. "The only person who has ever made me really angry is the Dowager Duchess of Daingerfield. The mere thought of her, however, enrages me."

She heard it in his voice, and wanted to argue again that such feelings were wrong. She knew better than to raise that problem at the moment, however.

"I don't like my anger," he said. "But it feels worse if I bottle it up. So I let it out." He laughed. "Now, it's mostly an act for the servants. They put ugly items in my room, and I obligingly smash them. But I also get rid of the rage, and I think that's wise."

It was a strange concept to her. "But it means you live surrounded by ugly things. That's enough to turn anyone sour."

"Customs die hard. We all have to play our parts on the stage of life. To fulfill the expectations of others." He turned his head sensuously against her palm. "I was hoping to spend a great deal of time in my wife's apartments. Especially as she has one of my favorite paintings on her wall."

"Which one?" she asked, but she knew.

"The Vermeer."

"It is lovely. So calm and tranquil." She had to add, "I didn't think you'd like it."

"Don't forget, I like Turner, too. And Fuseli."

She laughed. Mr. Chancellor had been right. Sax was Sax.

And he was nuzzling her palm with wicked intent.

Meg flexed her hand against his mouth, but said, "Don't seduce me again, Sax. We do need to talk." As if in warning, St. Margaret's church clock began to chime. She counted ten strokes. It felt more like the middle of the night.

He licked her palm. "I can talk while seducing."

"I'm not sure I can hear, though."

He laughed, and separated them. "Very well. Let's lie apart and make sense of it all. But Meg"—and he caught her hand for one last kiss—"I promise I won't be angry. No matter what you've done. I promise."

"Why?"

"Because you're my wife. So tell me the truth."

Meg drank in the feel of his warm lips against her knuckles, and could imagine them against her lips. A touch of sadness made her sigh, however. For the briefest moment there she'd thought he might say his tolerance was because he loved her.

She was beginning to fear that she might be falling into love with him. It was a very weakening condition, especially if one-sided. "Where shall I start?" she asked.

"Tell me all about the visit to Sir Arthur's."

* * *

Tea was just being cleared when Pringle ushered in the limping footman. Laura remembered that his name was Clarence.

"I regret," the man said, "that the news of the dowager duchess does appear to be true. Two doctors are in attendance, and straw has been laid in the streets to lessen the noise."

Laura shared a dismayed look with her brother, sure he was feeling the same discomfort. The duchess was an old woman, and apparently a mean one, but still, she wished she hadn't made light of the message, or said harsh things.

Daphne rose. "Then I must certainly go to her."

"I will order the carriage," said Pringle and left.

"Did you learn anything else?" Jeremy asked the footman.

"Well, sir," the man said, relaxing now the butler had left, "I asked about a bit. The duchess travels with her own servants, so the hotel people don't get to see much of what goes on there, but there was questions asked about when and how Lady Daphne left. And also some about another young woman who was with the duchess. Turns out," he said with a smile and a wink, "a disreputable couple was seen leaving the back of the hotel."

"Disreputable!" Laura declared. "Cousin Sax would hate that." But she laughed in relief. Wherever she was, Meg was with the earl. He'd take good care of her.

"You clearly don't know Saxonhurst," said Daphne with a sniff. "He doubtless thought it great fun. He has always lacked a sense of the dignity of his position."

Laura and Jeremy shared another look.

"My outdoor clothes," Daphne demanded of the footman, doubtless with the dignity of her position. Laura didn't think she'd ever be comfortable making such curt demands, and she doubted Meg would, either. Would that be a terrible problem?

Daphne was staring into nothing, biting her lip, and pressing her damp handkerchief occasionally to her eyes. Laura tried to imagine how it felt to be losing someone who had almost been a mother, but not a loved one.

"Would you like me to come with you?" Laura impulsively asked.

Daphne started. "Would you? It's silly, but I will feel so strange. After all, I did run away. You needn't . . . needn't come in to see the duchess, but . . ." A smile fought through. "You're a very kindhearted girl."

Laura shrugged it off. "It's not a sacrifice. It will give me something to do. I can't go to bed without knowing what's happened. In fact, perhaps I'll be able to do a little snooping and find out more."

"Laura," said Jeremy in a warning tone.

"Nothing out of line," she assured him. "I'll just talk to people. You know that people talk to me. Tell me things."

She saw Daphne flash her a sharp look, obviously wondering what she'd said. For her part, Laura couldn't understand why some people were so intent on keeping secrets.

Still ill at ease with summoning servants, she went to the door and politely asked a hovering servant for her outdoor clothes. Turning back, she asked, "Why don't you come, too, Jeremy?"

"Because someone should stay here in case." He patted Brak, who was still circling the room restlessly, even whining now and then.

Laura pulled a face at her brother's tone. "I'm sure Mr. Chancellor will return soon to take care of things. What can he be doing at this time of night?"

"He had meetings at the Home Office, and with Bow Street. I think he said someone connected to Carlton House had asked to be kept informed. He's trying to solve the murder, after all. He asked to be informed of developments here, so I'll send a message. If you do find out anything interesting, send a message here immediately. But don't do anything foolish! It's not enough to find Meg. We have to clear her of this murder."

"Murder. It's so ridiculous!"

"But serious. Even if Cousin Sax can stop the legal process, the scandal will hang over her forever."

Chapter 21

Meg told Sax the whole story of her visit to Sir Arthur's house. She tried to think of a way around telling him about the whip, but in the end, blurted it out.

His hand touched her shoulder. "Pity he's dead."

"I felt so soiled by it," she whispered.

"I can imagine."

"I didn't know. . . ."

"No."

Though his touch was light and almost impersonal, his understanding and sympathy was like an extra blanket, one for the soul.

"Have you ever . . . ? No, of course not."

After a moment, he said, "I have, actually. Once. Truth is, my dear, I'm done nearly everything once. Seems a shame not to. Flagellation, giving or receiving, didn't do a thing for me. Except hurt."

She lay there, trying to absorb that. She realized he had rolled onto his side to face her, even though in the deep dark neither of them could see.

"Upset?" he asked.

"No. Yes. I don't know. It just seems strange. I can imagine wanting to try different things. But . . . but some things are so unlikely. You wouldn't try cutting off your hand, would you?"

"Hardly. I avoid things likely to lead to permanent damage. As for unlikely, it's a common enough erotic game, and needn't even hurt much. And it's a necessity for some people. Like your Sir Arthur."

"Necessity?"

"You didn't really understand, did you? Some people can't find sexual release without pain. Some men can't perform at all without it, giving or receiving."

"But then, why bother at all?"

Silence stretched, then he said, "I mustn't have pleased you as much as I thought."

Dear lord, she'd offended him! "Of course, you did. I—"

His hand covered her mouth. "No lies. Perhaps it was just because you were a virgin. But sex is, at its best, worth sacrifice."

She twisted her head free. "Worth hurting others?"

"No. But I can understand the temptation if there's no other way." He stroked down the side of her cheek. "Perhaps we need to clarify the appeal of lovemaking before going on with our explanations. . . ."

Part of Meg swooned toward him, and the pleasure he offered. Why had she implied it wasn't special? Physically, however, she edged away. "No. I don't think so. Later perhaps."

He laughed, and stopped touching her. "Later, then. You do like anticipation, don't you? Didn't the clock strike eleven a while ago? When it strikes midnight, I'm going to educate you on the overwhelming beauty of sexual love."

"I'm not sure—"

"Go on with your story," he insisted, a smile in his voice. "You may not have much time. After Sir Arthur staggered off to rut with his child-servant, what did you do?"

Meg realized she was gaping, and quietly closed her mouth. The impossible man was doing it again. He'd excited her body with a touch and a few words, started a process that would end, she knew, at midnight.

"I decided to search for the *sheelagh*," she said in as firm and cool a voice as she could muster. "I can usually sense it if I'm close. It's a kind of hum that gets under my skin, if that makes sense."

"Oh yes. Like you, now. A hum under my skin. You didn't find it?"

Meg swallowed. "No. And I went through every room except the bedroom. And even there, I think I'd have sensed it if it had been present.

"And then you left. By the back way?"

"Yes."

"Who saw you?"

"Some servants in the kitchen. Sitting around in idleness. It was not a well-run household." After a moment, she added, "And the man with the housekeeper."

"What?"

She was glad for darkness to hide her blushes. "I said I checked every room. That included the housekeeper's room. At first I thought she was just sitting astride a man's lap, which would be strange enough. But then I realized . . ."

"Yes?" he said as if puzzled, though she was not deceived.

"Wretch. You know just what I mean."

"Mmmm. And you'll like it. So the housekeeper was riding one of the servants, and he saw you? But she didn't."

"Her back was toward the door."

"Did he do anything?"

"He looked startled. But then he grinned," she added. "It . . . it wasn't a nice grin."

"He doubtless wasn't a nice man. Next?"

"By then, I just wanted to get out of the house. I suppose I didn't check every room. There were probably some pantries I missed. But I couldn't sense the *sheelagh* at all, and I couldn't bear any more."

"So you staggered past the servants, looking dazed. Unfortunate, that."

"I know."

He tucked her into his arm, in a way that was just comforting. "At least you weren't covered with blood."

"No, of course not."

"I'm sure someone who'd just cut two throats would have to be. I wonder if Monk kept your cloak. Unfortunate if he didn't. Did anyone see you outside?"

"Not that I noticed. Then I found Monk, and we were leaving. And someone started the hue and cry."

After a moment, he asked, "Exactly how did that happen?"

"How?"

"Yes. When someone found the bodies, you'd expect confusion, wouldn't you? But from what Monk said, they were after you almost immediately."

Meg thought back. "It must have been one of the servants from the kitchen who pointed me out to the crowd." Suddenly, irresistibly, she shuddered. "They were like hounds. Baying."

He held her close. "Thank heavens for Monk's quick wits."

"But they'll be after me again, as soon as I appear on the street!"

"Nonsense. But," he said, nuzzling her ear, "we can always stay snuggled up here forever."

"That's physically impossible."

"Shame." He kissed her again, then suddenly he moved away from her. She felt the covers shift as he reached out, felt cold air seep in.

"What are you doing?"

"Finding my pocket watch."

"It's pitch dark!"

He said nothing, but then settled back, straightening the covers. "It's still hellishly cold out there."

"And not likely to change."

"You mean no servant's going to creep in to make the fire? Plague take 'em all. Let's stay in bed until Owain comes to find us." A chime startled her.

"What's that?"

"My watch. It tells the time, even in the dark. Listen."

Eleven high-pitched chimes, then a tinkle. Then another.

"Half past eleven," he said, but the watch kept going in a lower *ding*. He counted. When the clock went silent, he said, "You have exactly eighteen minutes to finish your story, my dear. On you go."

Meg was gaping again, and had a strong urge to punch him. She wasn't sure why. Probably because he was turning glossy. She hadn't even known watches like that existed, and she was sure they were fabulously expensive. "I suppose that's enamelled by a master hand and set with jewels," she muttered.

"Not at all. It's plain chased silver." His hand found her again, and played lazily with her hair.

"You're a mystery to me, Sax."

"As you are to me. We have a lifetime. So, how did you end up in the dragon's lair?"

"The dragon?" She gathered her wits. "You mean the dowager duchess? I thought she'd be bound to help me. To avoid scandal. And at first, it seemed she would." She turned her head toward him. "Why wouldn't she?"

He stroked her hair for a moment. "That comes to my tale. I think I had better take Owain's advice and tell you all about the duchess. What did he tell you?"

Meg hoped she wasn't going to get Mr. Chancellor into trouble. "About your parents' marriage and death. He said it was public knowledge."

"True enough. I was ten." Abruptly, he moved away, leaving a few bleak inches between them.

"I was feeling upset in general. My father had recently become earl and our lives had changed. We'd had to leave Bankside, which was the only home I'd known, and move into Haverhall, which is a lovely house, but enormous. Being second son, my father had never expected it, or wanted it. He was fond of my uncle, too, so he was unhappy with everything, even months later. I remember that. That everyone was in poor spirits. For some reason I feel it might have been better if they'd been snatched from me when things were going perfectly. But perhaps not."

"I don't think it makes any difference." She longed to hold him, but gave him privacy from her touch.

"I was sick as well. Just a cold, but my parents insisted that I stay home. It was our first visit to the London town house—my first visit to London at all—so I was sulking about being left behind. That's what lingers with me most sharply. That I was angry with them when we said good-bye. Then this stranger arrived—it was the Bishop of London recruited for the task—come to tell me that my family were all dead, and that I was now Earl of Saxonhurst. And that since there seemed to be no suitable person on the Torrance side, and my father had not named a guardian, my mother's family had been informed."

Meg rolled toward him, having to offer at least that much closeness. "How did they die?"

He moved slightly toward her. "They were visiting an aunt—Daphne's mother, actually—who was staying at a house in Kensington. It is assumed that they were accosted by a highwayman."

"So close to town?"

"It's still a little wild on the far edges of Hyde Park, but the military keeps order now. Fifteen year ago"—she felt him shrug—"I gather it was much less orderly. But no one was ever sure quite what happened, except that my father was shot. He was driving them in a phaeton, and the horses must have bolted. Damn careless . . ."

She was trying to understand that strange remark when, faintly, the distant church clock sounded the three quarters. He slid a hand over her left breast.

"To lose them all like that," she said, swaying closer. "So young. And to be so alone. My parents made no provision, either. And they had less excuse, since my father was so ill. But I don't suppose my mother thought to die. And anyway, they knew I would take care of them all. . . ."

She was tempted then to tell him her fears about the *sheelagh* and her parents' death. But he still didn't believe, and anyway, this was his story.

He moved closer, and found her lips with his. "Remind me, as soon as we are out of this, to have our affairs very competently taken care of."

"Very well." She could sense his resistance, his resistance to telling her all, but she thought he needed to. She stroked his thick, silky hair. "So, you were taken to live with the Duke and Duchess of Daingerfield."

She thought he wouldn't respond, but then he said, "At the time it hardly mattered. I was numb. I remember, however, the wrongness of everything. Even my name—" His voice broke and he pressed his head briefly into her neck.

Then he continued. "I had been Lord Ireford for so little time. And anyway my parents had told everyone to keep calling me Master Frederick. But now everyone addressed me as Lord Saxonhurst. That was my grandfather. Or my uncle. Or my father. Not me. But the duchess insisted on it. It was as if Master Frederick Torrance had ceased to exist."

Meg closed her eyes, overwhelmed by this picture of the devastated little boy, no older than Richard, surrounded by strangers in a strange house. Having met the duchess, she could imagine how cold and unsympathetic she must have seemed, even though she was doubtless grieving for her beloved daughter.

"It *was* your title," she said gently. "It would have been wrong for them to call you anything else." When he didn't say anything, she asked, "So, how did you come to be called Sax?"

He stirred, moving slightly away again. "Later. When I began to put myself together. I didn't want to go back to being Frederick. He was dead. So I began to encourage the people I felt closest to to call me Sax. Owain in particular."

"He was there back then?"

"My tutor's son. Owain was allowed to attend lessons with Cobham and me."

"Cobham?"

"Another cousin. Next in line to the dukedom now. Pompous and spineless. And rather dull-witted. Dr. Chancellor's attempts to drill basic knowledge into his head gave Owain and me a certain amount of leisure, as long as we never let our games come to the duchess's attention. Some of the servants were our allies. We tried not to endanger their positions. Didn't always work . . ." After a moment, he continued, "When I came of age, I hired those I could find. Pringle. Cook. Clarence was turned off with a pittance because of his leg, even though it was the duke who'd run over him.

A picture was opening for Meg, but it felt like a butterfly struggling out of the chrysalis. Fragile, as if the wrong word, the wrong movement could destroy it.

"I can see that it was a terrible time for you, and that the duchess was rigid in her ways, but surely that isn't why you hate her. Was she cruel?"

"Cruel?" He seemed to roll the word around his mouth like brandy. "Physically, no. I was punished when I offended, but not cruelly. Some of the offenses were unfair in my mind, but I wouldn't hate her for that." He was silent for a while, then said, "She tried to wipe out my life."

"She tried to *kill* you?"

"No. My former life. She hated my father, you see.

Loathed and detested him because he'd stolen her favorite daughter. She couldn't accept that my mother avoided her only because the duchess hated my father. Instead, she chose to think that my father kept my mother away. She tried to break the marriage. When that failed, she tried to ruin him in society. Had some success, too, since he was a Torrance and had been a wild young man. But she didn't break him or the marriage, and that she could not bear. So she tried to do it after their deaths. She had all pictures of him destroyed. I don't have one. She forbade me to speak of him. I could speak of my mother and my sister, but not my father."

Meg was almost shaking with horror at this tale. "How could she stop you? With punishment?"

"I would have taken daily beatings. But if I transgressed in this way, I wasn't beaten. Owain was. She's a devilishly clever woman. I paid her back by never speaking of my mother and sister, either. I acted as if my former life had never existed. Except once a year. On the anniversary of their deaths, I made a formal statement of remembrance, and Owain was beaten for it."

Meg lay there, trying to imagine being a grieving ten-year-old forbidden to speak of his dead loved ones, all visual memory of his father destroyed. The horror of those years. No wonder he was not rational about all this. It was astonishing how mild Mr. Chancellor seemed about the duchess.

"But still," she said, having to clear her throat, "that's all in the past. Can you not put it behind you now?"

"Perhaps I have done that too well."

That was a strange thing to say, too.

"The duchess was obliged to surrender control when I turned twenty-one," he continued, "but she has never given up her mission."

"What did you mean, you have put it behind you too well?"

"I have left her in peace."

"Sax," she said, turning to him, "revenge will do you no good."

"But what of justice?"

"Justice? Perhaps that is served. She is not a happy woman."

"True enough. It sweetens my bitter moments."

But he still had those moments. Meg sighed. She understood better now, though she still thought he hurt himself more than his grandmother by his hatred. She no longer thought she could change him, or heal the breach. She stroked him gently. "At least she can't hurt you any more."

He stirred. "Meg, she's attacking me through you."

"It's just that she planned to marry you to Daphne. Did you know poor Daphne has a wedding dress all ready?"

"Poor Daphne, indeed. She came to me, you know. To save you."

"That was kind, then. And needed courage. I think she's terrified of the duchess."

"With reason. The woman would throw her out into the street if it suited her mood. Throw her into the Thames if it came to that. Or have her thrown, more likely. A duchess does not soil her hands."

His still hand on her breast was managing to be torment, but Meg tried to ignore it. "You should take care of her."

"Daphne? Perhaps. She's right, in a way, about being promised in the cradle. Her mother was my mother's older sister, and they kept in touch in defiance of the duchess. Since we're almost of an age, they did talk of us marrying, and apparently we did share a nurse and cradle sometimes, amusing the adults by playing with one another's toes and such. On my parents' side, at least, any talk of marriage was entirely in fun.

"The duchess, however, took up the idea. When I was moved to Daingerfield Court, she had Daphne make frequent, long visits, treating her as my promised bride. We'd have been at the altar at sixteen if I would have agreed. When I resisted, she found the most tempting lure. If I accepted my fate, she would acknowledge my parents. She argued that my marriage to Daphne had been my parents' dearest wish, and that I was honor bound to go through with it. And if I'd marry Daphne,

I could speak of my father whenever I wished. She even produced a family portrait I'd thought long gone."

"Yet you still held out?"

"She made me watch it burn."

Meg bit her lip, tears stinging at her eyes.

"And she brought Daphne to live permanently at the Court, and made her wear the ring."

"The ring," Meg prompted.

"The Torrance betrothal ring. My mother's ring. She always wore it."

Meg absorbed the fact that it had been taken from his mother's hand after death. That was usual in the case of such family treasures that must be passed on, but she could imagine the pain it caused for him to see it every day on Daphne's hand.

"Daphne didn't resist?"

"It takes a touch of madness to fight someone like the duchess, I think. And Daphne liked the idea of being countess. Mostly, however, compliance was the price of escaping her life with a gouty father who was usually sunk in a bottle and vicious with it."

"Then are you not rather cruel to her? She is as much a victim as you."

"Cruel?" He laughed shortly. "It was war, Meg. She even tried to seduce me once or twice, but thanks to her stern virtue, she was very bad at it. Which wasn't true of some of the others."

"The others?" Meg didn't want to hear of his youthful conquests, but she would listen to anything he felt driven to say.

"It was a struggle, but I left the duchess's care a virgin."

"She . . . ?"

"She found some very tempting specimens, yes. Especially for a young, healthy male whose body was hungry for experience." One finger gently circled her nipple. "I made up for it later."

"So I gather," Meg breathed, then managed to speak more clearly. "But why? I would have thought the duchess honest in her stern morality at least. Why try to debauch you?"

"To weaken me." He snuggled down and put his mouth to her breast. "It is very weakening, isn't it?"

"Very. Which is why we were going to wait until midnight."

He moved away and his watch began its chiming message. "Four minutes, Meg."

She resisted the temptation to roll toward him, to consign four tedious minutes to the devil. "Very well. How would your marriage to Daphne have served the duchess's purpose?"

"She's obsessed. Daphne was her choice, shaped by her, and under her control. My marriage to Daphne would correct my mother's rebellious and unsuitable marriage to my father. She could also expect that Daphne would stay under her thumb, so my children would be hers to mold in what she considers a suitable manner, not in the unruly way—her opinion favored by my parents. It is all just a matter of a tyrant's maniacal insistence on control."

"But in the end, she lost everyone. Couldn't she see what she was doing?"

"Apparently not. She is always right, her actions are always just, and if things go awry, it is always the fault of someone else."

"But—"

The distant clock began to chime, and his watch blended in with a merry count of twelve. "Abandon hope, fair lady. Your time of liberty is over."

Meg was tempted to protest, just on principle, but instead, she rolled toward him. "So is yours, my lord."

Chapter 22

When the carriage was announced, Laura and Daphne almost ran through the bitingly cold midnight air and into its warmth. Laura envied her companion her fur-lined cloak, and prayed that Meg had found a warm haven. Well, of course, she had. The earl had her safe, doubtless tucked away in luxury somewhere.

After all, he lived in luxury. Even his carriage floor was set with warm tiles beneath the carpet. It was almost as warm as in her drawing room. Lady Daphne had to un-clasp her fur-lined cloak in the heat.

It wasn't a long trip to the hotel, and soon she and Lady Daphne were being led reverently down a hushed corridor. No, this was no trick. The duchess must indeed be deathly ill.

They were ushered into a bedchamber before Laura had time to think about staying outside. The dowager duchess lay in the big bed, old face sagging with sleep and sickness. She looked like a frail old woman, but the coverlet was richly embroidered with a crest, surely the ducal one. Laura thought it strange for anyone to haul such trappings around.

A middle-aged woman in black sat beside her. That was probably the dresser. A white-haired, slender man sat farther away, looking rather bored. He was doubtless the doctor, obliged to stay because of his patient's high rank, but having nothing to do to save her.

Another servant stood in a corner. A man. Just there in case he was needed.

The room was so hot that Laura wanted to immedi-ately shed her cloak, but it seemed somehow out of place.

Daphne crept forward, and the dresser rose to remove

her cloak and muff. It was all done without an order, without Daphne's seeming aware of the service. Laura watched with interest. If she was going to move in high circles, she'd have to learn the way of it.

Daphne touched a pale, be-ringed hand. "Grandmother?"

The eyelids fluttered. The old lady's mouth worked a little, but then she just turned her hand to squeeze Daphne's. Laura felt tears. How sad that these two hadn't been more loving in life. She was sure Daphne had wanted to love. In fact, she couldn't imagine that the earl hadn't wanted to love his grandmother. He was not a cold person.

The dowager duchess was clearly one of those people who turned every relationship to vinegar and never realized it was their own fault.

"Who's with you?" the duchess whispered. The words were faint and slurred a little, but quite understandable.

"Miss Gillingham," Daphne said in a hushed voice. "The countess's sister."

Though the lids hardly parted, Laura felt the eyes on her, quite sharply. Clearly, people didn't change that much on their deathbed. "What's she doing here? Where's Saxonhurst?"

"He went to find the countess. Don't agitate yourself, Grandmother!"

The old woman's teeth were bared like Brak's. "I'll leave," said Laura, dropping a curtsy. "This is a family time. I'll wait elsewhere."

"No." Though raspy, it was a bark of command. "Come closer, gel. You are a distant connection now."

Laura didn't want to go closer, but she couldn't refuse. She wished the dresser would unobtrusively remove her cloak, but she didn't. In the end, she pushed it off herself and draped it over a chair, along with her muff.

"Where is your sister, then? Where's my grandson?"

"I don't know, Your Grace."

"I had the silly gel safe here, so she couldn't cause more trouble. Trouble for my grandson. Trouble for the family. Scandal . . ." One hand clutched the ornate bedcover and the doctor came over.

"Your Grace, you must not upset yourself."

"I'm not upsetting myself, Wallace," she said with surprising asperity. "Everyone else is upsetting me."

He clasped her wrist to test her pulse. "Then perhaps we should send everyone away—"

"What point? You go away. Go!"

The doctor stepped back. "Do I understand that you wish me to leave the room, Your Grace?"

"Leave the room. Leave the hotel." Her voice grew louder and less coherent. "Go. Someone'll come for you when . . . something for you to do."

The man bowed stiffly, picked up his bag, and stalked out. Laura wanted to roll her eyes. What an impossible, rude old woman.

The duchess looked between Daphne and Laura. "Sit. Can't stand people hovering. Like vultures. Stop looking tragic, Daphne. If I die, I die."

The dresser rose to give Daphne her chair. Laura turned to fend for herself, but the manservant had come forward. He removed her cloak and muff from the nearby chair, replacing them on the one vacated by the doctor. She flashed him a smile of thanks and sat, wishing she'd not come, and yet fascinated.

The duchess, however, was staring beyond Laura. "Stafford, what are you doing here?"

"Don't distress yourself, duchess." He moved to stand by the bed, facing them. "Where will your sister have hidden herself, Miss Gillingham?"

"Don't answer him! Waterman, get him out of here. . . ." The agitated old woman began to choke, and the dresser hurried to offer some sort of cordial.

"Don't, Your Grace. You must be calm."

Most of the liquid dribbled out of the poor woman's lips and she lay back, still muttering. "Stafford. . . . Out . . ."

Laura looked up at the man, who seemed unmoved, though he turned to the duchess and said, "Don't agitate yourself, Your Grace. Trust me to carry out your wishes with respect to your family."

The duchess looked dreadful, but she did seem to calm.

The man—Stafford—turned back to Laura. "As you

see, we must try to find her family for her. Can you help, Miss Gillingham?"

"I'm sorry, no. If I knew, I would go there myself and find her. We are all very worried."

"But the earl is with her?"

"Yes."

"Pshaw!" the duchess spat, now even opening her eyes. "Running to set a murderess free like a hero in a bad play. Probably in disguise. I wash my hands of him. Do you hear that, Stafford? I wash my hands of him."

"Yes, Your Grace," said the man with a bow toward the bed, as if the old woman wasn't spitting nonsense.

He turned back to Laura. "People have checked the inns and hotels. Checked the earl's friends, those who are in town. On such a cold night, they must be somewhere. Where would you hide, Miss Gillingham?"

Laura was out of her depth and knew it, but it probably was right to find Saxonhurst and inform him of his grandmother's state. She was very ill, that was clear.

"The earl asked me the same question. I don't know. We have friends, yes, mostly around Mallett Street, but I'm not sure they would take in fugitives. And Meg has been a governess for the past four years, living in the country."

"Perhaps she has gone there."

"I don't think she could throw herself on their mercy, and it would be too far."

"True." The man certainly seemed to be taking his task seriously. "What about empty places then? Are any of the properties near your old home empty?"

"Only our old home," she replied.

His eyes widened slightly, and the silence was very loud.

"You think . . . ?" Laura rose. "It might be. I must go and—"

"Sit!" The duchess's command was surprisingly strong, and Laura automatically obeyed.

"It must be checked," the old woman whispered. "Stafford . . ."

"There's no need for you to go, Miss Gillingham," the man said. "What number?"

Laura wished she didn't feel that everything in this

room was discordant, like music out of tune. "Number thirty-two. But perhaps I should . . ."

"It's bitter out, miss," Stafford said easily. "You'd need a carriage and that would take time. I can get there quickly by hackney and bring them back. I'm sure the earl would want to know about his grandmother."

"Yes, I suppose. I don't mind a hackney, though. . . ."

"It's not necessary."

"Go, Stafford," said the duchess as if every word was precious. "Go and do my will. Or by heaven, I'll haunt you!"

The man bent to kiss the clawlike, frantic hand. "You know me, Your Grace. I'm sure we'll meet again."

Laura watched the man stride out, knowing there were things going on here that she did not understand. She looked at Daphne, but Daphne gave her a slight, reassuring smile.

The duchess rolled her head on her pillow. "Go . . ." She twitched a hand toward an adjoining door. "Can't talk. Come when Helen comes back. Helen . . ."

Laura was happy enough to escape into a cooler, fresher room. "Who's Helen?"

Daphne hugged herself. "Saxonhurst's mother."

"But she's dead, isn't she?"

"I gather people do that when they're dying. Slip into the past. I hope Stafford brings Saxonhurst back."

Laura wasn't sure it would be a pretty scene. "I can't like that man."

"No. He's coarse. I don't know why Grandmother keeps him about. He's even steward of one of her smaller properties."

Laura wished she hadn't come. She didn't like any of these people and something in the air frightened her. "What if the earl won't come?"

Daphne sat and held out pale, net-gloved hands to the fire. "Then she'll probably be served right. She's never thought of others, only of herself. She's a duke's daughter, you know, and married a duke. And her husband was a mere cipher. Their son is the same, and she made sure he married a mouse. And his son. Cobham was married at sixteen to the girl of her choice. Saxonhurst is the only person who's ever crossed her."

"Good for him." Laura thought about going out to question servants, but it was late and there wouldn't be anything to learn here about the murder.

She sat down, too, hoping Stafford did find Sax and Meg so they could all go home.

The clock struck the half hour, and though she still trembled slightly with memories of passion, Meg's stomach rumbled.

Sax rubbed it. "Hungry?"

"A bit. It's all right." She moved closer and rubbed against his sweaty body just for the heaven of it.

"No it's not. I want to dress you in silk and surround you with every luxury. I want you to never have a care again."

She laughed. It was totally dark, and yet he was clear to her through every other sense. Clear and beloved. "That sounds very dull."

"Very well." His face rubbed softly in her hair. "We'll take to the road as vagabonds, and have endless adventures."

"You, my lord earl, are a creature of extremes. I prefer the middle path."

"I'm not fond of discomfort, either, especially after this brief brush with it. And I think you'll come to like the occasional wild adventure, as long as it's all in fun."

"Yes, I think I might. What are we going to do, though, if we can't clear my name?"

"Live in scandal."

"I don't think I'd like that."

"I know. That's why we'll have to clear it up."

"How?"

"By trusting in Owain."

Meg laughed. "You are impossible, you know."

"What irritates people is that I am entirely possible— I exist—and I am happy with my foibles. I'm unnatural."

She cuddled even closer. "You're magical." But that sparked a memory. "I do have to get the *sheelagh* back."

He shrugged. "If your Sir Arthur didn't hide it in his house, it's a needle in a haystack. We can't search the whole of London."

"Remember I can sense it. It's almost like music, but

too low to hear." She shook her head against his chest. "That must sound like madness to you."

"No more so than the statue itself. I confess, if you had it here, I'd ask you to wish for some food."

Meg *tsked,* but then became very still. "Sax . . ."

"Yes?" After a moment, he said, "Meg?"

"This is strange. I thought it was you."

"What?"

"Since we arrived here, I've felt something. I thought it was you. The *sheelagh*—don't laugh—it feels like, like you make me feel."

"Should I be jealous?"

She poked him in the ribs. "To be blunt, it feels like sexual arousal. Faintly."

"I don't usually think of faintly and arousal in the same sentence."

"Stop it. The fact is, I can feel it now."

"Oh, good." His hand moved.

She wriggled away. "Sax! I think the *sheelagh* is in this house! Think. It's a logical place for him to hide it, if he didn't want to use his own home. He probably never took it away, just moved it to a different room."

"Then why didn't you sense it when you came to look for it?"

"I was in such a panic. Sneaking out of your house, then into here. Not finding it. Then hearing someone coming into the house. . . . The sense of the *sheelagh* is very faint, and I've been used to it in this house all my life."

"Are you sure?"

Meg lay there and concentrated on the elusive music, then shivered. "It's here. It really is."

She would have scrambled out of bed, but he held her back. "No rush. If it's here, we'll find it. Then you can keep your mind on more important matters."

"Like my being suspected of murder? I suppose I *could* ask it to sort things out. I don't know, though. . . ."

"That wasn't particularly what I had in mind." He moved his body against hers.

"Sax, you're *impossible*!"

"Women usually say it with more reverence."

She pushed and he obligingly rolled off her.

She sat up, then slid down again. "It's so cold out there!"

"You don't want to look?"

Meg just fumbled for her dress, grateful to have remembered to put it under the covers. She could feel him doing the same with his clothes, then they bumped and wriggled together as they struggled into them.

"I'm very glad you're not wearing boots," she said. "Which reminds me. Tell me about duchessing. You promised."

"Ah. It's slang for hasty sex, where the man doesn't even take time to get out of his boots. Comes from a note in the diary of the first Duchess of Marlborough that her husband came home from war and pleasured her with his boots on."

Meg paused. "Pleasured. I like that word. I can't be bothered with my corset."

"Good. As for pleasure, it can be our word. Every time I ask, 'What is your pleasure, my lady?' you will know exactly what I mean. What's on my mind."

Meg laughed and slid out from under the covers, shivering in the icy air, and at the awareness of the *sheelagh*. How astonishing that Sax had swamped the stone's song.

"I think I'll do without the boots," he said. "Then we can make a quick dash back into bed once you've found the statue. I suspect having it in the bed with us might be interesting."

"Lord, you're wicked! Do you believe me, then?"

After a moment, he said, "I honestly don't know. You clearly believe it, but call me Thomas."

"I'm not going to use it to prove it to you."

"I won't ask you to. But you can't expect me to believe such a thing without proof."

"Just let me keep it and guard it."

"Of course."

"Right, then." Before leaving the room, Meg turned back to feel at the bed.

"What are you doing?" he asked.

"Pulling your covers up to keep the heat in. Here, take an eiderdown, or you'll only end up shivering again."

"My, if ever I'm caught in this situation again, I will be well prepared."

"You have an unpleasant edge to your voice, my lord."

In a moment, he touched her, drew her into his arms. "I'm sorry, love. I'm not used to being so inept. It stings."

"I didn't much care for the feeling of being an infant in your world."

He kissed her. "Any chance of a candle? This infant doesn't care for wandering a strange house in the pitch dark. I don't suppose the *sheelagh* is in this room?"

"No. I'm sure it's not. I think there are still candles in my parents' room next door."

"And I did think to put the lighter in my pocket."

"Well done." She knew he hated feeling like an infant, but in many ways, that was what he was in her world.

Hand in hand, they groped their way out of the room, along the corridor, and into her parents' room. She halted for a moment, for it still held an ambience whose memory stretched back to her childhood. If anything, the memories sang stronger now, lacking sight. She could almost imagine her parents in the bed, there to be wakened if she had a bad dream.

She shook herself and worked her way to the chest of drawers. She pulled open the top drawer, and her fingers found the three partly burned candles. The red ones, kept for the *sheelagh.* Another fumble located the brass holder on the top. When she had one candle set firmly in it, she said, "Perform your magic, sir."

He'd have to work by touch, and she suspected she'd be more adept at the task than he was, but she knew she had to let him do it. Sparks flew from the flint, and then the first precious glow from the tinder. With a breath, he coaxed flame, then lit the candle.

The sudden light startled them after so many hours of darkness. She looked at him, newly precious. Perhaps he felt the same, for he reached out to touch her cheek, just a light brush of fingers against her skin. Seeing the disorder he was in, she knew she must be the same or worse. Her hair must be a tangled nest down her back, and her clothes a creased disaster. It didn't matter at all.

"Right," he said, picking up the candle. "Follow your music, my pretty witch."

Meg turned away, needing to try to block the music that was Sax in order to find the *sheelagh's* song. It was hopeless. After a while, she turned back. "You'll have to go away. You drown it."

He waggled his eyebrows. "I think I like that. All right, I'll go back into our room. But call out where you're going." He picked up the extra candles and lit one. "I'll put this in the other holder."

Once he left, she began to sort things out. She'd never tried to trace the *sheelagh* in this way, so it was hard, but slowly she began to distinguish a hum along her nerves that could only be from the wishing stone.

Owain Chancellor walked into Sax's house, ready to share his triumphs, despite an unease that had been prickling him all evening. "Where's the earl?" he demanded of an exhausted-looking Pringle.

"He's sent no word, sir. And Miss Gillingham and Lady Daphne have gone to Quiller's—the duchess is on her deathbed. And the parrot is in a state."

"'Struth! The duchess is dying?" Then he put that aside. "Damn Sax. He was supposed to send word. What's wrong with Knox?"

"He just keeps calling his lordship's name, sir, and trying to get out of the cage."

Owain ran up the stairs. Sax would blister everyone if the damn bird came to harm. Even before entering the room, he could hear Knox screeching, *"Sax! Want Sax. Sax home."*

In the warm dressing room, he found the bird clinging to the cage door, picking at the catch, Nims and Babs in attendance, wringing their hands. "Oh, Mr. Chancellor, thank heavens you're here! What should we do?"

Sax was always saying the bird was intelligent, so Owain went to the cage. "Come on now, Knox. Sax is out."

The bird stilled, tilting its head to eye him. Then: *"No! Sax. Bad, bad, bad."*

Owain looked at Nims. "Did Sax do something to Knox before he left?"

"No, sir. As if he would. And anyway, he never came up here. He changed, if you remember, below stairs." It was clearly a lingering wound.

"Knox doesn't usually get like this if Sax is away for most of a day, does he?"

"Not at all, sir, though he makes his annoyance clear later."

The bird was still crying its owner's name. "Shut up!" Owain snapped at it.

Knox went silent, then said, *"Damn dragon."*

"Jupiter!" Sensible Owain could hardly believe that the bird might be talking sense, never mind showing psychic powers, but then again his own neck had been prickling despite the feeling of success. The duchess was dying, though, wasn't she? "All right, Knox. I'll go and check."

As he walked toward the door, however, the parrot started an ear-splitting screech. When he turned back, it was clinging to the door and glaring at him balefully.

"It's freezing out there, you stupid bird!" But then he unlocked the cage, praying the damn bird wouldn't try to take his finger off. "Come on, then."

The bird hopped onto his hand. *"Sax?"* It was a distinct question.

"Yes, we'll go and find Sax."

Feeling three-quarters idiot, he tucked the large bird inside his jacket for warmth, repressing all thought of droppings, and hurried downstairs. He thought he knew who'd done the murder, though no one at Jakes's house knew the man's name or address. He had a description, though, of the man who'd been asking questions about the Gillinghams.

In the hall, Jeremy stood waiting, Brak whining at his side.

"Don't tell me the dog's uneasy, too."

"It won't settle. What's going on, sir?"

"I'm not sure, but I'm going to Quiller's Hotel."

Jeremy was staring at his chest. "Excuse me, sir, but . . ."

"Yes, I've Knox in here. Unless he's run totally mad, he's predicting danger."

"Predicting, sir. But . . ."

"Believe me, I know. Pringle, my riding cloak! Do you want to come?"

Jeremy rolled his eyes, but said, "I suppose so."

"Damn dragon," muttered the bird. *"Bad. Bad."*

Owain fastened his heavy cloak, covering the parrot as best he could. He knew the world had turned topsyturvy when cowardly Brak insisted on coming with them.

Meg circled her parents' room carefully just in case, but the sense of the *sheelagh* was no stronger in any spot. Sir Arthur would never have hidden it here, anyway. Too obvious. Where, then? She headed for the stairs up to the attic.

"Is it upstairs?" Sax called from her room.

Meg paused at the top of the attic stairs. "I don't think so. I'm going down instead."

As soon as she was halfway down, she knew. "It's downstairs. I'm sure."

She paused in the front hall, trying to find some sense of direction, but the swirling, maddening song was too ethereal for that. "I'm checking the rooms down here," she called, entering the bleak study. "Nothing so far."

She followed what she thought was a thread to the kitchen, but ended up frustrated and went slowly back to wander the hall.

Then she halted, swamped as if the *sheelagh* had suddenly decided to summon her. "The parlor," she said, knowing by the light that he was on the stairs.

"Is it dangerous?" He kept his distance.

"No, why?"

"You sound frightened."

"No. Just . . . it overwhelms me."

"Can I help?"

"I don't think so. Not until I've found it. Then you can carry it."

She went cautiously into the room, hoping to see the *sheelagh* in the open. She'd point it out to him, and need never touch it at all. It wasn't visible, however, and the sense of it was still without direction. She worked her way around the room, increasingly dazzled by sensations so like those Sax could bring to her, and yet unlike. Inferior.

Tainted.

Or perhaps just lacking the trust and closeness that made sex into love. She wished she could call to him to come to her, to hold her, but the *sheelagh's* song working with Sax's magic was already building an excruciating chord.

Frozen in the center of the room, she made herself focus instead of fleeing. Then, shaking, she forced her feet toward the heavy chair that had been her father's favorite. She knelt and peered underneath.

"It's here," she said unsteadily. "Can you come and get it, please?"

"Perhaps you'd better do that, Lady Saxonhurst."

Meg turned to see a stranger there, a stranger with a pistol pressed to Sax's head.

Chapter 23

"As you see," Sax said at his glossiest, "we have a guest, my dear. Would you care to introduce yourself, sir?"

"No."

"What do you want?" Meg demanded, standing up.

"The treasure."

"Treasure? What treasure?"

"Whatever's under that chair."

"It's a stone statue. It has no value."

The stranger grinned, and she recognized the man she'd seen with the housekeeper in Sir Arthur's house. "A stone statue that can give riches," he was saying. "Don't give me any trouble, my lady. I know all about it and you. You're going to wish me up riches, and then we can all go on our way."

Like an icy stream, she realized the man was probably the murderer. She saw Sax read her. He winked.

It was all very well for him to wink. The man was a killer. He'd shoot without hesitation. He'd *kill* him!

She had no idea whether the *sheelagh could* produce instant riches. Even if it did, would this man let them live?

Perhaps everyone could read her. The man said, "You don't have to worry, Lady Saxonhurst. I only kill when I'm paid my price. Once I have what I want, I'll be off and out of the country before anyone can find me."

"How did you find out about my wife's magical stone?" Sax asked, still sounding as if this was a social occasion.

"Wouldn't you like to know?"

The sneer flowed off Sax like oil. "Yes."

Meg could almost have laughed at the familiar expression of exasperation on the man's face.

Sax was Sax.

"Hell, why not? It's nothing to me and no one's rushing to your rescue. Sir Arthur talked a lot to his housekeeper, and she talked a lot to me. You remember me, don't you, Lady Saxonhurst. You saw me . . . conversing . . . with Hattie when you were there killing Sir Arthur."

"You killed Sir Arthur." There was no point in pretending.

"Perhaps I did at that. I was sent here to kill you two, but I don't reckon I'll get paid for it."

Meg saw Sax become serious. If he'd had his quizzing glass, it would have come into play. "Who's your employer?"

"Who do you think, my lord?"

"The Dowager Duchess of Daingerfield, of course."

"Bull's-eye. Countess, get that statue and get on with it!"

"Have you been in her employ long?" Sax asked, as if the man hadn't issued the command.

"Quite a while, aye."

"Steward of one of her estates, I hear."

"So?"

Meg wondered if she could launch an attack, but at a movement, the man's eyes flickered back to her. She slid a look around. The fireplace and poker were too far away. All that lay to hand were some tiny ornaments and the man had his pistol still pressed to Sax's head.

"Though I don't suppose you started as steward," said Sax, his voice chilly as the air.

"Don't suppose anyone does, my lord. Countess—"

"Fifteen years ago, perhaps?"

A strange silence hung in the air. "You've always known, have you?" He gave a sharp laugh. "No wonder you've set yourself against her."

The two men seemed totally focussed on each other. Meg began to inch toward the poker.

"You killed my father at her command."

Meg froze, and turned to stare at Sax.

"Water under the bridge," said the man, and turned to Meg. "Get back there and get on with it. Believe it or not, I only kill for pay. Shower me with wealth and you'll never see me again."

"Did you get a bonus for the deaths of my mother and sister?"

"Damn near got scragged. But I'd stashed away some evidence about the others. Your uncles. Unlucky lot, the earls of Saxonhurst. Mad, you know."

Sax stood like a statue of ice, perhaps shocked insensible by all this. But he'd known. All along, he'd known his grandmother had killed his family. And Meg had thought he was overreacting.

"Get on with it, Countess!" The man jabbed the pistol into Sax's head so he jerked.

"It's not that easy!" Meg protested.

"Tell me what we have to do then. And be quick about it. It'd be dead easy to put a ball in my Lord Saxonhurst where it'll cripple but not be fatal."

"You have to be careful what you wish for," Meg said quickly. "Once I pick up the *sheelagh*, I'll be under its power. We have to form the wish first."

"You make up the poxy wish, or I swear to heaven he'll never be the same!"

"What do you want, then? Tell me what you want!"

"I told you. Riches!"

"Just riches?"

"Just riches," he sneered. "Fine for you who've lived in luxury all your lives. Riches, lovey. Shower me with it. Jewels. Coins. Anything."

Meg looked at Sax. He was burning with icy rage. This man had killed his family, and he wanted his blood. His eyes met hers, and it was as if he spoke. *Kill him for me, Meg.*

Did he believe? Or was it just a wild hope?

If he did believe, could she risk the *sheelagh's* sting for murder?

And what would happen once he did believe, and knew she'd trapped him?

Whatever, she burned as fiercely as he. She thought of the child, blighted by murder, of a family hounded by a vicious, possessive woman. "Careless," he'd said earlier, of his father's death. Of course, they'd only intended to kill his father, leaving his mother to be dragged back into the dragon's claws.

She wished the horrible, twisted duchess were here, too.

Meg bent down and pulled out the bag. The power began and she wasn't touching it yet. She almost giggled when she realized they'd used the red candles. She didn't know if they mattered, but now two of them lit this moment.

"Shower you with riches," she repeated, loosening the drawstring. She glanced at Sax, trying to send a message, though she had no way of knowing whether the *sheelagh* could grant an instant wish. Always before it had taken time for a wish to come true.

"Lots and lots of riches," said the man. "Get on with it."

Meg sat on the chair, and drew the cloth down off the statue.

"What is it, then?" asked the man. "Show me."

She turned it, keeping cloth between her hands and the stone, watching the men's faces.

Despite his fury, Sax laughed. "Jupiter, Meg, no wonder you're not easily shocked!"

Surprisingly, the murderer protested. "There ought to be a law against it! Turn it away, and get on with it."

Meg obeyed, and couldn't see any excuse to delay. With a final, meaningful look at Sax, she said, "On your head be it," and let the cloth fall. She put her hands to the cold, rough stone of the *sheelagh* and braced herself.

It was worse than before.

Worse!

Sucked into a ravaging whirlwind, she remembered her wish, and cried it into the void. "A shower of riches on him!"

Then, because she truly feared that this time she would die, she cried, "Keep Sax safe! Let him be happy!"

The whirlwind smashed things, crashed things, ripped her in and out of torment. She screamed. People screamed. Everything groaned as if the whole world around her was being mangled apart.

Christ, Meg prayed, hoping Christ and the pagan gods

were not antagonists, *help me! Don't let it kill me now, not now I've found Sax.*

It hurt. Hurt more than before, with a tearing of muscle and a breaking of bones, and a terrible, final agony in her head. Her flesh slowly turned liquid and puddled on a bloody floor. . . .

Christ!

"Christ, Meg, come back to me."

Meg forced open leaden lids, aching in every joint and muscle, to see a white-faced Sax staring down at her. She was so sorry to be dying. Then she vomited all over him.

When she could speak, while Sax wiped her face with a damp cloth—where had that come from?—she gasped, "Did it work?"

"Something did," he said in a shaken voice.

"What happened?" He was keeping his body between her and the rest of the room, but she had a vague sense of voices. Many voices. And groans. Had the groans been real?

"What you wished for," he said. "A shower of riches. A huge shower of pennies that battered him to the ground. But—"

"But?"

"But . . . Meg, the ceiling above him gave way. I suppose there must have been a leak and the plaster rotted. Perhaps someone stashed the coins up there."

Meg laughed weakly. Trust the *sheelagh*. And it didn't matter whether he believed or not.

"Meg?" Astonishingly, Laura appeared, pale, wide-eyed, but looking rather excited. "Are you all right?"

Meg struggled to sit up straighter. Was she dreaming? Was she dead? She looked around the room, lit now by a couple of lamps as well as candles, and knew she was not. There were a lot of people here, though.

Someone—it sounded like Sax himself—was muttering, *"Sax. Bad. Dragon. Bad."*

At her look, Sax said, "Knox is here. And Brak. And your brother and sister. I'll explain later."

"That man was sent to find you!" Laura exclaimed. "But I didn't like him. I didn't feel easy about it. I was so glad when Mr. Chancellor turned up and brought us over here. And the parrot is so clever! It knew."

"Lots and lots of riches," the bird suddenly exclaimed in a passable imitation of the villain's voice, then it emitted a scream.

Meg shuddered, and Sax gathered her into his arms. "Don't think about it. It's still freezing here. Let's get you back to Marlborough Square."

She was indeed shivering, though it wasn't entirely with cold. "Yes, please. Laura, don't forget the *sheelagh.*"

He stood with her in his arms. They were both crumpled and dirty, and stinking of her vomit. She saw a couple of angry marks on his temple, showing he hadn't entirely escaped her deadly shower.

Safe in his arms, she looked at last at what she had done. His parents' killer lay groaning among his wished-for wealth, guarded and tended by Sax's servants and a snarling Brak.

Even though she'd envisioned it, she hadn't been sure that coins would do that much damage. Each copper penny weighed half an ounce, though, and there were a lot of them. The man's skull was surely cracked, and he was bleeding from mouth and nose.

She wasn't sorry, but she looked at Sax.

"Thank you," he said. "Thank you for everything. Especially, for summoning me to your side."

She rested her head against his shoulder. "You believe?"

"I'd be a clod not to, though the stone covers its tracks remarkably well. I find it fascinating."

Meg groaned. The impossible man was probably going to want to play with it like a scientific toy!

"What about the duchess?" she asked as he carried her out of the room.

"She really is dying. I think she sent him here to kill me because she wanted to take me with her. I'm tempted to go and tell her she's failed, but I'll let God and the devil take care of creating an appropriate hell for her."

Meg rested her head on his shoulder and gave thanks to gods, Christian and pagan.

Chapter 24

The Marlborough Square house was decorated to welcome them home.

That was Meg's first thought as she walked over the threshold on Sax's arm and saw that festoons of rich materials and gilded ornaments had been added to the Christmas greenery. Despite the hour, servants seemed to be everywhere, adding to the display.

It was the sort of idiocy that could only happen in Sax's domain.

She was probably gaping, for he said, "The Twelfth Night ball, I suppose? Time's short."

She stared at him. "That's going on?"

"Of course, though it'll be a little tricky if the duchess dies between now and then. I suspect, however, that the main reason for this industry is to give everyone an excuse to be in the hall when we arrive home."

Meg looked around at the servants, who had all stopped work to smile at them. As Owain Chancellor had said, Sax was Sax, and his household was his household.

She burst out laughing, and the servants gathered around to welcome them home and pelt them with questions, like family not employees. How many of them, she wondered, had Sax rescued from poverty and unemployment because they were small, or fat, or crippled, or had had an unfortunate brush with the law?

Which had lost their excellent places in the ducal household for helping him? He wouldn't have been able to do anything for them immediately, and she knew that must have added agony to his years in the dragon's claws.

He held up a hand. "I'm pleased to see you all so very

devoted to your work," he remarked, looking around at the decorations. "Has anything been done to the ballroom yet, or was it essential that you all work in the front hall?"

"Tomorrow, milord," someone said. "Promise."

"I'm sure you have it all in hand. Now, the brief summary of events you've been waiting for. The countess, of course, had nothing to do with the death of Sir Arthur Jakes, and the real culprit has been found. People at Sir Arthur's house have been persuaded to tell the truth, so we can put that behind us. However, I'm sure the scandal will guarantee that anyone who is in town will want to attend our celebration, so let's do the Torrances proud."

Meg felt rather sick at the thought of everyone coming to the ball, especially with her scandalous self as the attraction, and he squeezed her hand as if he knew. "Any questions?"

"What about the people hanging around outside still, milord? The magistrate came and read the Riot Act to get rid of 'em, but some came back."

"And have doubtless seen what they waited to see. They'll disperse now on such a cold night. Mr. Chancellor is having a word with the official watchers. Perhaps, out of Christian charity, someone should go and tell the duchess's minions that the game is up. By the way, the Dowager Duchess of Daingerfield appears to have suffered a serious seizure and to be on her deathbed."

Meg noted that he didn't dress it up with regrets, and she thought she heard a couple of faint cheers. It was terribly unchristian, but she understood. Some of these people had witnessed the woman's harshness firsthand, and she wondered how many of them had shared his suspicions about the woman's true evil.

"Now," he was saying, "you should all be off to your beds. I do expect normal service tomorrow. Having endured life without you, I need extra special care."

They all chuckled.

"But before that, the countess and I require baths and food. Good solid food as quickly as possible."

At this, the servants exploded into action. Meg and Sax were swept up to their rooms. Meg found herself in the hands of Susie and another maid, who stripped her messy clothing off her, put her in a bath like a baby, washed her thoroughly, then dressed her tenderly in nightgown and robe.

She wondered if they knew she and Sax had made love. Probably. It didn't matter. Perhaps she was getting used to the lack of privacy, or perhaps she was too exhausted to care.

She wanted to be with him again.

At that moment, she wasn't sure how she was going to endure being apart for even short periods, though common sense told her this degree of madness would pass.

Clean and neat, with her hair loose and damp on her shoulders, she was guided into the room that held Knox's cage. Sax was already there, addressing a tableful of food with enthusiasm, devoted parrot on his shoulder being fed with tidbits.

"Did Knox really sound the warning?"

"Remarkable, isn't it? I'm sure Owain would have acted eventually, and, of course, you took care of the villain, but it was convenient to have help turn up. Sit."

Meg sat opposite him. He was in his gold-and-brown banjan and looked unbelievably wonderful. Food, however, looked even better, and she fell on cheese, bread, and cold meats, then upon mince pies and apple tarts, each crowned with a mound of thick cream.

She drank the wine he'd poured for her. "I'm always gulping down food in front of you!"

"I was gulping along with you." He held out his glass and chinked it against hers. "Welcome home, Meg."

"Women. Aaaargh!"

"No, Knox. Be nice, Say, 'Pretty lady.' "

The bird shifted, glowering, but then it said, exactly in Sax's voice, *"Pretty lady."*

Meg smiled and fed him a crust. "And I think you're a pretty lady. And clever, too. Thank you, Knox."

"Thank you. Thank you." But then the parrot turned its back.

"He'll come around," Sax said.

Meg sipped her wine, looking at him across the table. "You truly don't mind me wishing you into this?"

His smile could brighten a coal pit. "How could I mind anything so delightful? Give me your hand."

Brows raised a little, Meg held it out, and he slipped a ring above her wedding ring. The Saxonhurst ring that Daphne had worn.

"Didn't she mind?"

"Somewhat, but I substituted another just as valuable. That is yours by right. My chosen bride."

She laughed softly, likely to be overwhelmed by tenderness.

He glanced over into a corner. "Laura brought the stone and left it there. Do you mind if I look at it?"

"No." Meg tasted the *sheelagh* in her mind, and could sense it, but it was, in a way, muted by Sax, by the effect he could have on her. Perhaps it had been the same for her parents.

He picked up the bag and pulled out the stone. Though she knew it didn't affect others, it still startled her to see it handled so casually.

"It really is deliciously risqué. Laura said they have them in churches in Ireland?"

"So I'm told."

He touched the *sheelagh's* open mouth, then her open vulva, in a stroke that caught Meg's breath. "I have power of my own, you old witch," he said, "and I forbid you to charge a price for what my wife did today."

Meg shivered. "What power?" she whispered, though she did not doubt it.

"I have no idea. Perhaps the powers of a man who is not afraid of women. I just know she will obey." He propped the *sheelagh* upon a chair. "I also don't think she likes being hidden away. No wonder she's become a little bitter."

"Rescuing statues now? Sax, you're—"

"Impossible. I know." He gave her his most glorious smile. "But it's true. She wasn't made to be hidden."

"We can hardly leave her out on view!"

"I don't see why not. See, even Knox approves."

Indeed, for some strange reason the misogynistic parrot had flown off his shoulder onto the chair by the *sheelagh* and was exploring it with its beak as if fascinated. Exploring a rather improper place!

Meg knew propriety would make no impression on Sax. "It's always possible someone else might have the power."

"Ah, that's true. But I think you should have her in your bedroom. I assume you're not intending to invite strangers to your bedroom?"

"Not if you don't."

He laughed. "I remember my promise. I don't think I will have any trouble keeping it."

"I certainly won't. You're likely to exhaust me!"

His smile was his special one, his precious one. "It was good, wasn't it, our midnight tryst? Worth suffering for?"

Meg fussed with her dressing gown, knowing she looked foolish, but unable to help herself. "I don't want to talk about that sort of thing."

"Very well," he said amiably.

She rolled her eyes at him, but then frowned at the *sheelagh*. "I can't keep her in my room. She'd drive me mad."

"Mmmmm. I do want to try lovemaking with it in the bed with us."

"Sax!"

"One day. But we'll keep it in here with Knox. They seem to be becoming fast friends."

"Don't ever ask me to use it again."

He came back to sit beside her. "Of course not. It terrified me to watch."

She fiddled with her wineglass. "It's not just that. I think it killed my parents. It's dangerous."

"Why? I thought you said your father was ill."

"Yes, but . . ." She'd hardly had time to work this out in her mind. "My mother said it shouldn't be used lightly, but I think she did. Looking back, I can see that we lived better than we could afford, and my parents were always so carefree about things. It drove me distracted, and was part of the reason I left home. I think she was wishing anytime they needed something."

"And is that bad?"

"There's always a sting. I don't know how it works, but there always is. Or was. I hope you've curbed her. Perhaps it accumulated, and caused my father's sickness.

I don't know. But I'm sure that at the end she tried to
wish death away. Sir Arthur . . . he said he'd found the
sheelagh on the bed between them. And that Father had
been worried she might use it."

"You think she wished for her own death?"

"No! No, I don't think she'd do that. I don't think
she'd wish to abandon the young ones." But Meg fal-
tered there.

He took her in his arms. "You're not sure?"

She rested against him, so grateful to have someone
at last to lean on. "No. It's terrible, but they loved each
other so much. Love can be a dangerous force."

"A kind of magic, yes, and often with a sting in the
tail."

She wished again that he might love her.

"So you think she wished to go with him?" he added.

After a moment, Meg said, "No. She was too much
the optimist. I'm sure she wished for his recovery. But
perhaps there are some things the *sheelagh* cannot do.
Or perhaps she just worded it carelessly."

"Such as a wish that they not be parted."

She stared at him. "Yes! But I'm sure if that was her
wish, it was deliberate. She'd hope it would lead to his
recovery, but be ready to die with him if necessary. She's
doubtless been pacing the clouds of heaven impatiently,
urging me to get on with it and use the *sheelagh* to save
her children!"

He grinned and kissed her hand. "I've just realized,
I'm the answer to a maiden's prayer!"

Meg groaned. But then she asked, "Are you all
right?"

He didn't pretend to misunderstand. "It's an astonishing relief, in fact. I always suspected the truth—a
highwayman on that road wasn't likely, and my parents'
trip there had been arranged by my aunt, who generally
did what the duchess said. But what could a ten-year-
old boy do? Who would believe him? There were times
when I thought perhaps I was the one who was mad,
who had a distorted view of reality.

"Once I escaped, the trail was cold, and I knew with
an adult's eye that proving anything against the duchess
would be impossible. Even if I found the person she'd

used, it would stop there. So I just continued to refuse her any reward from her crimes."

"I'm glad you're not seeking revenge."

"Don't think me too saintly. If I didn't believe she was going straight to hell, I'd be at her beside making her last moments miserable."

"Sax!"

He met her eyes. "That's the truth, Meg. She tried to ruin my parents' lives, and then she killed them. She tried to ruin my life in many ways, and partially succeeded. She killed my uncles, for heaven's sake, out of spite. Then, in the end, she tried to kill me and you. I'm not Christian enough to forgive all that, but I'm God-fearing enough to believe that He will deal with her."

"It all started with love. Doesn't love frighten you sometimes?"

"It terrifies me."

Despite her own words, that was not what she wanted to hear. "And yet you've surrounded yourself with love. Even if it meant so many meddling fingers in your life."

He laughed, perhaps with a touch of embarrassment. "Perhaps I have a hunger for love, then. Feed me, Meg?"

She looked at him, wondering if she misunderstood. She seized her courage and took the first step. "It's early days yet, but I do believe I love you, Sax."

He drew her into his arms. "You have to. I don't think I could endure unrequited love, and I've decided to give up smashing things."

She was so overwhelmed, she couldn't think of anything beautiful to say. "Pity. I'd like to have one last clear-out."

"What a marvelous idea!" He snatched Knox from his adoring attentions to the *sheelagh* and popped him in his cage. Then he led Meg into his bedroom, and together they happily destroyed every trace of ugliness.

With a final, satisfied survey of the shambles, they staggered off to her bedroom and collapsed in exhausted sleep.

Meg thought perhaps the whole of London *had* come to Sax's Twelfth Night Ball, and most of them were curious about her. She would have hated it except that he stayed by her side and he was magic enough to drive away any fear or doubt.

Also, Laura was attending, and she was distracting most of the male attention. The twins were watching from a quiet corner, nipping out—she was sure—to filch delicacies from the supper display. They'd already had traditional Twelfth Night cake in the servants' hall earlier.

Meg was in the "apricot thing" which was truly a fairy-tale gown of cream silk under a tunic of embroidered apricot gauze set with small russet stones and seed pearls. And she was wearing her mother's pearls.

When Sax had come to escort her down to the ball-room, he'd brought two boxes. One held an exquisite parure of diamonds—necklace, earrings, brooch, bracelets, and tiara. The other contained her mother's simple pearl set, her locket, and her rings.

"I put Owain to finding some of your property that first day. Your family helped. Thus far, we have some of your father's books and these." He looked almost uncertain. "If you'd rather wear the diamonds, I brought them in case. . . ."

Meg burst into tears and tried to crush him with a hug. "Sax, you're impossible!"

"Impossible, like magic?"

"Wickedly magical," she'd said, and they might have been late if Susie hadn't bullied them into behaving themselves.

Her mother's simple jewels kept her feet on the ground, but her real confidence came from Sax, from the deep, true feeling that ran between them. It was early days yet, and there was much they didn't know about each other, much to learn. But they loved, and their love was something wonderful added to the world.

They'd slept together last night, but only slept. He hadn't needed words to tell her that they wouldn't only sleep tonight. Or tomorrow, for the ball would go on into the early hours of the morning.

Perhaps they'd both be too tired.

She doubted Sax was ever too tired, and he'd make sure she wasn't either. Or perhaps, as he'd first suggested, he would sleep with her to be ready when she felt more rested.

So here she was, greeting people as the Countess of Saxonhurst. The scandalous Countess of Saxonhurst, which was the last thing sensible Meg Gillingham had ever expected to be. And here beside her was her husband, the handsome, charming, magical earl, stealing her breath with his beauty in his stark, dark evening clothes, his yellow hair and eyes shining, touching her heart with his kindness and his need for love.

And here he was leading her down to open the ball with the first dance, but pausing, despite all eyes upon them, to lean his head close to hers.

"Tonight," he murmured, "in your room. Do not undress, for I intend to strip you layer by layer in candlelight, and discover every one of your magical secrets."

Meg knew she was blushing, but as the first bars of music started and she sank into a grand curtsy, she looked him in the eye. "It will be my pleasure, my lord. Truly my pleasure."

Author's Note

Writing is magical fun! Sax came to me first—a crazy earl trashing his room because of a letter from his grandmother. Then Meg revealed her racy underwear. By the time the *sheelagh,* the parrot, and the snarling, cowardly dog arrived, I knew I had trouble on my hands. But wonderful trouble.

The *sheelagh* came about because of a lot of thought, actually. I needed a magic item, and I didn't want it to be anything trite like a medallion. Also, I needed it to be something not easily carried and hidden. I was getting desperate, and even thinking of major items of furniture, when I remembered an on-line discussion about *sheelagh-ma-gigs.* That discussion had been about whether they were remnants of pagan goddess-worship, or Christian warnings about the evils of women. (My own, inexpert opinion is that there are two sorts and two purposes: the ones giving birth to leaves and flowers which are of the goddess; and the ones exposing themselves, which are the warning. It won't be the first time the Christian faith took something pagan and turned it to its own use.)

The *sheelagh* suited my purposes perfectly because it gave Meg another reason to keep her secret. Any well-bred Regency lady would be hesitant to reveal that they owned and treasured such a scandalous item!

However, I thought I was using something very obscure. Imagine my surprise to open my paper one Sunday and find a full-page item with a picture, because there was a major exhibition of *sheelagh-ma-gigs* on in Dublin. Writing, as I said, is a strange and sometimes magical business.

The pets came when I realized that a man like Sax

would acquire some needy animals. What should they be? An unattractive dog sounded good, as did a bird. What would make a parrot an unwanted pet, though? Parrots that talk dirty have been done too often, and so I came up with the idea of a misogynistic parrot passed on when its owner married. That was clearly going to create a few awkward moments!

I was intending to use Knox as a plot device for only a few cute moments. I can't resist research, however, so off I went on the Internet to see what I could find. What a fascinating subject, and what wonderful stories bird people have to tell. Soon I saw that Knox needed more attention, and he became a secondary character.

The really strange thing, however, was that it was as if he'd been there all along. From first writing, the heroine had noted how warm the hero kept his house. Now, anyone who has ever lived in a house without central heating will know that's not easy to do. Anyone who's spent December and January in England will know that though the temperature rarely drops low, the damp climate makes it miserable, and that damp chill seeps in everywhere.

Sax clearly isn't delicate, so why the warm house? Of course, for Knox!

As I said, creating fiction is magical.

Is Knox possible? Today, yes, even to his psychic powers. Many animals show them. Unfortunately, back in the Regency, he is unlikely because people didn't understand the needs of these tropical birds and they died of cold, of lack of water, from being fed the wrong foods, and being deprived of light. But this is fiction and Sax is a hero, so Knox thrives.

Perhaps it's just the power of love.

Many thanks to the many on-line people who shared their bird knowledge with me, especially Whitney Walters in the Genie Romex, and the newsgroup rec.pets.birds.

Unlike all my recent books, this is not linked to any previous ones. I decided it was time to do my first, true Regency historical. The Regency period, which lasted from 1811 to 1820, was a mostly prosperous time of aristocratic elegance and gracious, rather idle living, peopled by astonishing eccentrics. It is, of course, the period of Jane Austen's later works, and though she wrote of her own gentry class, the atmosphere is much the same.

The Georgian, on the other hand (my other main period), is a more racy, full-blooded age. The aristocratic elegance is often blended with rampant immorality, and a zest for learning, expansion, and new ideas.

I enjoy hearing from readers. Please address letters c/o The Alice Orr Agency, 305 Madison Ave # 1166, New York, NY 10165, and enclose a SASE if you want a reply.

Or send e-mail to jobeverley@poboxes.com

My web page is http://www.sff.net/people/jobeverley and contains, among other items, a complete annotated list of my books.

I have signed bookplates for all my books. Send a SASE and a list of the books you own and I will be happy to provide them.

And remember, romance readers know how to value love, joy, courage, and triumph. More power to us!

SUSAN KING

□LAIRD OF THE WIND   0-451-40768-7/$5.99

In medieval Scotland, the warrior known as Border Hawk seizes the castle belonging to the father of the beautiful Isabel Scott, famous throughout the Lowlands for her gift of prophecy. During the battle, Isabel is injured while fighting alongside her men, and placed under Border Hawk's protection. As the border wars rage on, the warrior and prophetess engage in a more intimate conflict, discovering their love for the Scottish borderlands is surpassed only by their love for each other.

Also available:
□THE ANGEL KNIGHT   0-451-40662-1/$5.50
□THE BLACK THORNE'S ROSE   0-451-40544-7/$4.99
□LADY MIRACLE   0-451-40766-0/$5.99
□THE RAVEN'S MOON   0-451-18868-3/$5.99
□THE RAVEN'S WISH   0-451-40545-5/$4.99
Prices slightly higher in Canada